BIG DATA
IN COMPLEX
AND SOCIAL
NETWORKS

T0312704

Chapman & Hall/CRC
Big Data Series

SERIES EDITOR
Sanjay Ranka

AIMS AND SCOPE

This series aims to present new research and applications in Big Data, along with the computational tools and techniques currently in development. The inclusion of concrete examples and applications is highly encouraged. The scope of the series includes, but is not limited to, titles in the areas of social networks, sensor networks, data-centric computing, astronomy, genomics, medical data analytics, large-scale e-commerce, and other relevant topics that may be proposed by potential contributors.

PUBLISHED TITLES

BIG DATA COMPUTING: A GUIDE FOR BUSINESS AND TECHNOLOGY MANAGERS
Vivek Kale

BIG DATA IN COMPLEX AND SOCIAL NETWORKS
My T. Thai, Weili Wu, and Hui Xiong

BIG DATA OF COMPLEX NETWORKS
Matthias Dehmer, Frank Emmert-Streib, Stefan Pickl, and Andreas Holzinger

BIG DATA : ALGORITHMS, ANALYTICS, AND APPLICATIONS
Kuan-Ching Li, Hai Jiang, Laurence T. Yang, and Alfredo Cuzzocrea

NETWORKING FOR BIG DATA
Shui Yu, Xiaodong Lin, Jelena Mišić, and Xuemin (Sherman) Shen

BIG DATA
IN COMPLEX
AND SOCIAL
NETWORKS

EDITED BY

MY T. THAI
UNIVERSITY OF FLORIDA, USA

WEILI WU
UNIVERSITY OF TEXAS AT DALLAS, USA

HUI XIONG
RUTGERS, THE STATE UNIVERSITY OF NEW JERSEY, USA

CRC Press
Taylor & Francis Group
Boca Raton London New York

CRC Press is an imprint of the
Taylor & Francis Group, an **informa** business

A CHAPMAN & HALL BOOK

CRC Press
Taylor & Francis Group
6000 Broken Sound Parkway NW, Suite 300
Boca Raton, FL 33487-2742

© 2017 by Taylor & Francis Group, LLC
CRC Press is an imprint of Taylor & Francis Group, an Informa business

No claim to original U.S. Government works

Printed on acid-free paper
Version Date: 20161014

International Standard Book Number-13: 978-1-4987-2684-9 (Hardback)

Visit the Taylor & Francis Web site at
http://www.taylorandfrancis.com

and the CRC Press Web site at
http://www.crcpress.com

Printed and bound in the United States of America by
Edwards Brothers Malloy on sustainably sourced paper

Contents

Preface

In the past decades, the world has witnessed a blossom of online social networks, such as Facebook and Twitter. This has revolutionized the way of human interaction and drastically changed the landscape of information sharing in cyberspace nowadays. Along with the explosive growth of social networks, huge volumes of data have been generating. The research of big data, referring to these large datasets, gives insight into many domains, especially in complex and social network applications.

In the research area of big data, the management and analysis of large-scale datasets are quite challenging due to the highly unstructured data collected. The large size of social networks, spatio-temporal effect and interaction between users are among various challenges in uncovering behavioral mechanisms. Many recent research projects are involved in processing and analyzing data from social networks and attempt to better understand the complex networks, which motivates us to prepare an in-depth material on recent advances in areas of big data and social networks.

This handbook is to provide recent developments on theoretical, algorithmic and application aspects of big data in complex social networks. The handbook consists of four parts, covering a wide range of topics. The first part focuses on data storage and data processing. The efficient storage of data can fundamentally support intensive data access and queries, which enables sophisticated analysis. Data processing and visualization help to communicate information clearly and efficiently. The second part of this handbook is devoted to the extraction of essential information and the prediction of web content. By performing big data analysis, we can better understand the interests, location and search history of users and have more accurate prediction of users' behaviors. The book next focuses on the protection of privacy and security in Part 3. Modern social media enables people to share and seek information effectively, but also provides effective channels for rumor and misinformation propagation. It is essentially important to model the rumor diffusion, identify misinformation from massive data and design intervention strategies. Finally, Part 4 discusses the emergent application of big data and social networks. It is particularly interested in multilayer networks and multiparty systems.

We would like to take this opportunity to thank all authors, the anonymous referees, and Taylor & Francis Group for helping us to finalize this handbook. Our thanks also go to our students for their help during the processing of all contributions. Finally, we hope that this handbook will encourage research on the many intriguing open questions and applications in the area of big data and social networks that still remain.

My T. Thai
Weili Wu
Hui Xiong

Editors

My T. Thai is a professor and associate chair for research in the department of computer and information sciences and engineering at the University of Florida. She received her PhD degree in computer science from the University of Minnesota in 2005. Her current research interests include algorithms, cybersecurity and optimization on network science and engineering, including communication networks, smart grids, social networks and their interdependency. The results of her work have led to 5 books and 120+ articles published in various prestigious journals and conferences on networking and combinatorics.

Dr. Thai has engaged in many professional activities. She has been a TPC-chair for many IEEE conferences, has served as an associate editor for *Journal of Combinatorial Optimization (JOCO)*, *Optimization Letters*, *Journal of Discrete Mathematics*, *IEEE Transactions on Parallel and Distributed Systems*, and a series editor of *Springer Briefs in Optimization*. Recently, she has co-founded and is co-Editor-in-Chief of *Computational Social Networks* journal. She has received many research awards including a UF Research Foundation Fellowship, UF Provosts Excellence Award for Assistant Professors, a Department of Defense (DoD) Young Investigator Award, and an NSF (National Science Foundation) CAREER Award.

Weili Wu is a full professor in the department of computer science, University of Texas at Dallas. She received her PhD in 2002 and MS in 1998 from the department of computer science, University of Minnesota, Twin City. She received her BS in 1989 in mechanical engineering from Liaoning University of Engineering and Technology in China. From 1989 to 1991, she was a mechanical engineer at Chinese Academy of Mine Science and Technology. She was an associate researcher and associate chief engineer in Chinese Academy of Mine Science and Technology from 1991 to 1993. Her current research mainly deals with the general research area of data communication and data management. Her research focuses on the design and analysis of algorithms for optimization problems that occur in wireless networking environments and various database systems. She has published more than 200 research papers in various prestigious journals and conferences such as *IEEE Transaction on Knowledge and Data Engineering (TKDE)*, *IEEE Transactions on Mobile Computing (TMC)*, *IEEE Transactions on Multimedia (TMM)*, *ACM Transactions on Sensor Networks (TOSN)*, *IEEE Transactions on Parallel and Distributed*

Systems (TPDS), IEEE/ACM Transactions on Networking (TON), Journal of Global Optimization (JGO), Journal of Optical Communications and Networking (JOCN), Optimization Letters (OPTL), IEEE Communications Letters (ICL), Journal of Parallel and Distributed Computing (JPDC), Journal of Computational Biology (JCB), Discrete Mathematics (DM), Social Network Analysis and Mining (SNAM), Discrete Applied Mathematics (DAM), IEEE INFOCOM (The Conference on Computer Communications), ACM SIGKDD (International Conference on Knowledge Discovery & Data Mining), International Conference on Distributed Computing Systems (ICDCS), International Conference on Database and Expert Systems Applications (DEXA), SIAM Conference on Data Mining, as well as many others. Dr. Wu is associate editor of *SOP Transactions on Wireless Communications (STOWC), Computational Social Networks,* Springer and *International Journal of Bioinformatics Research and Applications (IJBRA).* Dr. Wu is a senior member of IEEE.

Hui Xiong is currently a full professor of management science and information systems at Rutgers Business School and the director of Rutgers Center for Information Assurance at Rutgers, the State University of New Jersey, where he received a two-year early promotion/tenure (2009), the Rutgers University Board of Trustees Research Fellowship for Scholarly Excellence (2009), and the ICDM-2011 Best Research Paper Award (2011).

Dr. Xiong is a prominent researcher in the areas of business intelligence, data mining, big data, and geographic information systems (GIS). For his outstanding contributions to these areas, he was elected an ACM Distinguished Scientist. He has a distinguished academic record that includes 200+ referred papers and an authoritative *Encyclopedia of GIS* (Springer, 2008). He is serving on the editorial boards of *IEEE Transactions on Knowledge and Data Engineering (TKDE), ACM Transactions on Management Information Systems (TMIS)* and *IEEE Transactions on Big Data.* Also, he served as a program co-chair of the Industrial and Government Track for the 18th ACM SIGKDD International Conference on Knowledge Discovery and Data Mining (KDD), a program co-chair for the IEEE 2013 International Conference on Data Mining (ICDM-2013), and a general co-chair for the IEEE 2015 International Conference on Data Mining (ICDM-2015).

I

Social Networks and Complex Networks

CHAPTER 1

A Hyperbolic Big Data Analytics Framework within Complex and Social Networks

Eleni Stai, Vasileios Karyotis, Georgios Katsinis, Eirini Eleni Tsiropoulou and Symeon Papavassiliou

CONTENTS

D ATA management and analysis has stimulated paradigm shifts in decision-making in various application domains. Especially the emergence of big data along with complex and social networks has stretched the imposed requirements to the limit, with numerous and crucial potential benefits. In this chapter, based on a novel approach for big data analytics (BDA), we focus on data processing and visualization and their relations with complex network analysis. Thus, we adopt a holistic perspective with respect to complex/social networks that generate massive data and relevant analytics techniques, which jointly impact societal operations, e.g., marketing, advertising, resource allocation, etc., closing a loop between data generation and exploitation within complex networks themselves. In the latest literature, a strong relation between hyperbolic geometry and complex networks is shown, as the latter eventually exhibit a hidden hyperbolic structure. Inspired by this fact, the methodology adopted in this chapter leverages on key properties of the hyperbolic metric space for complex and social networks, exploited in a general framework that includes processes for data correlation/clustering, missing data (e.g., links) inference, social network analysis metrics efficient computations, optimization, resource (advertisements, files, etc.) allocation and visualization analytics. More specifically, the proposed framework consists of the above hyperbolic geometry based processes/components, arranged in a chain form. Some of those components can also be applied independently, and potentially combined with other traditional statistical learning techniques. We emphasize the efficiency of each process in the complex networks domain, while also pinpointing open and interesting research directions.

1.1　INTRODUCTION

Data processing and analysis was one of the main drivers for the proliferation of computers (processing) and communications networks (analysis and transfer). However, lately, a paradigm shift is witnessed where networks themselves, e.g., social networks and sensor networks, can create data as well, and, in fact, in massive quantities. Indeed, gigantic datasets are produced on purpose or spontaneously, and stored by traditional and new applications/services.

Characteristic examples include the envisaged Internet of Things (IoT) paradigm [1], where pervasive sensors and actuators for almost every aspect of human activity will collect, process and make decisions on massive data, e.g., for surveillance, healthcare, etc. Similarly, the Internet, mobile networks, and overlaying (social) networks, i.e., Google, Facebook and others described in [2], [3], are responsible for the explosion of produced and transferred data. Collecting, processing and analyzing these data generated at unprecedented rates has concentrated significant research, technological and financial interest lately, in a broader framework popularly known as "big data analytics" (BDA) [2]. The current setting is only expected to intensify in the future, since the expanding complex and social networks are expected to generate much more massive amounts of complexly inter-related information and impose harsher data storage, processing, analysis and visualization requirements.

1.1.1 Scope and Objectives

Given the aforementioned setting and the fact that significant research and technological progress has taken place regarding the lower level aspects, e.g., storage and processing, this chapter focuses more on aspects of data analytics. It aspires to provide a framework for combining traditional methodologies (e.g., statistical learning) with novel techniques (e.g., communications theory) providing holistic and efficient solutions.

More specifically, we adopt a radical perspective for performing data analytics, advocating the use of cross-discipline mathematical tools, and more specifically exploiting properties of hyperbolic space [4], [5]. We postulate that hyperbolic metric spaces can provide the substrate required in data analytics for keeping up with the pace of data volume explosion and required processing. The main goal is to briefly describe a holistic framework for data representation, analysis (e.g., correlation, clustering, prediction), visualization, and decision making in complex and social networks, based on the principles of hyperbolic geometry and its properties. Then, the chapter will touch on several key BDA aspects, i.e., data correlation, dimensionality reduction, data and networks' embeddings, navigation, social networks analysis (SNA) metrics' computation and optimization, and show how they are accommodated by the above framework, along with the associated benefits achieved. The chapter will also explain the salient characteristics of these approaches related to the features and properties of complex and social networks of interest generating massive datasets of diverse types. Finally, throughout the chapter, we highlight the key directions that will be of great potential interest in the future.

1.1.2 Outline

The rest of this chapter is organized as follows. In Section 1.2 the relation between complex networks-big data processes and their emerging challenges are presented, while in Section 1.3 the proposed hyperbolic geometry based approach is introduced and analyzed. Section 1.4 describes how to perform data correlation, and dimensionality reduction over hyperbolic space. In Section 1.5 several types of data embeddings on hyperbolic space, along with their properties especially related to complex networks are studied. In Section 1.6, we examine the navigability of complex networks embedded in hyperbolic space via greedy routing techniques. In Section 1.7 optimization methodologies over large complex and social network graphs using hyperbolic space are described, while applications on advertisement and file allocation problems are pinpointed. In Section 1.8, visualization techniques based on hyperbolic space and their proporties/advantages versus Euclidean based ones are surveyed. Finally, Section 1.9 concludes the chapter.

1.2 BIG DATA AND NETWORK SCIENCE

1.2.1 Complex Networks, Big Data and the Big Data Chain

Diverse types of complex and social networks are nowadays responsible for both massive data generation and transfers. The corresponding research and technological progress has been cumulatively addressed under the *Network Science/Complex Network Analysis (CNA)* domain [6].

It has been observed that several types of networks demonstrate similar, or identical behaviors. For example, modern societies are nowadays characterized as *connected, inter-connected* and *inter-dependent* via various network structures. Communication and social networks have been co-evolving in the last decade into a complex hierarchical system, which asymmetrically expands in time, as shown in Figure 1.1. The interconnecting physical layer expands orders of magnitude faster than the growth rate of the overlaying social one. This leads to the generation of massive quantities of data from both layers, for different purposes, e.g., data transferred in the low layer, control and peer data at the higher, etc., in unprecedented rates compared to the past. This form of "social IoT" (s-IoT) [7] is tightly related to the big data setting, as storage, analysis and inference over gigantic datasets impose stringent resource requirements and are tightly inter-related with the structure and operation of the complex and social networks involved. Various forms of BDA are applied nowadays in diverse disciplines, e.g., banking, retail chains/shopping, healthcare, insurance, public utilities, SNA, etc., where diverse complex networks produce and transfer data.

Computers have revolutionized the whole process chain of data analytics, allowing automation in a supervised manner. Nowadays, such a chain is part of a broader BDA pipeline that includes *collection, correlation, management, search & retrieval* and *visualization* of data and analysis results, in

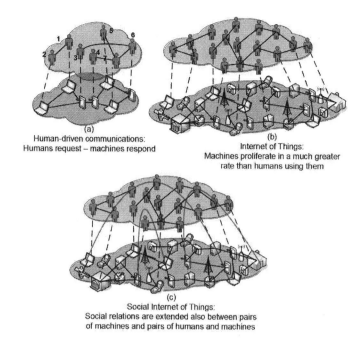

(a)
Human-driven communications:
Humans request – machines respond

(b)
Internet of Things:
Machines proliferate in a much greater
rate than humans using them

(c)
Social Internet of Things:
Social relations are extended also between pairs
of machines and pairs of humans and machines

FIGURE 1.1 Communication (complex) – social network co-evolution.

unprecedented scales compared to the past [2]. More specifically, the BDA pipeline consists of **data generation, acquisition, storage, analysis, visualization** and **interpretation** processes.

Data generation involves creating data from multiple, diverse and distributed sources including sensors, video, click streams, etc. Data acquisition refers to obtaining information and it is subdivided into *data collection, data transmission,* and *data pre-processing.* The first refers to retrieving raw data from real-world objects, the second refers to a transmission process from data sources to appropriate storage systems, while the third one to all those techniques that may be needed prior to the main analysis stage, e.g., *data integration, cleansing, transformation* and *reduction.* Data integration aims at combining data residing in different sources and providing a unified data perspective. Data cleansing refers to determining inaccurate, incomplete, or unreasonable data and amending or removing (transforming) these data to improve data quality. Data reduction aims at decreasing the degree of redundancy of available data, which would in other cases increase data transmission overhead, storage costs, data inconsistency, reliability reduction and data corruption.

Analysis is the main stage of the BDA pipeline and can take multiple forms. The goal is to extract useful values, suggest conclusions and/or support decision-making. It can be descriptive, predictive and prescriptive. It may use data visualization techniques, statistical analysis or data mining techniques in order to fulfill its goals and interpret the results. All the pre-analytics, analytics and post-analytics stages (i.e., visualization and interpretation) of BDA described above can only become more diverse and very informative within the complex and social network ecosystems considered in this chapter. Thus, even though BDA is characterized by the four V's — *Volume* (of data), *Velocity* (generation speed), *Veracity* (quality) and *Variability* (heterogeneity) — the above settings create a new "V" feature for BDA, namely *Value*, rendering them essentially a new and in fact "expensive" commodity for our information societies.

1.2.2 Big Data Challenges and Complex Networks

Several challenges emerge due to the fact that big data carry special characteristics, e.g., heterogeneity, spurious correlations, incidental endogeneities, noise accumulation, etc. [2], which become even more intense within the complex/social network environment. Challenges related to BDA can be distinguished in *challenges related to data*, and *challenges related to processes* of the BDA pipeline. Table 1.1 summarizes these two types of challenges.

Data-related challenges correspond to the four "V's" of BDA with the addition of privacy that relates more to personal data protection. The first two deal with storage and timeliness issues emerging from the explosion of data generated/collected, and the following two with the reliability and heterogeneity of data due to multiple sources and types of data.

Additional challenges emerging with respect to the big data pipeline deal with the data collection and transferring requirements imposed, the preprocessing and analysis of data with respect to the associated complexity, accurate and distributed computation, the accumulated noise, as well as other peripheral issues, such as data and results visualization, interpretation of results and issues related to cloud storage, computing and services in general.

TABLE 1.1   Big Data Challenges

Big Data Challenges	
Data-Related	BDA Pipeline-Related
Volume	Collection Transferring
Velocity	Pre-processing Analysis
Veracity	Complexity Distributed operation
Variety	Accuracy Noise Visualization
Privacy	Cloud computing Interpretation

1.3   BIG DATA ANALYTICS BASED ON HYPERBOLIC SPACE

The aforementioned challenges will require radical approaches for efficiently tackling the emerging problems and keeping up with the anticipated explosion of produced data. In this chapter, we describe a methodology that is capable of addressing holistically the above challenges and provide impetus for more efficient analytics in the future. The framework is conceptually shown in Figures 1.2 and 1.3 and it is mainly based on the properties of hyperbolic metric spaces (a brief summary of which is included in the forthcoming subsection 1.3.1). This approach provides a generic computational substrate for data representation, analysis (e.g., correlation and clustering), inference, visualization, search & navigation, and decision-making (via, e.g., optimization). The proposed framework builds on primitive pre-processing operations of traditional BDA techniques, e.g., statistical learning, and further complements them in terms of analytics and interpretation/visualization to allow more scalable, powerful and efficient inference and decision-making.

Figure 1.2 shows the observed evolution of data volumes until today, where nowadays more than big, i.e., "hyperbolic", data require processing. The proposed framework suggests a lean approach for tackling with such scaling. Input data may take either raw or networked form, where the latter corresponds to correlated data (nodes) and their correlations/relations (links between nodes) drawn from combinations of complex/social networks. Their analysis leads to sophisticated decision-making for challenging problems over large data sets,

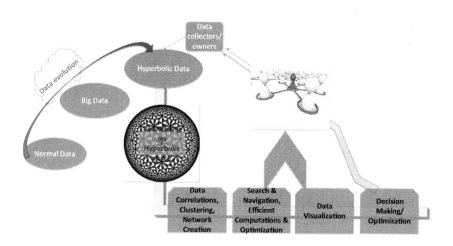

FIGURE 1.2   Evolution of data volume (from data to "hyperbolic" data), proposed framework's functionalities and interaction with complex and social networks.

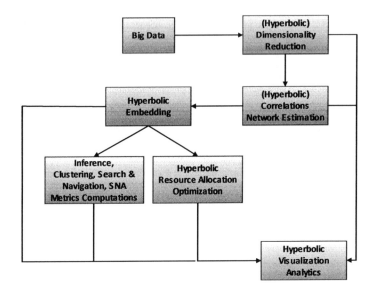

FIGURE 1.3 The workflow of the proposed hyperbolic geometry based approach for BDA over complex and social networks.

e.g., resource allocation and optimization, thus eventually having an impact on the networks themselves, closing the loop of an evolutionary bond between networks (humans, IoT)-data-machines (analytics)(Figure 1.2).

The role of the term "hyperbolic" in the proposed approach is twofold. On one hand, it successfully indicates the passage from "big data" to even more, i.e., "hyperbolic data", denoting the tendency of growth of the available data to be handled and analyzed in the future. On the other hand, it emphasizes the benefit of the use of hyperbolic geometry for BDA. The core of this approach is the fact that, as it is shown in the literature, networks of arbitrarily large size can be embedded in low-dimensional (even as small as two) hyperbolic spaces without sacrificing important information as far as network communication (e.g., routing) and structure (e.g., scale-free properties [50]) are concerned [8], [9], [5]. Thus, hyperbolic spaces are congruent with complex network topologies and are much more appropriate for representing and analyzing big data than Euclidean spaces.

The specific workflow of the proposed framework is shown in Figure 1.3. It starts with obtaining data and determining a suitable data representation model. Input (big) data from complex and social networks might be in raw (e.g., list) form, or in the form of a data network representing their correlations. Pre-processing of data follows, consisting of dimensionality reduction, correlations and generation of networks over data that may be performed either following traditional techniques or using hyperbolic geometry's properties. The data representation after their pre-processing (e.g., network or raw form) will either lead to or determine the appropriate methodology for the following data embedding into the hyperbolic geometric space (subject of Section 1.5). Data embedding is the assignment of coordinates to network nodes in the hyperbolic metric space. Properly visualizing the accumulated and inferred data following the analysis bears significant importance. The proposed framework will leverage on flexible (systolic) hyperbolic geometry based mechanisms for data visualization, in order to allow their holistic and simultaneously focused view and more informed decision-making. This is capable of providing visualization tools that capture simultaneously global patterns and structural information, e.g., hierarchy, node centrality/importance, etc., and local characteristics, e.g., similarities, in an efficient and systolic manner, which hides/reveals detail when this is required by the decision-making in a scalable manner. The latter approach can be very useful in applications and studies of CNA/SNA.

In this chapter, we also describe techniques for extracting useful information from the data under processing and analysis for different application domains. Following and depending on the data embedding, further data correlation/clustering and inference may be attained, in which various forms of (possibly hierarchical) data communities/clusters will be built and missing data (e.g., links) will be predicted from the input data within accuracy and time constraints imposed. Leveraging the hyperbolic distance function and greedy routing techniques, efficient SNA metrics computations (such as centralities, the computation of which becomes hard over large data sets) will be studied and proposed. The proposed framework also allows performing efficient and suitable for large data sets optimization for advertisements' allocation and other — mainly of discrete nature — resources' allocation problems (e.g., file allocation over distributed cache memories in a 5G environment).

In the following, we first present some background on hyperbolic space and then present the proposed framework in more detail. Following, we describe in more detail techniques enabled by the framework for performing and exploiting the analytics over the embedded data.

1.3.1 Fundamentals of Hyperbolic Geometric Space

Non-Euclidean geometries, e.g., hyperbolic geometry [4], emerged by questioning and modifying the fifth (parallel) postulate of Euclidean geometry. According to the latter, *given a line and a point that does not lie on it, there is exactly one line going through the given point that is parallel to the given line.* As far as hyperbolic geometry is concerned, the parallel postulate changes as follows: *Given a line and a point that does not lie on it, there is more than one line going through the given point that is parallel to the given line.*

The n-dimensional hyperbolic space, denoted as $\mathbb{H}^n$, is an n-dimensional Riemannian manifold with negative curvature c which is most often considered constant and equal to $c = -1$. Several models of hyperbolic space exist such as the Poincare disk model, the Poincare half-space model, the Hyperboloid model, the Klein model, etc. These models are isometric,[1] i.e., any two of them can be related by a transformation which preserves all the geometrical properties (e.g., distance) of the space. We will describe in detail and use in our approach the Poincare models (disk and half space) which are mostly used in practical applications.

For instance, the Hyperboloid model realizes the $\mathbb{H}^n$ hyperbolic space as a hyperboloid in $\mathbb{R}^{n+1} = \{(x_0, ..., x_n)|x_i \in \mathbb{R}, i = \{0, 1, ..., n\}\}$ such that $x_0^2 - x_1^2 - ... - x_n^2 = 1, \quad x_0 > 0$. Hyperbolic spaces have a metric function (distance) that differs from the familiar Euclidean distance, while also differs among the diverse models. In the case of the Hyperboloid model, for two points $x = (x_0, ..., x_n)$, $y = (y_0, ..., y_n)$, their hyperbolic distance is given by [4]:

$$\cosh d_H(x, y) = \sqrt{\left(1 + \|x\|^2\right)\left(1 + \|y\|^2\right)} - <x, y>, \qquad (1.1)$$

where $\|\cdot\|$ is the Euclidean norm and $< \cdot, \cdot >$ represents the inner product. The Hyperboloid model can be used to construct the Poincare disk/ball model, where the latter is a perspective projection of the former viewed from ($x_0 = -1, x_1 = 0, \ldots, x_n = 0$), projecting the upper half hyperboloid onto an $\mathbb{R}^n$ unit ball centered at $x_0 = 0$.

Specifically, focusing on the two dimensions, the whole infinite hyperbolic plane can be represented inside the finite unit disk $\mathbb{D} = \{z \in \mid \|z\| < 1\}$ of the Euclidean space, which is the 2-dimensional Poincare disk model. The hyperbolic distance function $d_{PD}(z_i, z_j)$, for two points z_i, z_j, in the Poincare disk model is given by [4], [11]:

$$\cosh d_{PD}(z_i, z_j) = \frac{2\|z_i - z_j\|^2}{(1 - \|z_i\|^2)(1 - \|z_j\|^2)} + 1. \qquad (1.2)$$

The Euclidean circle $\vartheta \mathbb{D} = \{z \in \mid \|z\| = 1\}$ is the boundary at infinity for the Poincare disk model. In addition, in this model, the shortest hyperbolic path between two nodes is either a part of a diameter of $\mathbb{D}$, or a part of a Euclidean circle in $\mathbb{D}$ perpendicular to the boundary $\vartheta \mathbb{D}$, as illustrated in Figure 1.4(a). Note that these shortest path curves differ from the cords that would be implied by the Euclidean metric.

Let us now consider the following map in the two dimensions, $z = \frac{w-i}{1-iw}$, where z, with $\|z\| < 1$, is a point expressed as a complex number on the Poincare disk model and i is the imaginary unit. Then w is a point (complex number) on the Poincare half-space model. This map sends $z = -i$ to $w = 0$, $z = 1$ to $w = 1$ and $z = i$ to $w = \infty$ (note that the extension to more dimensions is trivial).

According to the Poincare half-space model of $\mathbb{H}^n$, every point is represented by a pair (w_0, w) where, $w_0 \in \mathbb{R}^+$ and $w \in \mathbb{R}^{n-1}$. The distance

---

[1]Isometry is a map that preserves distance [10] between metric spaces.

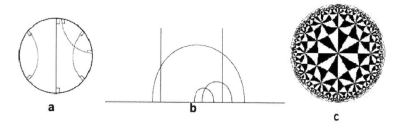

FIGURE 1.4 Poincare disk (a) and half-space (b) models along with their shortest paths in two dimensions: part of a diameter of $\mathbb{D}$ or a part of a Euclidean circle in $\mathbb{D}$ perpendicular to the boundary $\partial\mathbb{D}$ for the disk model and vertical lines and semicircles perpendicular to $\mathbb{R}$ for the half-space model. (c) shows the Voronoi tesselation of the Poincare disk into hyperbolic triangles of equal area.

between two points (w_0^1, w^1), (w_0^2, w^2) on the Poincare half-space model is defined as [12]:

$$\cosh d_{PH}((w_0^1, w^1), (w_0^2, w^2)) = 1 + \frac{(w_0^1 - w_0^2)^2 + \left\|w^1 - w^2\right\|^2}{2w_0^1 w_0^2}. \tag{1.3}$$

Figure 1.4(b) depicts indicative shortest path curves for the Poincare half-space model similarly with the Poincare disk model in Figure 1.4(a).

A remarkable advantage of hyperbolic space, regarding its application in BDA (see Sections 1.5 and 1.8), is its property of "exponential scaling" with respect to the radial coordinate. Specifically, the circumference C and area A of a circle of radius r in the 2-dimensional (2D) Poincare disk model are given by the following relations [46], [4], [8]:

$$C(r) = 2\pi \sinh(r), \quad A(r) = 4\pi \sinh^2(r/2). \tag{1.4}$$

Therefore, for small radius r, e.g., around the center of the Poincare disk, the hyperbolic space looks flat, while for larger r, both the circumference and the area grow exponentially with r. The exponential scaling with radius is illustrated in Figure 1.4(c) which shows a tesselation of the Poincare disk into hyperbolic triangles of equal area. The triangles appear increasingly smaller the closer they are to the circumference in the Euclidean visual representation of the triangulation. In the following, we describe the different components synthesizing the proposed framework, even though several parts can be combined and employed jointly.

1.4 DATA CORRELATIONS AND DIMENSIONALITY REDUCTION IN HYPERBOLIC SPACE

In this section, we describe two basic functionalities of the proposed framework (Figures 1.2 and 1.3). The first deals with inferring correlations among data, yielding network structures representing such relations (nodes-data, correlations-edges). The second deals with a distance-preserving dimensionality reduction approach over the hyperbolic space (i.e. multidimensional scaling [12], [13]) with multiple practical applications, e.g., various efficient computations, efficient data visualization, etc. Each functionality of course can be applied independently.

We assume generic forms of "data items", each of which can be unrolled in a set of features. The set of features will be common for all data items, e.g., customer's parameters such as payment information, demographic information, etc., when customers correspond to data items. Before analytics one needs to apply a method for clustering/reduction of these features to a set of latent features (considered important to fully describe each data item). Examples of such methods include spectral clustering [principal component analysis (PCA)] [14], [15] singular value decomposition (SVD) [14], [15], etc., where each can be appropriately sped up to scale with large datasets, as in [15], [16], [17]. Following, correlations may be inferred via the application of similarity/distance metrics to quantify similarities on various data aspects (e.g., between pairs of data items). A thorough survey of similarity metrics such as cosine, Pearson, etc. is performed in [18]. Another widely accepted approach for computing similarities is the one that identifies distribution functions in the parameters of interest and then exploits an appropriate distribution comparison metric, e.g., Kullback-Leibler divergence [19], [20] for probabilistic distributions. Hyperbolic distance may also serve as a similarity measure, as described in the following. Other ways of clustering and network estimation include [14] partitional algorithms (k-means and its variations, etc.), hierarchical algorithms (agglomerative, divisive), the "lasso" algorithm and its variants that are based on convex optimization [21] producing a graph representation of the data, etc. In the case of the proposed framework, it is beneficial to consider hierarchical clustering of data for allowing efficient visualization using the two- or three-dimensional hyperbolic space (Section 1.8).

Data correlations in hyperbolic space can be achieved via the hyperbolic distance function over the hyperbolic space of a suitable dimension — e.g., equal to the number of important features of users/products — applied on pairs of data items to reveal their hidden dependencies/correlations with respect to their features to a controllable extent. As an example, if having only two latent features describing the data items, we can assign the radial and angular coordinates of the 2D Poincare disk model according to the values of each feature correspondingly. Then, we consider linking two nodes together only if their hyperbolic distance (e.g., Equation (1.2) for the Poincare disk model) is less than a predefined upper bound. By controlling this upper bound, one can control the "neighborhood" of each node and thus the extent to which the correlations among data reach. In other words, important correlations may be considered up to a controllable extent via a threshold value over hyperbolic distance. This is a simple model of data correlation; however, its effectiveness lies in its simplicity and the fact that it can lead to a simultaneous data correlation, analysis and visualization.

After embedding the data pieces/nodes on the k-dimensional Poincare half-space model (k corresponds to the number of latent features), one can apply a dimension reduction distance-preserving technique over the hyperbolic space, such as the one proposed in [13], [12]. Importantly, if choosing the dimension of the final metric space equal to 2 or 3, we will be able to achieve simultaneously a visualization of the data set and its analysis/navigation (Sections 1.6 and 1.8). Particularly, regarding the dimensionality reduction over hyperbolic space, we provide the following two theorems from the literature [12], [22]. Given an n-point subset S of the hyperbolic space, let T be its projection on $\mathbb{R}^{n-1}$ (i.e., the Poincare half-space model, Section 1.3.1). By Johnson-Linderstrauss Lemma [22], there exists an embedding of T, determined by a function f, into the $O\left(\frac{(logn)}{\varepsilon^2}\right)$-dimensional Euclidean space such that for every points x_1, $x_2 \in T$, $\|x_1 - x_2\| \le \|f(x_1) - f(x_2)\| \le (1 + \varepsilon)\|x_1 - x_2\|$, $\varepsilon > 0$.

Theorem 1.1 *(Dimension reduction for $\mathbb{H}^n$)*
Consider the map $g : \mathbb{H}^n \to \mathbb{H}^{O(logn)}$ defined by $g(w_0, w) = (w_0, f(w))$. Then for every two points (w_0^1, w^1), (w_0^2, w^2) at hyperbolic distance Δ, we have:

$$\Delta \le d_{PH}(g(w_0^1, w^1), g(w_0^2, w^2)) \le \left(1 + \frac{3\varepsilon}{1 + \Delta}\right)\Delta. \qquad (1.5)$$

Dimensionality reduction can be performed efficiently via the Fast Johnson-Linderstrauss Transform of Ailon and Chazelle [22], which is a low-distortion embedding of d-dimensional hyperbolic space to $O(\log n)$-dimensional hyperbolic space (n is the number of points to be embedded) based on the preconditioning of a sparse projection matrix with a randomized Fourier transform.

Note that n will be equal to the number of data items, and this will be achieved by assigning the zero value to all dimensions of each data piece after the kth dimension in raw up to the $n - 1$ one.

Theorem 1.2 *(Embedding into the hyperbolic plane (for visualization purposes))*
Assume that the distance between every two points in S is at least $\frac{ln(12n)}{\varepsilon}$, then there exists an embedding of S into the hyperbolic plane $\mathbb{H}^2$ with distance distortion at most $1 + \varepsilon$.

1.4.1 Example

A similar methodology of data correlation over hyperbolic space is applied in [9], where the new nodes added in the network embedding in the hyperbolic space form connections with existing ones. The popularity of the latter and the similarity of the new nodes with the existing ones is taken into account in determining the connections of the new nodes in the embedding. More specifically, newcomers choose existing nodes to connect via optimizing the product of similarity and popularity with them. In [9], the procedure of the simultaneous data embedding/visualization and correlation in hyperbolic space is as follows, starting with an initially empty network.

1. At time $t \geq 1$, a new node t is added to the embedded network and it is assigned the polar coordinates (r_t, θ_t) where the angular coordinate, θ_t, is sampled uniformly at random from $[0, 2\pi]$ and the radial coordinate, r_t, relates to the birth date of node t via the relation $r_t(t) = \ln t$. Every existing node $s < t$ increases its radial coordinate to $r_s(t) = \beta r_s(t) + (1 - \beta)r_t(t)$, $\beta \in [0, 1]$.

2. The new node t connects with a subset of existing nodes $\{s\}$, where $s < t$, $\forall s$. This subset consists of the m nodes with the m smallest values of product $s \cdot \theta_{st}$, where m is a parameter controlling the average node degree (i.e., the extent of the correlations among nodes), and θ_{st} is the angular distance between nodes s and t.

Actually, by following the above steps for a network construction over data, it turns out that new nodes connect simply to their closest m nodes in hyperbolic distance. The hyperbolic distance in the Poincare disk (Equation (1.2)) between two nodes at polar coordinates (r_t, θ_t) and (r_s, θ_s) is approximately equal to $x_{st} = r_s + r_t + \ln(\theta_{st}/2) = \ln(s \cdot t \cdot \theta_{st}/2)$. Therefore, the sets of nodes $\{s\}$ minimizing x_{st} or $s \cdot \theta_{st}$ for each newcomer t are identical. At the second step above, in order to reduce network clustering [23], the newcomer node t instead of connecting with its m closest nodes may select randomly a node $s < t$ and form a connection with s with probability equal to $p(x_{st}) = \frac{1}{[1+e^{(x_{st}-R_t)/T}]}$, where T is a temperature parameter and R_t is a threshold value. This step is repeated until m nodes are selected to connect to node t.

Here, the radial coordinate abstracts the popularity of a node. The smaller the radial coordinate of a node (the closer the node in the center of the Poincare disk) the more popular it is, thus the more likely it is for it to attract new connections (we will elaborate more on this fact in Section 1.5, see also the hyperbolic distance functions in Section 1.3.1). The increase of the radial coordinate expresses any attenuation of nodes' popularity with time, which is equal to zero when $\beta = 1$. Note that, in complex networks the time presence of a node in the network is strongly related to its popularity. Specifically, the scale-free structure of complex networks is mainly due to the preferential attachment of newcomers, as the network grows, to existing nodes with high degree. Thus, nodes of high degree continue to increase their connectivity, and these nodes are with higher probability older nodes assuming that initially all nodes have the same degree. Therefore, in the above mapping of nodes to hyperbolic coordinates, the similarity characteristic is mapped to the angular coordinate (here assigned randomly), while the popularity characteristic is mapped to the radial coordinate and hyperbolic distance is used to predict/infer connections between pairs of nodes based on their characteristics. As a result, hyperbolic distance serves as a convenient single-metric representation of a combination of popularity (radial) and similarity (angular).

1.5 EMBEDDING OF NETWORKED DATA IN HYPERBOLIC SPACE AND APPLICATIONS

In this section, in order to perform data embedding, it is assumed that data items are already available in network form. Thus, the focus shifts on obtaining different embeddings into latent hyperbolic coordinates in conjunction with several applications over complex large-scale networks, such as graph theoretic and SNA metrics' computation (e.g., centrality metrics), missing links' prediction, etc. Two types of embedding in the low-dimensional hyperbolic space are presented. In the first (Subsection 1.5.1), the latent node coordinates in hyperbolic space are determined so that the hyperbolic distances between node pairs are approximately equal to their graph distances initial network. Towards this objective, multidimensional scaling (MDS) is applied [24]. Given n the number of network nodes (data items), MDS has a running time of $O(n^3)$ and requires space $O(n^2)$ (distance matrix between all node pairs). Since the complexity of MDS is extremely high for large-scale networks, landmark-based MDS has been introduced [24], based on the graph and hyperbolic space distances among k chosen landmarks and the rest of nodes. With landmark-based MDS, the running time reduces to $O(kn)$ and the space to $O(dkn + k^3)$, where d is the dimension of the hyperbolic space and it should also hold $d < k << n$. By considering d, k as small constants, landmark-based MDS has a linear running time complexity. The second type of embedding (Subsection 1.5.2), applies statistical learning methods to embed a complex network graph in hyperbolic space by constructing a new network graph trying to mimic with high probability the initial graph structure [5]. Contrary to the first approach the node pairs' hyperbolic distances may differ significantly from their initial graph distances. The statistical learning techniques applied are based on maximum likelihood estimation for the node coordinates' inference, while global (i.e., for the whole network) and local (i.e., for every node) likelihood functions are defined and maximized, where local likelihood functions serve to approximate the global ones for complexity reductions.

1.5.1 Rigel Embedding in the Hyperboloid Model

Several complex and social network analysis problems such as computation of node centralities, community detection, etc., are based on node distances which appear hard to compute within large-scale graphs such as online social networks with millions of nodes. However, for marketing purposes, such computations become necessary or even critical for companies, e.g., to locate the more influential/central node for achieving efficient marketing. Therefore, several works in literature [24], [12] have attempted to propose algorithms for network embeddings (e.g., in Euclidean or hyperbolic space) so that the inferred coordinates can be used for approximating node distances in the initial graph. We will focus on large-scale network embedding in hyperbolic space and specifically on the Rigel embedding proposed in [24], which achieves low distortion (of distance) error and answers to queries for node distances and shortest paths in microseconds even for up to 43 million nodes compared to the order of seconds of a traditional breadth-first-search (BFS) algorithm. Importantly, Rigel allows for parallelization in computations which is a great advantage in the field of BDA. Experimental results in [25], [8], focused on embedding Internet distances in hyperbolic space, have shown less distortion with respect to the node distances in the initial graph, compared with other embeddings in Euclidean coordinates. This fact is also verified in [26] via empirical computation of distortion metrics for diverse coordinate systems where it is shown that hyperbolic space achieves significantly more accurate results than Euclidean and spherical ones.

Let us assume that the network consists of N nodes. Rigel employs the Hyperboloid model of hyperbolic space with distance function given by Equation (1.1). Rigel applies landmark-based MDS, where $L << N$ nodes are chosen as landmarks in the network graph. Landmarks may be chosen as high-degree nodes, if the given network is scale-free, otherwise they can be chosen randomly. First, the hyperbolic coordinates of the landmarks are computed with the aid of a global optimization algorithm aiming to achieve that the distances between the landmarks in the Hyperboloid are as close as possible to their matching path distances in the graph. This is the bootstrapping step of Rigel. Then, the hyperbolic coordinates of the rest of the nodes are calibrated, so that each node's distances to all landmarks in the Hyperboloid are very close to the corresponding actual path distances in the network graph. Note that the authors of [24] studied the accuracy of Rigel with respect to the dimensions of the hyperbolic space and showed that the former increases with the increase of the latter. However, the number of landmarks should be higher than the dimension of the embedding space, thus leading to a trade-off between accuracy and complexity [24].

Importantly for large-scale network graphs, a parallel version of Rigel is proposed in [24], offering great improvement in the complexity of Rigel, the latter increasing linearly with the network size. Both steps of Rigel (bootstrapping and embedding in the Hyperboloid model) can be parallelized in a number of servers at most equal to the number of landmarks. One or more landmarks are assigned to each server and the rest of the nodes are distributed in a balanced way across servers. It is shown that parallel Rigel performs similarly with respect to accuracy as Rigel.

Concerning the effectiveness and efficiency of Rigel in computing SNA [27] and graph analysis metrics, experiments and comparisons with existing schemes are performed in [24]. Regarding the graph analysis metrics of radius, diameter and average path length, which are applied in identifying the small-world property of a network [6], [51], Rigel resulted in values extremely close to the ground truth. Note that distances in Rigel are given by Equation (1.1). Rigel's performance in computing node centralities that constitute an important SNA metric for industries is also examined in [24]. Closeness centrality [27] is considered, according to which the most central node is the one that has the lowest average distance to all other nodes in the network. Rigel achieved a high accuracy in identifying the node ranking with respect to closeness centrality and outperforms existing schemes.

1.5.2 HyperMap Embedding

This section uses statistical learning methods to embed a social graph in hyperbolic coordinates, focusing on the HyperMap embedding algorithm introduced in [5]. HyperMap leverages the emerging relation between complex network topologies and hyperbolic geometry [8]. Due to their scale-free property, complex networks exhibit hierarchical, i.e., tree-like structure [28], while hyperbolic geometry is the geometry of trees. More specifically, the similarity between an infinite tree graph and the hyperbolic space provides an intuition about the hidden hyperbolic structure of complex networks. The exponential scaling of a circle and an area of a disk in hyperbolic space (explained in Section 1.3.1) coincides with the scaling of the number of nodes with respect to their distance from the root of the tree in an "e-ary" tree [8]. To make this clearer, let us examine a b-ary tree which is a tree with branch factor equal to b. The number of nodes located at distance exactly R from the root of the tree is $(b+1)b^{(R-1)} \sim b^R$ and the number of nodes being at distance at most R from the root of the tree is $\frac{(b+1)b^R - 2}{(b-1)} \sim b^R$. As a result, hyperbolic space can be seen as a continuous version of a tree, a fact realized as the exponential expansion property of the hyperbolic space. Scale-free complex networks are characterized by heterogeneity regarding the node degree, where the majority of nodes is assigned low node degree (power-law degree distribution), implying a tree-like network organization indicating the existence of a hidden hyperbolic metric space [28].

The example of the simultaneous embedding and creation of a growing random network provided in Subsection 1.4.1 leads to the formation of network graphs with the following two characteristics: (i) they appear to be highly clustered [23] since the links added between close nodes in hyperbolic distance lead to the formation of a large number of triangles and (ii) they have power-law degree distribution, i.e., two basic properties of complex networks' structure. These statements further support the existence of an underlying hidden hyperbolic space in complex networks' structure. On one hand, a random network created over hyperbolic space as in Subsection 1.4.1 emerges to be scale-free while on the other hand, a scale-free network is proven to have negative curvature [8] (similarly to hyperbolic metric spaces).

Based on these studies and observations, HyperMap aims at embedding a given complex (social) network in hyperbolic space in a way that is congruent with the embedding of an extended version of the model of Subsection 1.4.1. The extension lies basically in providing the possibility to add links between existing nodes, while in Subsection 1.4.1 new links can be added only between a newcomer and an existing node. Precisely, HyperMap finds nodes' angular and radial coordinates such that the probability that the given complex network is produced by this extended model of Subsection 1.4.1 is maximized.

HyperMap assigns hyperbolic coordinates to the nodes inside the Poincare disk by maximizing approximately but in an efficient manner a globally defined likelihood function over the node pairs' hyperbolic distances (which are functions of nodes' hyperbolic coordinates) expressed considering the given complex network's links. Specifically, in order to mimic the network creation/hyperbolic embedding of Subsection 1.4.1, it first performs a maximum likelihood estimation of the appearance (i.e., birth) times of the given network's nodes (let t denote their number). Then, after estimating the time sequence of nodes' arrivals, it replays the hyperbolic growth of the network roughly similarly to the steps of the model of Subsection 1.4.1. The difference lies in the computation of the angular coordinates where HyperMap computes the angular coordinate θ_i of node i, i.e., with sequence number i, via maximizing a local likelihood function defined for node i equivalently to maximizing the aforementioned global likelihood function with respect to θ_i. Specifically, the HyperMap embedding algorithm receives as basic input the adjacency matrix of the given complex network and performs the following steps:

1. It sorts nodes in decreasing order with respect to their degree in the given complex network, where node 1 corresponds to the one with the highest node degree. Node 1 receives $r_1 = 0$ and a random angular coordinate $\theta_1 \in [0, 2\pi]$ (i.e., it is placed on the center of the Poincare disk model).

2. For $i = 1$ to t do

   (a) Node i arrives (is born) and is assigned the radial coordinate $r_i = \frac{2}{\zeta} \ln i$, where $\zeta = |c|$ (Subsection 1.3.1) is the constant absolute curvature value of the hyperbolic space provided as input to HyperMap. Usually, $\zeta = 1$. Every existing node $s < i$ increases its radial coordinate to $r_s(t) = \beta r_s(t) + (1 - \beta)r_i(t)$, $\beta \in [0, 1]$, where β is provided as input to HyperMap.

   (b) The angular coordinate θ_i is computed via maximizing a local likelihood function defined for node i.

HyperMap embedding also provides the possibility to predict missing links of the given complex network, efficiently and with high accuracy. Link prediction is a very important process on the study of large-scale networks since topology measurements for inferring their structure may miss part of the links. In HyperMap, prediction is based on the aforementioned possibility of internal link addition, i.e., between pairs of existing nodes. Specifically, two (non-neighboring) existing nodes k, l are connected at time t (i.e., prediction of a missing link in the initial complex network) with probability equal to $p(x_{kl}) = \frac{1}{[1+e^{\zeta(x_{kl}-R_t)/2T}]}$. HyperMap's performance to predict missing links is evaluated according to diverse indices and shown to be very satisfactory, while it outperforms several well-known classical link prediction methods such as Common-Neighbors, Katz Index, Hierarchical Random Graph Model, Degree-Product, Inverse Shortest Path, etc. [5].

1.6 GREEDY ROUTING OVER HYPERBOLIC COORDINATES AND APPLICATIONS WITHIN COMPLEX AND SOCIAL NETWORKS

This section mostly concerns the navigability of networks embedded in hyperbolic space [28]. A network embedded in a geometric space is navigable, if one can perform efficient greedy routing on the network using the node coordinates in the underlying geometric space [5].

After embedding the network graph (or the correlated data) in the hyperbolic geometric space, greedy routing over hyperbolic coordinates can be used to navigate or route messages from source to destination. Specifically, each node forwards the message to its neighbor closer in hyperbolic distance to the destination. As a result, greedy routing uses only local information, i.e., each node's necessary knowledge is limited to the hyperbolic coordinates of its neighbors and the destination. Due to this fact, greedy routing can be adapted and applied for performing efficient search and navigation in large data sets [24], [26], [29], while we foresee its applications in SNA metrics' computation and in recommender systems [30]. A disadvantage of greedy routing lies in the case of failure to deliver a message to the destination when a node does not have a neighbor closer to the destination than itself (local minima of distance). In this case, the message gets blocked in the specific node [11] with no further forwarding via greedy routing.

With respect to networks with hidden hyperbolic structure (i.e., scale-free complex networks), greedy routing based on hyperbolic coordinates/distances achieves a very high success rate (close to 100%), as it is shown through experimental examination in literature. Also, in this case the paths obtained via greedy routing are very close to the global shortest paths between the corresponding node pairs. Specifically, in [8], [9], the performance of greedy routing is studied over the synthetic networks constructed similarly to the example of Subsection 1.4.1 (in a way congruent to the exponential expansion of hyperbolic space) and it is shown to achieve success rate close to 100% and stretch with respect to the shortest paths close to 1. This is a very important property showing the small-world navigability of this particular category of networks [31]. The success of greedy routing over hyperbolic space is strongly tied with the fact that hyperbolic space has a tightly connected core, where all paths between nodes pass through. This is the reason why shortest paths in hyperbolic space can be found efficiently and with high accuracy [8]. In [5], the performance of greedy routing in the AS Internet graph is examined when using the HyperMap inferred hyperbolic coordinates (Section 1.5). Note that the AS Internet graph exhibits a scale-free structure [6], [23]. Due to the congruency between the scale-free network topology and hyperbolic geometry, the success of greedy routing over hyperbolic coordinates is much improved compared to the case when the real coordinates are used, while the length of the paths paved by greedy routing is roughly the same with one of the shortest paths. HyperMap actually estimates the node coordinates that best fit a given network.

"Greedy embeddings" in other than Euclidean metric spaces [11], [49] have been proposed to optimize greedy routing techniques. In the case of a greedy embedding of any network (not only scale-free) in hyperbolic space, the success rate of greedy routing becomes exactly 100%. In [11], a distributed implementation of a greedy embedding in two-dimensional hyperbolic space is proposed, which also can be applied in dynamic network conditions, by assigning hyperbolic coordinates to new nodes without re-embedding the whole network. The greedy embedding is constructed by choosing a spanning tree of the graph of the initial network and then embedding the spanning tree into the hyperbolic space according to the algorithm of [11]. Following this algorithm, after having assigned hyperbolic coordinates to the root of the tree inside a specific area of the Poincare disk model, each node computes its own coordinates using the ones of its parent, in such a way that the hyperbolic bisector of the embedded spanning tree edge between the node and its parent does not intersect any other embedded edge of the spanning tree. The greedy embedding of a spanning tree of a graph implies the greedy embedding of the whole graph. Importantly, it is proven that every graph has a greedy embedding in two-dimensional hyperbolic space [49]. For all these reasons, hyperbolic geometry dominates over the Euclidean one for performing greedy routing. Note that a greedy embedding basically ensures the existence of at least one greedy path between each source-destination pair, thus 100% success of greedy routing. Greedy embeddings have been applied successfully in communications networks, e.g., [11], [32], [33], however, in the case of large scale networks their implementation may impose challenges due to the need of a spanning tree of the whole graph, thus opening new research directions in BDA. The average length of the paths paved by greedy routing is a crucial performance factor to evaluate. In the case of greedy hyperbolic embedding, different choices of spanning tree and the root of the spanning tree (e.g., shortest path spanning tree rooted at the node with highest degree, or spanning tree derived via a random walk) will lead to different routing paths and path lengths between pairs of sources and destinations [34].

Greedy routing can become node-degree aware by exploiting the node degree metric available in network graphs [26]. This enhancement may improve its performance, since apart from the reason that high degree nodes are "more connected" to other nodes, they also tend to be embedded nearer to the core of the network (e.g., center of the Poincare disk) than the lower degree nodes. Other enhancements of greedy routing (e.g., Gravity-Pressure Greedy Forwarding [11]) have been also proposed to enhance its performance for dynamic network conditions, e.g., random node arrivals and departures [11]. Based on all the advantages of greedy routing techniques over hyperbolic coordinates, we envision their suitability and efficiency for the computation of SNA metrics that demand knowledge of paths between node pairs, e.g., betweenness centrality [27] often used for defining most influential nodes for information propagation purposes.

1.7 OPTIMIZATION TECHNIQUES OVER HYPERBOLIC SPACE FOR DECISION-MAKING IN BIG DATA

1.7.1 The Case of Advertisement Allocation over Online Social Networks

Analysis of big data leads to problems of large-scale optimization. Since optimization involving large data sets is not only expensive but suffers from slow numerical rates of convergence, new approaches are required. Throughout this subsection, we will describe and study the advertisement (ad) allocation problem and how it can be significantly simplified computationally leveraging hyperbolic space's properties for large-scale networks, following the approach of [35]. A common advertising mechanism used by, e.g., an online social network (OSN) platform for the distribution of advertisements over its users is of auction-style where the advertisers place bids on users' impressions (e.g., clicks) based on their budget constraints, while the platform's owner seeks to maximize its revenue. In an OSN, users' impressions are not *ad hoc* since users get influenced by their acquaintances and, therefore, the social influence should be taken into consideration in the optimization. This is due to the fact that a user's engagement may influence other users depending on the influence strength of the former. According to [35], a fairness constraint should be added in the optimization problem so that "a similar users' influence distribution becomes assigned to each advertiser".

Initially, we review the conventional way to formulate an advertisement allocation problem over an OSN, which is the following (Equations (1.6)-(1.9)) Integer Programming (IP) problem.

$$\max_{S,I} \sum_{j=1}^{|A|} p_j \sum_{u_i \in S_j} I_{i,j} g(u_i) \text{ subject to:} \tag{1.6}$$

$$p_j \sum_{u_i \in S_j} I_{i,j} g(u_i) \leq b_j, \ \forall a_j \in A \text{ (budget constraint)} \tag{1.7}$$

$$\sum_{j:u_i \in S_j} I_{i,j} \leq I_i, \ \forall u_i \in V \text{ (impression constraint)} \tag{1.8}$$

$$I_{i,j} \in \mathbb{N}, (S, I) \in R_D \text{ (domain constraint)} \tag{1.9}$$

where a_j is an advertisement (corresponding to an advertiser), A is the set of all advertisements, p_j the bid of the advertiser j which is considered homogeneous over all users, u_i is a user of the OSN (node of the network) with maximum number of impressions assigned to all advertisers ($\sum_{j:u_i \in S_j} I_{i,j}$) equal to I_i and social influence given by $g(u_i)$. R_D is a feasible set expressing domain constraints, e.g., fairness or priority constraints among advertisers. Furthermore, S, I are the optimization variables where $S = \{S_1, S_2, ..., S_{|A|}\}$ is the allocation strategy, i.e., the set of users assigned to each advertiser and $I = \{I_{i,j} | u_i \in S_i, a_j \in A\}$ is the users' impressions allocation strategy, i.e., the number of impressions of a user assigned to each advertiser where $I_{i,j} = 0$ if $u_i \notin S_j$. Also, V stands for the set of users. Note that the total number of impressions of a user is upper bounded due to the limited time that a user spends on OSNs daily.

The IP problem formulation has two significant disadvantages. Firstly, the decision variable I has an order of $|A| \cdot |V|$, implying an extreme increase in dimensionality for the modern OSNs consisting of billions of users. Secondly, the domain constraints mentioned above are hard to express in such an IP formulation setting. The most common and important domain constraint (R_D) is the fairness one as it constitutes a requirement and business model of most OSN platforms. Except fairness, several other kinds of domain constraints are described and handled in [35], such as the priority model and the hybrid model that combines fairness with priority. In this chapter, we will focus only on the fairness constraint, as it is very representative on indicating the computational efficiency when utilizing the properties of hyperbolic space in the ad allocation problem for large-scale OSNs.

In [35], an alternative problem formulation of the advertisement allocation problem is proposed based on the mapping of the OSN in hyperbolic space (performed as in Sections 1.4 and 1.5). Following the new methodology the disadvantages of the IP problem formulation are tackled in a significant degree as (i) the discrete nature of the advertisement allocation problem (due to I, S) becomes continuous leveraging region-wise integrals on the continuous hyperbolic geometric space, allowing for dimensionality reduction reaching a final one of order $O(|A|)$, (ii) in many cases the domain constraints can be efficiently represented and visualized. For the latter and considering the fairness domain constraints, note that two fan (or pie) shapes on the Poincare disk indicate the same distribution of user influence due to the properties of a complex network's (e.g., OSN) mapping in hyperbolic space (Section 1.5) that will be also pinpointed below.

For the network mapping in hyperbolic space, the HyperMap scheme (Section 1.5) is used. The mapping exhibits the important properties of OSNs, such as the power-law degree distribution (scale-free property), the community structure, and the efficient network navigability via greedy routing using local information (related to small-world phenomenon, Section 1.6). One important aspect is that after the mapping of the network on the Poincare disk, the expected node degree, $p_d(r)$, depends on the radial coordinate and is given by $p_d(r) \propto e^{-\frac{r}{2}}$, while the node density is expressed as $p_n(r) \propto e^r$. This means that every circle on the Poincare disk has uniform node density, while the node degree-node density is exponentially distributed along the radius. This exponential dependence of node degree and node density on the radius can be exploited for capturing the users' influence factor discussed above, while the continuity of the hyperbolic space can be leveraged for approximating the sum over users of the advertisement allocation problem with integrals over certain areas where users are mapped to. In this case, the advertisement allocation problem seeks an optimal allocation strategy that assigns to each advertiser a region of population and a maximum revenue is achieved.

Considering all the above, the advertisement allocation problem, after the mapping of the OSN in hyperbolic space, becomes:

$$\max_{S,I} \sum_{j=1}^{|A|} p_j f_j(S, I) \text{ (volume assignment) subject to:} \tag{1.10}$$

$$p_j f_j(S, I) \leq b_j, \ \forall j \in \{1, ..., |A|\} \text{ (budget constraint)} \tag{1.11}$$

$$\sum_{j=1}^{|A|} \sigma_i(S_j, I) \leq I_i, \ \forall u_i \in V \text{ (impression constraint)} \tag{1.12}$$

$$I_{i,j} \in \mathbb{N}^+, \ \forall u_i \in S_j : a_j \in A \tag{1.13}$$

$$S \in R_D \text{ (domain constraint)} \tag{1.14}$$

where $f_j(S, I)$ is a function of the impressions assigned to the advertisement a_j, $\sigma_i(S_j, I)$ is the amount of the impressions of user u_i that become assigned on advertisement a_j. According to this meta-formulation, an allocation strategy or a shape design is given for S (e.g., fan-shape for the fairness model, ring-shape for the priority model [35]) which also determines the $f_j(S, I)$ function. The dependence of the f_j, σ_i functions on I is due to the multiple impressions that a user has and may assign to different advertisers. Therefore, the areas assigned to different advertisers over the hyperbolic space may be overlapping complicating the optimization problem (Equations (1.10)–(1.14)). However in [35], this issue is resolved via a methodology denoted as Unit Impression Decomposition that leads to a multi-stage optimization problem with unit impressions (and nonoverlapping areas among advertisers) at each stage. For simplicity, suppose that $I_i = 1, \forall \ u_i \in V$. Thus, f_j, σ_i depend only on S. In the following, we will study the case of the fan-shape allocation strategy that expresses fairness with respect to social influence in users' allocation among advertisers. Then, the allocation area S_j for the advertiser j has a fan-shape or pie-shape of angle θ_j in the Poincare disk (as shown in Figure 1.5). Then, $f_j(S_j)$ is computed as follows:

$$f_j(S_j) = f_j(\theta_j) = a \int_0^R e^\tau \int_0^{\theta_j} (1 + w \cdot \delta(\tau)) dl d\tau = q \cdot \theta_j, \tag{1.15}$$

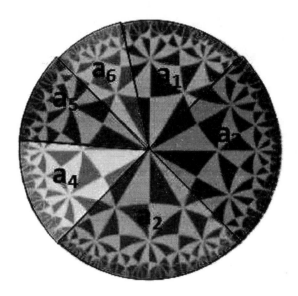

FIGURE 1.5 An example of an OSN's users' allocation to six advertisers considering fairness with respect to the social influence (node degree). Each advertiser is assigned a pie-shaped area over the Poincare disk, on which the users' OSN is embedded.

where $R < 1$ the radius of the disk inside the Poincare disk where the embedded OSN network lies in and q a constant appropriately determined after tedious computations. Also, the quantity $a(1 + w \cdot \delta(\tau))$ of the integral represents the profit that each node lying on radius τ attributes to its assigned advertiser where w, a constants and $\delta(\tau)$ the node degree, where $\delta(\tau) = g \cdot e^{\frac{\tau}{2}}$, g a constant. Thus, the advertisement allocation problem (for one stage in case of non-unit users' impressions) with fairness domain constraints attains a linear programming (LP) form as follows:

$$\max_{\Theta} \sum_{j=1}^{|A|} p_j q \theta_j \text{ subject to:} \tag{1.16}$$

$$p_j \cdot q \cdot \theta_j \leq b_j, \ \forall j \in \{1, ..., |A|\} \tag{1.17}$$

$$\theta_j \geq 0, \ \forall j \in \{1, ..., |A|\} \tag{1.18}$$

$$\sum_{j=1}^{|A|} \theta_j \leq 2\pi \tag{1.19}$$

In this problem formulation (Equations (1.16)–(1.19)), the optimization variable is $\Theta = \{\theta_1, ...\theta_{|A|}\} \in [0, 2\pi]^{|A|}$, which has only $|A|$ dimensions, a significant reduction to the $|A| \times |V|$ dimensions of the conventional problem formulation (note that $|V|$ is potentially in the order of billions). Each advertiser a_j is assigned a sector of angle θ_j in the Poincare disk. Note that the variable S is not needed anymore in the problem formulation. Also, it is a convex problem that can be solved efficiently [35]. Two more observations that further support the efficiency of the last problem formulation are the following. Since the regions can be arranged very tightly close to each other, all the users' impressions will be utilized as long as the demand (budget of advertisers) is more or equal to the supply (users' impressions). Also, due to this fact all the stages of the unit impression decomposition (in the case of non-unit users' impressions) can be performed in parallel to reduce the computation time [35] which is a very important advantage of this approach for big data analysis and computations.

1.7.2 The Case of File Allocation Optimization in Wireless Cellular Networks

In modern wireless cellular networks the shift from the reactive to proactive networking paradigm is a common trend [36]. The need for a smarter network that incorporates proactive mechanisms is driven by the increasing mobile data traffic [37]. One type of mechanism for proactive network operation which has already been proposed in the literature [36, 38] is the file/content caching at the edge of the network, i.e., at the evolved NodeBs (eNBs), small cell base stations (Home eNBs) or at the user equipment (UE) devices. Pushing content at the edge of the network alleviates the network from redundant data traffic and serves users requests at lower transmission delays.

In this subsection, we focus on the problem of optimal file placement in different cache memories lying at various components of a mobile cellular network. This problem can be cast in a form similar to the problem of Subsection 1.7.1 for achieving efficiency, since it bears similar social and complex characteristics, as well as a similarly large-scale nature, as will be explained in the following. The size and especially the number of the available files becomes extremely large and the number of the connected devices is increasing [39]. In this subsection, we describe a formulation of an optimization problem for distributing files having a complex networked structure over a large number of heterogeneous caches in a fair way, targeting at reducing the system delay of file downloading. Fairness is meant in terms of the popularity of each file, e.g., a particular cache should not monopolize all popular files. For example, consider the WWW graph [23], where an edge represents a link from a webpage to another. Therefore, high (in-) degree [6] of a page implies high popularity, since this webpage is pointed by many others, thus it is more likely to be visited, i.e., requested. In this context, the following file placement optimization problem is formulated (Equations (1.20)–(1.24)), aiming to determine in an optimal way the allocation of files in cache memories.

$$\max_{I,S} \sum_{f_i \in F, j \in M} \frac{l_i}{c_j} \cdot I_{i,j} \cdot g(f_i) \text{ subject to} \tag{1.20}$$

$$\sum_{j=1}^{|M|} I_{i,j} \leq I_i, \forall i = 1, 2, ..., |F| \tag{1.21}$$

$$\frac{1}{c_j} \sum_{i=1}^{|F|} l_i \cdot I_{i,j} \cdot g(f_i) \leq s_j, \forall j = 1, 2, ..., |M| \tag{1.22}$$

$$I_{i,j} \in \{0,1\}, \ \forall i = 1, 2, ..., |F|, \ \forall j = 1, 2, ..., |M| \tag{1.23}$$

$$(S, I) \in R_D \ \text{(domain constraint)} \tag{1.24}$$

where c_j is the capacity of the transmission link between the memory cache j and the provider of the file f_i, l_i is the size of the file f_i, M is the set of the memory caches, F is the set of files, $I_{i,j}$ is the indicator variable of the placement of a file f_i in memory cache j and $g(f_i)$ is a social influence factor associated to file f_i. $I_{i,j}$ is either 1 if the file f_i is placed in memory cache j or 0 otherwise, while I_i stands for the maximum number of caches into which the file f_i can be stored and s_j relates to the capacity of cache j. Finally, $S = \{S_1, S_2, ..., S_{|M|}\}$ is the allocation strategy, i.e., the set of files assigned to each cache memory.

The placement of a file f_i at the memory cache j has a certain benefit for the network in terms of the average system delay improvement. Each placement of a file to a cache memory offloads the network from the time needed to download a file from the file/content provider. This benefit can be on average quantified by the term $\frac{l_i}{c_j}$. Thus, the above file allocation problem maximizes the total benefit in terms of the system delay improvement from the placement of certain files in the available cache memories. This problem is of integer programming form, thus being NP-hard, while also attaining large-scale characteristics, as mentioned before. Thus, alternative approaches need to be taken into account in order to tackle efficiently the large scale and discrete nature of this problem. It can be observed by the following mapping table (Table 1.2) that the file placement problem in memory caches is of a similar nature to the problem of advertisement allocation, presented in the previous section (Subsection 1.7.1). Following the arguments and analysis of

TABLE 1.2   Mapping of the file allocation problem to the advertisement allocation problem.

Advertisement allocation in users	File allocation in caches
Advertisement (A)	Cache Memory (M)
Users $(u_i,\ V)$	Files $(f_i,\ F)$
Price Bid (p_j)	The inverse of the capacity of the link between cache and the file provider $(1/c_j)$
Social factor $g(u_i)$	Social factor $g(f_i)$
Ad budget constraint (b_j)	Storage capacity constraint of the cache memory (s_j)

Subsection 1.7.1, the files' network graph can be embedded in the hyperbolic space. After this mapping the file allocation problem takes the following form:

$$\max_{I} \sum_{j \in M} \frac{1}{c_j} \cdot f_j(S, I) \ \text{(volume assignment) subject to} \tag{1.25}$$

$$\frac{1}{c_j} \cdot f_j(S, I) \leq s_j, \forall j = 1, 2, ..., |M| \ \ \text{(storage constraint)} \tag{1.26}$$

$$\sum_{j=1}^{|M|} \sigma_i(S_j, I) \leq I_i, \forall i = 1, 2, ..., |F| \tag{1.27}$$

$$I_{i,j} \in \{0, 1\}, \ \forall i = 1, 2, ..., |F|, \ \forall j = 1, 2, ..., |M| \tag{1.28}$$

$$(S, I) \in R_D \ \text{(domain constraint)} \tag{1.29}$$

where $f_j(S, I)$ is a function of the number (or size) of files and their social influence that are assigned to the memory cache j. Following the lines of Section 1.7.1, this formulation leads to a significant reduction of the dimensionality from $O(|M||F|)$ to $O(|M|)$, and provides the flexibility of applying the desired fairness policy with respect to the social characteristics of the available files.

1.8   VISUALIZATION ANALYTICS IN HYPERBOLIC SPACE

Visual analytics consists of analytical reasoning facilitated by the visual interface, integrating the analytic capabilities of the computer and the abilities of the human analyst. The visual analytics approach relies on interactive and integrated visualizations for exploratory data analysis in order to identify unexpected trends, outliers or patterns. By putting a human back into the loop to guide the analysis, interactive data visualizations have an important role to play, e.g., as in [41].

Large datasets challenge the ability to visualize, navigate and understand relationships among data. In general, displaying large collections of data (rolled out in many dimensions) within a limited display area requires caution to avoid missing the necessary details. Especially when data analytics yield graphs of nodes (data points) and edges (relations among data points), properly depicting such inter-relations is crucial for facilitating better analysis. Displays of large graphs (typically derived in BDA) in Euclidean spaces may not utilize efficiently the available space and impose limitations on the order of the graph that can be handled. Contrary to that, hyperbolic space offers significant advantages in this direction by allowing the display of an arbitrarily large structure within a bounded, finite space (e.g., Poincare disk model), simultaneously providing the possibility of changing the focus to specific areas, while retaining the whole picture of the data structure.

Hyperbolic-based visualization may significantly assist data analysis and corresponding decision making via a holistic rather than a focused view on the data structure and correlations. For example, it is possible to identify important/influential nodes, thus avoiding or reducing a significant amount of computations over large data sets, e.g., shortest paths for identifying node centralities (SNA metrics). The advantages of hyperbolic space with respect to data visualization and BDA can be summarized as follows:

i. The hyperbolic space grows exponentially with its radius around each point. This property is ideal for embedding hierarchical data represented as tree graphs, and consequently scale-free graphs often emerging in social network analysis and BDA (see Subsection 1.5).

ii. The Poincare disk model of hyperbolic space exhibits a fish-eye property of dynamic focus, allowing real-time interactive navigation, e.g., via the mouse.

There are many visualization techniques that utilize hyperbolic space embedding. Most of them focus on hierarchical or tree-like graph embedding. Generally, depending on the data representation, different techniques can be applied, as described in the following.

1.8.1 Adaptive Focus in Hyperbolic Space

The visualization of large datasets in general suffers from a difficulty to show both focus and global context. Adjusting the focus is an important advantage of using hyperbolic space for data visualization. In order to change the focus point in the Poincare disk, a translation operation can be applied that corresponds to a user's mouse click and drag events. This translation is denoted as Mobius transformation, symbolized by $T(z)$, where z is a point in complex conjugates in the Poincare disk. In this case, the isometric Mobius transformation for a point z can be written as [46]:

$$z' = T(z; c, b) = \frac{bz + c}{\bar{c}bz + 1}, |b| = 1, |c| < 1. \qquad (1.30)$$

The complex number b describes a pure rotation of the Poincare disk around the origin 0. The translation by c maps the origin to c, and c becomes the new center 0 (if $b = 1$). In Figure 1.4 (c), the triangles mapped in the center of the Poincare disk can be seen in detail, a fact that does not hold for the triangles mapped close to the periphery, although all triangles are of equal size. Applying such Mobius transformations (Equation (1.30)) can transfer the focus to other triangles of interest by moving them to the center of the Poincare disk.

1.8.2 Hierarchical (Tree) Graphs

Data visualization inside the Poincare disk (in 2D) can be performed by using successive applications of the Mobius transformation given in Section 1.8.1, Equation (1.30) [40]. Each tree node receives a certain open space, called "pie segment", where it chooses the locations of its siblings. This is denoted as a *treemap* [42]. Then, for all its siblings, it calls recursively the layout routine after applying the Mobius transformation. A similar visualization technique is developed in [43] in the 3D hyperbolic space, although navigation in 3D is more complex. Given a hierarchical structure of data (similar to a tree structure), large directed graphs can be efficiently visualized in 3D hyperbolic space, since due to its exponential increase the same room can be allocated to every embedded node no matter how deep it lies in the tree.

1.8.3 General Graphs

In this case, two basic visualization techniques in the 2D hyperbolic space can be identified. The combination of these two techniques in a hybrid scheme allows for a more efficient visualization.

Self-Organizing Map (SOM) in Hyperbolic Space (HSOM) [44]. Firstly, a feature map is built, composed by a lattice of nodes (neurons) while a reference vector (prototype vector) is attached to each node. The position of a new data vector in the visualization is determined by the discrete (best-match) node in the lattice chosen via minimizing the hyperbolic distance (Poincare disk) of the new vector over all existing prototype vectors (nodes) in the lattice.

Hyperbolic Multidimensional Scaling (HMS) [45]. This visualization technique suitably represents the proximity relations (dissimilarities) of N objects by distances between points in the Poincare disk model of hyperbolic space. Therefore, comparing the spatial positions of two nodes on the Poincare disk provides strong intuition for the similarity/dissimilarity of their corresponding features.

Hybrid Scheme [46]. Each one of the HSOM and HMS schemes has advantages and disadvantages. HSOM processes only vectorial data and scales linearly in the number of nodes and HMS uses dissimilarity data and grows as the square of the number of nodes. Thus, HSOM may accommodate higher data quantities, while HMS accommodates a more general data form, i.e., the dissimilarity one. The proposed hybrid scheme in [46] exploits the advantages of each isolated visualization technique. It firstly creates a coarse-grain theme map of the data via HSOM (which accommodates more data) and then uses HMS for detailed inspection of data subsets where data similarities are continuously reflected as spatial proximities. Importantly, the display paradigm employs in both cases the hyperbolic plane in order to profit from its focus and context technique (as explained above).

Finally, there are two existing applications for visualizing data in hyperbolic space, namely Hyperbolic Tree Viewer [47] and Hypertree [48]. Although many other examples exist, they all suffer from different shortcomings, in particular problems regarding the inclusion of additional data dimensions, and the absence of a means to guide the user to those regions of the data that might be called "interesting", calling for novel approaches.

1.9 CONCLUSIONS

In this chapter, we developed a big data analytics (BDA) and exploitation framework for complex and social networks leveraging significant properties of hyperbolic geometry in this field. Briefly, many scale-free complex and social networks are characterized by a hidden hyperbolic structure, and thus embedding their large-scale produced data in hyperbolic space emerges natural, also allowing for their efficient handling, processing and exploitation via information extraction. In this context, our proposed framework collects methodologies over hyperbolic coordinates for several processes concerning complex and social networks, such as correlations and clustering, missing links' inference, efficient SNA metrics' computations, optimized resource allocation and visualization analytics. We envision that the proposed framework will revolutionize BDA in complex and social networks and will maximize the benefit from data analytics generated from the latter, for the latter.

ACKNOWLEDGMENT

This research is co-financed by the European Union (European Social Fund) and Hellenic national funds through the Operational Program 'Education and Lifelong Learning' (NSRF 2007-2013).

FURTHER READING

1. D. Puccinelli, M. Haenggi, "Wireless Sensor Networks: Applications and Challenges of Ubiquitous Sensing", *IEEE Circuits and Systems Magazine*, Vol. 5, No. 3, pp. 19-31, 2005.

2. C.L.P. Chen, C.-Y. Zhang, "Data-intensive Applications, Challenges, Techniques and Technologies: A Survey on Big Data", *Elsevier Information Sciences*, No. 275, pp. 314-347, 2014.

3. K.-C. Chen, M. Chiang, H.V. Poor, "From Technological Networks to Social Networks", *IEEE Journal on Selected Areas in Communications/Supplement (JSAC)*, Vol. 31, No. 9, pp. 548-572, September 2013.

4. J. W. Anderson, *Hyperbolic Geometry*, 2nd ed. Springer, 2007.

5. F. Papadopoulos, C. Psomas, D. Krioukov, "Network Mapping by Replaying Hyperbolic Growth", *IEEE/ACM Transactions on Networking*, Vol. 23, No. 1, pp. 198-211, Feb. 2015.

6. V. Karyotis, E. Stai, S. Papavassiliou, *Evolutionary Dynamics of Complex Communications Networks*, CRC Press - Taylor & Francis Group, Boca Raton, FL, 2013.

7. L. Atzori, A. Iera, G. Morabito, M. Nitti, "The Social Internet of Things (SIoT) - When social networks meet the Internet of Things: Concept, Architecture and Network Characterization", *Computer Networks*, Elsevier, Vol. 56, No. 16, pp. 3594-3608, 2012.

8. F. Papadopoulos, D. Krioukov, M. Bogua, A. Vahdat, "Greedy Forwarding in Dynamic Scale-Free Networks Embedded in Hyperbolic Metric Spaces", *in. Proc. of IEEE INFOCOM*, pp. 14-19, March 2010.

9. F. Papadopoulos, M. Kitsak, M. A. Serrano, M. Bogu, D. Krioukov, "Popularity vs. Similarity in Growing Networks", *Nature*, Vol. 489, pp. 537-540, Sept. 2012.

10. F. S. Beckman, D. A. Quarles, "On Isometries of Euclidean Space", *Proc. Amer. Math. Soc.*, Vol. 4, pp. 810-815, 1953.

11. A. Cvetkovski, M. Crovella, "Hyperbolic Embedding and Routing for Dynamic Graphs", *IEEE INFOCOM*, pp. 1647-1655, April 2009.

12. I. Benjamini, Y. Makarychev, "Dimension Reduction for Hyperbolic Space", *American Mathematical Society*, Vol. 137, No. 2, pp. 695-698, Feb. 2009.

13. D. A. Tran, K. Vut, "Dimensionality Reduction in Hyperbolic Data Spaces: Bounding Reconstructed-Information Loss", *in Proc. of 7th IEEE/ACIS Int'l Conf. on Computer and Information Science*, pp. 133-139, May 2008.

14. R. Lior, O. Maimon, "Clustering methods", *Data Mining and Knowledge Discovery Handbook*, Springer US, pp. 321-352, 2005.

15. D. Yan, L. Huang, M. I. Jordan, "Fast Approximate Spectral Clustering", *in Proc. of the 15th ACM Conference on Knowledge Discovery and Data Mining (SIGKDD)*, Paris, France, 2009.

16. Y. Koren, R. Bell, C. Volinsky, "Matrix Factorization Techniques for Recommender Systems", *Computer*, Vol. 42, No. 8, pp. 30-37, August 2009.

17. A. K. Menon, C. Elkan, "Fast Algorithms for Approximating the Singular Value Decomposition", *ACM Transactions on Knowledge Discovery from Data (TKDD)*, Vol. 5, No. 2, Feb. 2011.

18. S.-H. Cha, "Comprehensive Survey on Distance/Similarity Measures between Probability Density Functions", *Int'l Journal of Mathematical Models and Methods in Applied Sciences*, Vol. 1, No. 4, pp. 300-307, 2007.

19. L. Lee, "Measures of Distributional Similarity", *37th Annual Meeting of the Association for Computational Linguistics*, pp. 25-32, 1999.

20. M.E.J. Newman, *Networks: An Introduction*, Oxford, UK: Oxford University Press, 2010.

21. T. Hastie, R. Tibshirani, J. Friedman, *The Elements of Statistical Learning*, Springer, 2008.

22. N. Ailon, B. Chazelle, "The Fast Johnson-Lindenstrauss Transform and Approximate Nearest Neighbors", *SIAM J. Comput.*, Vol. 39, No. 1, pp. 302-322, 2009.

23. R. Albert, A.-L. Barabasi, "Statistical Mechanics of Complex Networks", *Reviews of Modern Physics*, Vol. 74, No. 1, pp. 47-97, Jan. 2002.

24. X. Zhao, A. Sala, H. Zheng, B. Y. Zhao, "Efficient Shortest Paths on Massive Social Graphs", *IEEE Collaborate Communic.*, pp. 77-86, 2011.

25. Y. Shavitt, T. Tankel, "Hyperbolic Embedding of Internet Graph for Distance Estimation and Overlay Construction", *IEEE/ACM Trans. on Networking*, Vol. 16, No. 1, pp. 25-36, Feb. 2008.

26. X. Ban, J. Gao, A. van de Rijt, "Navigation in Real-World Complex Networks through Embedding in Latent Spaces", *ALENEX*, pp. 138-148, 2010.

27. S. P. Borgatti, "Centrality and Network Flow", *Social Networks* (Elsevier), pp. 55-71, 2004.

28. M. Boguna, D. Krioukov, K. C. Claffy, "Navigability of Complex Networks", *Nature Physics*, Vol. 5, pp. 74-80, 2009.

29. J. Zhang, "Greedy Forwarding for Mobile Social Networks Embedded in Hyperbolic Spaces", *in Proc. of the ACM SIGCOMM*, New York, NY, pp. 555-556, 2013.

30. J. Bobadilla, F. Ortega, A. Hernando, A. Gutierrez, "Recommender Systems Survey", *Knowledge-Based Systems*, Elsevier, Vol. 46, pp. 109-132, April 2013.

31. J. Kleinberg, "The Small-World Phenomenon: an Algorithmic Perspective", *In Proc. of the 32 Annual ACM Symposium on Theory of Computing (STOC '00)*, New York, NY, USA, pp. 163-170, 2000.

32. E. Stai, J. S. Baras, S. Papavassiliou, "Social Networks over Wireless Networks", *in Proc. of the 51st IEEE Conf. on Decision and Control (CDC)*, Hawaii, Dec. 2012.

33. E. Stai, S. Papavassiliou, J. S. Baras, "Performance-Aware Cross-Layer Design in Wireless Multihop Networks via a Weighted Backpressure Approach", *IEEE/ACM Transactions on Networking*, DOI: 10.1109/TNET.2014.2360942, October 2014.

34. E. Stai, S. Papavassiliou, J. S. Baras, "A Coalitional Game Based Approach for Multi-Metric Optimal Routing in Wireless Networks", *in Proc. of the 24th Annual IEEE Int'l Symposium on Personal, Indoor and Mobile Radio Commun. (PIMRC)*, pp. 1935-1939, London, UK, Sept. 2013.

35. P. Gao, H. Miao, J. S. Baras, "Social Network Ad Allocation via Hyperbolic Embedding", *in Proc. of 53rd IEEE Conference on Decision and Control (CDC)*, pp. 4875-4880, December 2014.

36. E. Bastug, M. Bennis, M. Debbah, "Living on the Edge: The role of Proactive Caching in 5G Wireless Networks", *IEEE Communications Magazine*, Vol. 52, No. 8, pp. 82-89, 2014.

37. Cisco, "Cisco Visual Networking Index: Global Mobile Data Traffic Forecast Update 2013-2018", *White Paper, [Online] http://goo.gl/l77HAJ*, 2014.

38. F. Pantisano, M. Bennis, W. Saad, M. Debbah, "In-Network Caching and Content Placement in Cooperative Small Cell Networks", *1st Int'l Conference on 5G for Ubiquitous Connectivity (5GU)*, 2014.

39. Ericsson, "5G Radio Access-Research and Vision", *White Paper*, June 2013.

40. J. Lamping, R. Rao, P. Pirolli. "A Focus+Context Technique Based on Hyperbolic Geometry for Viewing Large Hierarchies", *ACM SIGCHI*, pp. 401-408, 1995.

41. U. C. Turker, S. Balcisoy, "A Visualization Technique for Large Temporal Social Network Datasets in Hyperbolic Space", *Journal of Visual Languages and Computing*, Vol. 25, pp. 227-242, 2014.

42. H.-C. Lam, I.D. Dinov, "Hyperbolic Wheel: A Novel Hyperbolic Space Graph Viewer for Hierarchical Information Content", *ISRN Computer Graphics*, Volume 2012, article ID 609234, 2012.

43. T. Munzner, "H3: Laying out Large Directed Graphs in 3D Hyperbolic Space", *in Proc. of IEEE Symposium on Information Visualization*, pp. 2-10, 1997.

44. H. Ritter, "Self-organizing Maps on non-Euclidean Spaces", *In Kohonen Maps*, Elsevier, pp. 97-110, 1999.

45. J. Walter, H. Ritter, "On Interactive Visualization of High-Dimensional Data Using the Hyperbolic Plane", *in Proc. of ACM Int'l. Conference on Knowledge Discovery and Data Mining (SIGKDD)*, pp. 123-131, 2002.

46. J. Walter, J. Ontrup, D. Wessling, H. Ritter, "Interactive Visualization and Navigation in Large Data Collections Using the Hyperbolic Space", *in Proc. of the 3rd IEEE International Conference on Data Mining (ICDM)*, pp. 355-362, Nov. 2003.

47. J. Lamping, R. Rao, "Laying out and Visualizing Large Trees Using a Hyperbolic Space", *in Proc. ACM Symp User Interface Software and Technology*, pp. 13-14, 1994.

48. J. Bingham, S. Sudarsanam, "Visualizing Large Hierarchical Clusters in Hyperbolic Space", *Bioinformatics*, Vol. 16, No. 7, pp. 660-661, 2000.

49. R. Kleinberg, "Geographic Routing Using Hyperbolic Space", *in Proc. of IEEE INFOCOM*, pp. 1902-1909, May 2007.

50. A.-L. Barabasi, E. Bonabeau, "Scale-Free Networks", *Scientific American*, pp. 50-59, May 2003.

51. D. J. Watts, S. H. Strogatz, "Collective Dynamics of 'Small-World' Networks", *Nature*, Vol. 393, pp. 440-442, Jun. 1998.

CHAPTER 2

Scalable Query and Analysis for Social Networks: An Integrated High-Level Dataflow System with Pig and Harp

Tak-Lon (Stephen) Wu, Bingjing Zhang, Clayton Davis, Emilio Ferrara, Alessandro Flammini, Filippo Menczer and Judy Qiu

CONTENTS

E VERY day, vast amounts of data are being collected from social network (e.g., Twitter) applications, and in response there is a growing need for analysis methods that can handle this terabyte-size input. To provide an effective and advanced data processing environment for various types of social data analysis such as political discourses, trending topics, evolution of user behavior, social bots detection and orchestrated campaigns, we need to support both query and complex analysis efficiently. Use of high-level scripting languages to solve big data problems has become a mainstream approach for sophisticated data mining and analysis. In particular, high-level interfaces such as Pig, Hive, and Spark SQL are being used on top of the Hadoop framework. This simplifies coding of complex tasks in MapReduce-style systems while improving the flexibility of database systems through user-defined aggregations. In this chapter we will compare different approaches of building high-level dataflow systems and propose an integrated solution with Pig and Harp (a plugin to Hadoop) along with giving extensive benchmarks. The results show that Pig and Harp integration for sophisticated iterative applications runs at a factor of 2 to 10 times faster than Pig or Hive implementation executed on Hadoop.

2.1   INTRODUCTION

Social media represents a precious data source providing tremendous amounts of streaming information for analytics and research applications. Many research projects are involved in performing intensive analysis on such data, and the outcome of this analysis is drawing the attention of various applications, including market sales analysts, societal studies (including political polarization [10], congressional elections [14, 13], protest events [12, 11], and the spread of misinformation [47, 37]) and information diffusion [24]. Compared to other problems in computing, social media analysis is "special"; it normally focuses on a subset of data related to a target social event within a specific time frame. To further investigate the inter-relationship of such subsets of data, various sophisticated algorithms and complex data transformations may be applied into a series of stages [19]. Therefore, developing a programmable solution for social media data must include features like expressiveness, ability for data extraction, reusability and interoperability with different computation runtimes. Apache high-level languages and Apache Hadoop [1] ecosystem are some of the existing building block solutions that match the requirements for social network analysis.

   The use of high-level language platforms is not just limited to social media data. Other fields of research such as workflow provenance [7], network traffic analysis [26, 23], and geographic data analysis [6] have proved the adaptation of these solutions boosts and scales up their historical data analysis. However, the complex workflows characterizing existing platforms makes it difficult for users to decide what language and low level runtimes best match their needs. Motivated by these challenges, our goal is to provide a comprehensive survey of these high-level abstractions involving experiments with real social media data examples and common query and analysis applications.

The rest of the chapter is organized as follows. Section 2.2 gives an overview of Apache high-level languages, especially Pig [22], Hive [40] and Spark SQL [2, 44]. The first two build on Hadoop while Harp [47] and Spark [46] are Apache iterative MapReduce frameworks offering support to complex parallel data systems. Section 2.3 provides a comparison of these languages' features especially the important user-defined functions that make MapReduce a simplified and scalable solution. Sections 2.4 and 2.5 introduce applications that are used for benchmarking later in the chapter. Section 2.4 introduces the *Truthy project* and the types of queries that it needs to run on top of Twitter data, while Section 2.5 discusses three data analytics use-cases and how to express them in high-level languages. Section 2.6 presents the performance evaluation of the applications presented in Sections 2.4 and 2.5, and the technologies of Section 2.2. Section 2.7 draws our conclusions.

2.2 APACHE HIGH-LEVEL LANGUAGE, SYNTAX AND ITS COMMON FEATURES

Programming languages have been developed for more than 50 years. Each language has its own compiler/interpreter and executes a physical plan on top of the low level (operating) system. Apache high-level languages share the common features of traditional programming languages; in many cases, a compiler built for such a language supports several fundamental functions and operations: a syntax parser, type and compile time semantic checking, logical plan generator and optimizer, and physical plan generator and executor. Here ANTLR (ANother Tool for Language Recognition) [34] is the general syntax parser for Pig, Hive, and Spark SQL. Each language has its own types and plan generator and optimizer, but all of them use YARN [42] as their resource management tool. The next sections will discuss details of Apache Pig, Apache Hive and Apache Spark SQL.

2.2.1 Pig

Pig is a high-level dataflow system that yields simple data transformations in pipeline for large amounts of semi-structured data stored in Hadoop compatible file storage. Applications such as massive system log analysis and traditional Extract, Transform, and Load (ETL) data processing are performed regularly. Pig was first introduced by Yahoo!, and became one of the most

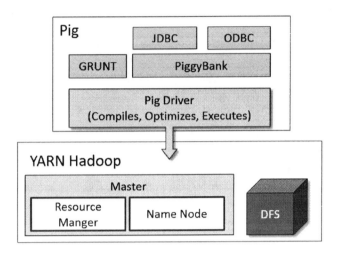

FIGURE 2.1 Pig's architecture.

popular Hadoop ecosystem projects in the Apache open source community. It uses its built-in procedural language, *Pig Latin* [32], designed for large-scale data analysis with Hadoop MapReduce. The syntax is straightforward so long as the developer is familiar with UNIX bash scripting. Pig hides complicated MapReduce programs with simple notations for a dataflow program. Internally, Pig scripts are compiled into sequences of MapReduce jobs, which automate parallelization and make the code easy to maintain. Pig also provides an interactive shell interface named GRUNT that generates MapReduce jobs which depend on the type-in lines. Figure 2.1 depicts an overall architecture of Pig. As shown, Pig is standalone and can run as a Java client on any worker node.

When a user submits their Pig scripts in a batch mode or enters line-by-line data transformation commands in an interactive mode, a default compiler handles the overall execution flows. This compiler translates the entered Pig scripts into operators and forms top-down Abstract Syntax Trees (AST) in different stages. It then visits the last compiled AST from the MapReduce operators plan compiler and constructs MapReduce jobs in order. Figure 2.2 shows the dataflow and lists all major steps. Similar to any programming language, Pig checks syntax by parsing the user-submitted script into a parser written in ANTLR. It then generates a logical LOP (Logical Operator Plan) for further optimization. Generally a logical rules-based optimization is performed without looking at the real data (this is different from traditional SQL or SQL-like technologies that take data schema as part of the rules-based optimization). Pig's main driver program converts each MapReduce operator from Map-Reduce Operator Plan (MROperPlan) objects into Hadoop JobControl

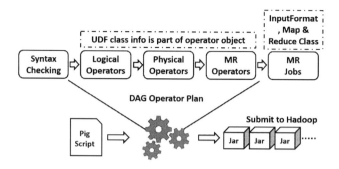

FIGURE 2.2 Pig high-level dataflow.

objects with detailed descriptions, input/output linkages, and other parameters, which are then passed along to each worker node with a configuration in xml format. These translations generate Java jar files that contain the Pig default Map and Reduce classes, including the user-defined functions. The packages of jar files are submitted to Hadoop Job Manager, and job progress is monitored until completion of the tasks.

An example of a WordCount program written in Pig Latin [32] is provided in Figure 2.3. In a Pig dataflow, each line of code has only one data transformation, which can be nested. The WordCount program consists of seven lines of code, and the syntax is straightforward and easy to understand. Generally, data is loaded as records in a relation/outer bag, and each field in a record is defined according to Pig's default data types: bag, tuple, and field. A bag is a set of unordered columnar tuples. A tuple is a set of fields, where tuples in a bag can contain flexible length of fields, and fields in the same column can have different data types. Lastly, a field is the basic type of a piece of data. Then, based on the supported data types, a developer applies the desired data transformation and generates their results.

In our example, the first line defines an outer bag input and loads a text document from HDFS. Each line of this text file is declared as string (chararray in Pig Latin). The second and third line further converts each line into English words and creates for each individual word a single tuple by using the

```
1 input     = LOAD 'input.txt'
              AS (line:chararray);
2 words     = FOREACH input GENERATE
              FLATTEN(TOKENIZE(line)) AS word;
3 filWords = FILTER words BY word MATCHES '\\w+';
4 wdGroups = GROUP filWords BY word;
5 wdCount  = FOREACH wdGroups GENERATE
              group AS word,
              COUNT(filWords) AS count;
6 ordWdCnt = ORDER wdCount BY count DESC;
7 STORE ordWdCnt INTO 'result';
```

FIGURE 2.3 WordCount written in Pig [5].

built-in function TOKENIZE and relational statement FILTER. The fourth line aggregates instances of the exact same word together and constructs a two-cell tuple for each word. Here, the first cell of this tuple stores the text of this word, while the second cell stores a list of the same word. The List length is the total number of occurrences of this word. The fifth line counts the amount of word items in the list and emits a word count pair for each word <word, occurrences>. Line six uses the built-in order statement and reorders the WordCount result with descending order. Finally, line seven stores the ordered result into default file storage. Other than the syntax shown in this chapter, Pig provides operations and syntax patterns for various data transformations, although the current version of Pig does not support optimized storage structures such as indices and column groups.

Pig performs well for ETL applications, but it does not directly support iterative computations. This implies that Pig can execute simple one-pass algorithms but not complex functions that need to apply a computation repeatedly (e.g., for loop) which exist in graph, linear algebra, and expectation-maximization computations. To write such general data analysis applications using Pig, the control flow should be similar to what is shown in Figure 2.4: an external wrapper script is required because Pig syntax does not provide control flow statements. This causes extra overhead of job startup and cleanup time when a program runs in several rounds of MapReduce jobs. Furthermore, inputs of iterative applications are normally unchanged and cacheable between iterations, whereas Pig has a DAG framework that does not cache those inputs in memory and reuses data efficiently.

To generalize the usage of Pig for scientific applications, we need to enable loop-awareness computation and in-memory caching; our research project yielded a version of Pig for scientific applications based on the DAG computation model. There are several iterative MapReduce frameworks available as candidates to integrate with Pig, including Twister [15], Spark [46], HaLoop [9], and Harp [47]. We chose Harp as it is a plug-in to Hadoop that supports our required iteration features, the result being referred to from here on as Pig+Harp [43]. With Harp integration, we replace the Hadoop Mapper interface with Harp's MapCollective, a long-running mapper to support conditional loops. Subsequently, iterative applications implemented in Pig+Harp can cache reusable data and replace the default GROUP BY operation with Harp's collective communication interface featuring high-performance data movement. Figure 2.5 shows a dataflow that can be applied to iterative applications.

2.2.2 Hive

Hive is a data warehouse solution for ad-hoc queries, from simple data summarization to business intelligence applications and high-latency queries for extremely large structured data sets stored on top of Hadoop related file storage. Initially developed by the Facebook data infrastructure team, it is used

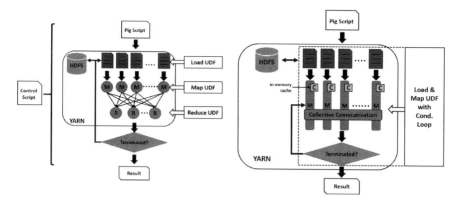

FIGURE 2.4 Iterative applications with Pig.

FIGURE 2.5 Iterative applications with Pig+Harp.

for filtering and summarization of information from their massive amount of stored social network data and support products associated with the collected data. Thousands of Hive jobs were submitted daily since 2010 [8]. Hive uses a SQL-like language named HiveQL which is very attractive for the traditional SQL community. Similar to Pig, HiveQL queries are compiled into MapReduce jobs and executed on top of Hadoop. Hive reintroduces a RDBMS technique —Metastore— that stores data schemas and statistics as a service of an in-memory system catalog to facilitate Hive's compiler and data scanning. Figure 2.6 shows the architecture of Hive.

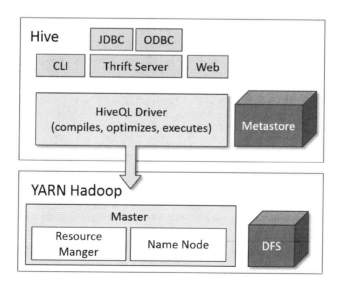

FIGURE 2.6 Hive architecture.

```
1. CREATE TABLE doc (line STRING);
2. LOAD DATA INPATH '$documentsPath'
   OVERWRITE INTO TABLE doc;
3. INSERT INTO OVERWRITE DIRECTORY '$outputPath'
   SELECT word, count(1) AS count FROM
   (SELECT explode(split(line, '\s')]
    AS word FROM doc) words
   GROUP BY word
   ORDER BY word;
```

FIGURE 2.7 WordCount written in Hive.

When a user submits HiveSQL statements via any supported APIs, Hive initially checks the syntax by an ANLTR parser, then cooperates with Metastore for further type checking and semantic analysis, and lastly generates an initial AST as a logical plan. This plan is then optimized through a rule-based optimizer involving the schema and indices metadata obtained from Metastore. Optimizations such as column pruning, pushdown, partition pruning, mapside joins, and join reordering are also performed. Finally, a physical plan is generated from the optimized logical plan and submits a sequence of MapReduce jobs to Hadoop cluster.

Hive supports nested statements, and each statement represents a single data transformation. In Figure 2.7, we see a WordCount program written in HiveQL. Hive supports nested statements, and each statement represents a single data transformation. The first line declares a table named doc with only a string column line. The second line reads files from the given path and overwrites the table doc. The third line is a nested statement that splits all words of each record of lines in table "doc", then groups all emitted (word, 1) pairs from the temporary table "words" in decreasing order with their occurrence. The overall syntax is very SQL friendly.

By default, Hive is compatible with local file systems HDFS [39] and HBase [4]. A user is required to provide data schema by creating tables before accessing the files in storage. For instance, prior to reading existing tables in HBase, users need an additional step to make tables in Metastore and link the schema of Hive to the HBase tables, such as row key and column families of the reading tables.

2.2.3 Spark SQL/Shark

Spark SQL [2] and Shark [44] are other open source projects directly inspired by Hive. Both use Spark runtime and RDD [45] as the core engine to execute their physical plan on top of YARN. Spark SQL is the latest release replacing Shark, now merged as a branch project under the Spark ecosystem.

Spark SQL reuses Hive's query parser to generate a logical operator plan. With this compatibility support, general Hive queries can run on Spark SQL without any changes to the execution script. Spark SQL has its own rule-based logical operator plan optimizer for matching the physical operators that run on Spark. As claimed by Spark runtime developers, this allows Spark SQL queries to run better on RDD operations and best match the Spark execution

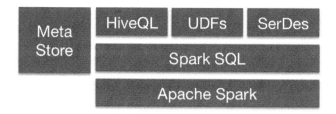

FIGURE 2.8 Spark SQL architecture [2].

model, rather than tuning Spark low-level execution to support Hive's Hadoop implementation. The architecture of Spark SQL appears in Figure 2.8. Spark SQL can support most of the HiveQL statements with several limitations; e.g., bucketed tables in Hive are not currently supported in Spark SQL.

2.3 PIG, HIVE AND SPARK SQL COMPARISON

Before comparing the differences between Pig, Hive and Spark SQL, we need to look into two fundamental terms: dataflow system and data warehouse system.

Dataflow system is a type of data processing system where data is transformed from one format to another via different processing units in a directed path. Data can be structured (with a predefined schema) or unstructured (e.g., logs); it therefore requires customized data selection and operations in order to extract meaningful information. Pig falls into this category. Data warehouse is a system that handles cleaned, structured and cataloged data in organized hierarchical data storage units. Data is available to observers for conducting data analysis. Hive and Spark SQL are designed for the data warehouse community.

Table 2.8 gives a comprehensive comparison between Pig, Hive and Spark SQL. Even though they are designed for different systems and applications, these three tools share many common features, operations and functions.

Pig can be used for unstructured raw data batch processing and simple statistical analytics, especially with massive logs for text mining. It is more like an alternative to Hadoop MapReduce applications in high-level abstraction with an extensible subset of general data operations. Data is stored in HDFS or HBase with high-latency data scanning operations. Pig scans data entirely (i.e., it must scan all data for filtering fields with numeric type less than 10) without the help of data indices. As such, it is considered "slower" in supporting ad-hoc queries than Hive.

Meanwhile, Hive and Spark SQL are SQL-like distributed systems that run high-latency queries for data sets stored on top of MapReduce (HDFS) file system. Hive still scans data from disk or HDFS directly for assigned map/reduce tasks. Metastore provides the data schema and indices while scanning the data. Spark SQL uses Hive's query parser and Metastore generates the operator plan, but it then uses Catalyst as its logical plan generator and optimizer (Shark uses Hive's query planner), executes with Spark, and stores the processed/queried data into DataFrame (columnar RDD in Shark) instead of files on HDFS. Here rule-based optimizations of Hive/Shark and Spark SQL are expandable. The use of RDD provides in-memory reusable access to the scanning data. It saves significant disk I/O and job restart overhead if the data is hit frequently, especially when the cases of mixing ad-hoc queries and further sophisticated applications are involved within the lines of the same submitted program. Spark SQL is still a newly released ongoing project, so some query plan optimizations of Hive/Shark are not included in Spark SQL such as block level bitmap indices and virtual columns. Catalyst is the core difference between Shark and Spark SQL. DataFrame is a special type of row objects RDD that has associated data schema such as column field name and data type as a collection of named and typed tuples. It can then support operations from the submitted relational queries in line. In addition, with the help of the known type of the row objects, DataFrame can be cached with better compression than general RDD objects.

All of Pig, Hive and Spark SQL introduce User-Defined Functions (UDF) for advanced tuple/record-based data transformation, which enables the possibility to implement special computation and sophisticated algorithms in addition to the basic queries.

2.4 AD-HOC QUERIES: TRUTHY AND TWITTER DATA

Ad-hoc queries are the most common benchmark for ETL applications. This also applies to Apache high-level languages, which are mainly designed to support ETL operations. Here we use Truthy project and Twitter-generated social media data to evaluate ad-hoc query performance among these runtimes.

Truthy [30, 21] is a public social media observatory developed as a research project at Indiana University. It analyzes and visualizes information diffusion on Twitter. Truthy monitors and collects Twitter data in real-time directly through the Twitter public steaming API. The overall size of compressed historical raw data from 2010 until April 2015 is about 3.2TB. IndexedHBase [19, 20] is used to store, load, and index this data as tables into HBase on a private large-storage, high-performance, and large-memory cluster called MOE. As of today, the overall data on HBase including the raw data tables and index tables (as well as the standard 3 replicas) occupies nearly 133TB of disk space. We expect to continue storing more historical data, as the Truthy team aims to perform innovative and large-scale social network research and analysis to understand how information propagates in complex socio-technical systems. Many researchers [14, 13, 12, 11, 47, 37] have built their prototypes, models and analyses based upon this complex infrastructure, which shows the capability to capture the spread of information, from political discourses to trending topics [17], the evolution of user behavior [41], and even the presence of social bots and orchestrated campaigns [16].

TABLE 2.1 TRUTHY'S AD-HOC QUERIES FOR SIMPLE TWEETS RETRIEVAL

Queries	Description	Index Table Name
get-tweets-with-meme	Search tweets with given memes such as hashtags, user-mentions, and URLs	memeIndexTable
get-tweets-with-text	Search tweets with given keywords	textIndexTable
get-tweets-with-user	Search tweets with given user information, e.g., user ID and screen name	userTweetsIndexTable
get-retweets	Search retweets with given tweet Ids	retweetIndexTable

The data collected from the Twitter streaming API consists of tweets containing various attributes. The most common attributes used for intensive analysis include hashtags, user metadata, text and media content, retweets information, user mentions, and specific time intervals. Truthy identifies this information and utilizes the concept of "meme" [25] (a piece of data that corresponds to specific topics, communication channels, or shared elements by people in a social network) to construct a set of temporal queries for extracting tweets' information for further data intensive analysis. These queries can be classified into two categories [20]: ad-hoc queries for simple tweet retrieval with the help of index tables, and combination of tweet retrieval with extra data transformation. We only discuss the ad-hoc queries here because it is the best practice for matching the common features of high-level languages. Table 2.1 shows four different queries that firstly search the related index table and then redirect the obtained tweets back to the user.

Previous research [10, 19] utilized the above queries on top of further data mining techniques, such as eigenvector modularity [31] and label propagation [36], on two datasets about political discussion collected during the six weeks leading up to the 2010 U.S. congressional midterm elections and 2012 U.S. presidential elections. The results shown in [10, 19] prove that the retweet networks exhibited a highly segregated partisan structure; users of those tweets are mainly split into two homogeneous communities corresponding to the political left and right leanings.

2.5 ITERATIVE SCIENTIFIC APPLICATIONS

Many domain scientists who work on scientific applications use programming languages such as Python, Matlab and R to perform standard data-analysis tasks. Oftentimes, such analysis involves sophisticated data mining and machine learning techniques that must run in several rounds of computation to complete a full task. With the built-in mathematics and statistical operations in Pig and Hive, these two runtimes could be candidate tools to support scientific applications run with very large-scale data. Due to the fact that Pig and Hive do not support iterative applications directly, we need to extend them with an external wrapper script/program to handle the loop control and link the program inputs from HDFS between iterations. On the other hand, Pig+Harp integrated Harp's collective communication API to support iterative application as well as single pass in common Hadoop jobs for both high-level language tools.

2.5.1 K-means Clustering and PageRank

We present two popular algorithms, K-means clustering and PageRank computing, as our standard benchmarks. K-means clustering [29] is one of the standard clustering algorithms that has been widely used for finding distance and similarity among a set of objects with multidimensional vectors. In addition to various applications in social media analysis [18], studies involving large-scale image classification [27, 35] have used this technique on high-dimensional (over 100 dimensions) SIFT descriptors [28]. This allowed for creating a training dataset of visual vocabulary to automatically determine specific characteristics of a given photo, e.g., whether it was taken in an urban or rural environment. Meanwhile, the PageRank [33] webpage-ordering algorithm was introduced by Google co-founders, Larry Page and Sergey Brin while they were researching the next generation of search engine in 1996. Eventually, this ranking algorithm became the key technology of the Google search engine, and it was applied to several general-purpose graph or network problems in bibliometrics, social network analysis, and recommendation systems. We show the difference in implementations below by using Pig and Hive.

Pig K-means consists of three components: a Python control-flow script, a Pig data-transform script for a single iteration, and two K-means user-defined functions written with a Pig provided Java interface. A single iteration of K-means written in Pig Latin is included in Figure 2.9. Our customized Loader yields the aggregated centroids into memory as vector objects loaded from the distributed cache on disk before computing the Euclidean distances for all data points at each iteration of the algorithm. Every loader outputs the assigned centroids and data points as fields in a single bag; each field in a bag is defined as string data type which further splits into tuples to match Pig's GROUP operation and collect partial centroid vectors from mappers. It then takes the average of all partitions, emits to a final centroids file and saves it to HDFS.

Hive K-means is written in SQL-like syntax and uses a UNIX bash script as the loop conditions wrapper for supporting iterations. Figure 2.10 depicts a single iteration of K-means written in HiveQL. Data points and centroids are originally stored on HDFS during each iteration, where they overwrite the intermediate centroids to HDFS. The default INPUT_FILE_NAME field provided by Hive is used, and our K-means UDF directly loads entire files for com-

```
1 raw     = LOAD $hdfsInputDir USING
            PigKmeans('$centroids',
            '$numOfCentroids') AS (datapoints
2 dptsBag = FOREACH raw GENERATE
            FLATTEN(datapoints) AS dptInStr;
3 dpts    = FOREACH dptsBag GENERATE
            STRSPLIT(dptInStr, ',', 5)
            AS splitedDP;
4 grouped = GROUP dpts BY splitedDP.$0;
5 newCens = FOREACH grouped GENERATE
            CalculateNewCentroids($1);
6 STORE newCens INTO 'output';
```

```
1 CREATE EXTERNAL TABLE IF NOT EXISTS
  $INPUTTABLE (filename String)
  LOCATION '$hdfsInputDir ';
2 DROP TABLE IF EXISTS interKmeansTable;
3 CREATE TABLE interKmeansTable(x double, y double,
  z double, beta double)
  LOCATION '$hdfsOutputDir;
4 INSERT OVERWRITE TABLE interKmeansTable
  SELECT SUM(KmeansTable.ret.x)/SUM(KmeansTable.ret.count),
  SUM(KmeansTable.ret.y)/SUM(KmeansTable.ret.count),
  SUM(KmeansTable.ret.z)/SUM(KmeansTable.ret.count),
  0.c
  FROM
  (SELECT explode(Kmeans(INPUT__FILE__NAME,
  '$initCentroidOnHDFS', '$centroidSize')) AS ret
  FROM $INPUTTABLE T) KmeansTable
  GROUP BY KmeansTable.ret.assignedcentroid;
```

FIGURE 2.9 Pig K-means for a single iteration.

FIGURE 2.10 Hive K-means for a single iteration.

putation instead of using Hadoop InputFormat with a series of input splits. General data aggregations such as GROUP BY and SUM are executed, while Euclidean distance computation is handled by the K-means UDF.

Pig+Harp K-means script in Figure 2.11 illustrates a similar idea using R. Users only provide the parameters, such as number of mappers, total amount of iterations, and communication patterns used for global data synchronization. In the case of executing Pig+Harp K-means, a customized Loader in each Mapper first loads the initial centroids and data points from HDFS to memory and caches the data points for all iterations. Then the UDF computes Euclidean distances and emits partial centroids locally. The Harp communication layer then exchanges these partial centroids in each mapper. By default, Pig+Harp K-means UDF uses AllReduce to synchronize among all partitions. The program reuses the same set of mapper processes until exit conditions have been reached.

For *Pig PageRank*, we use a model with fewer UDF functions by leveraging Pig built-in operators. Figure 2.12 has a single iteration of the PageRank algorithm, which is created and iteratively invoked by a Java wrapper. The script involves the following steps: (a) Load the given input file using the custom loader into variable raw; (b) extract the outgoing URLs and emit both outgoing URL and partial page rank from the source URL; (c) CO-GROUP above two aliases to calculate new page rank and store it in an alias newPgRank; (d) store new page rank in an HDFS temp file, which will be the input file for the next iteration. One drawback of this program is that

```
1 centds = LOAD $hdfsInputDir USING
           HarpKmeans('$initCentroidOnHDFS',
           '$numOfCentroids', '$numOfMappers',
           '$iteration', '$jobID', '$Comm')
           AS (result);
2 STORE centroids INTO '$hdfsOutputDir';
```

FIGURE 2.11 Pig+Harp K-means.

```
1 raw        = LOAD '$InputDir' USING
               CmLoader('$noOfURLs','$itrs')
               AS (source,pagerank, out:bag);
2 prePgRank  = FOREACH raw GENERATE
               FLATTEN(out) AS source,
               pagerank/SIZE(out) AS pagerank;
3 newPgRank  = FOREACH (COGROUP raw BY source,
               prePgRank BY source OUTER)
               GENERATE
               group AS source,
               (1-$dpFactor) +
               $dpFactor*(SUM(prePgRank.pagerank
               IS NULL?0:SUM(prePgRank.pagerank)
               AS pagerank,
               FLATTEN(raw.out) AS out;
4 STORE newPgRank INTO '$OutputFile';
```

```
1 CREATE EXTERNAL TABLE pageRankInput(line String)
  LOCATION 'SINPUTDIR';
2 CREATE TABLE PageRankComputeTable(pagerankCell
  struct<source:int,pagerank:double,outLinks:array<int>>)
  CLUSTERED BY(pagerankCell)
  INTO $MAP_SIZE BUCKETS
  LOCATION '$tmpPageRankResult';
3 INSERT OVERWRITE TABLE PageRankComputeTable
  SELECT InitialPageRank(line, '$numOfUrls') AS ret
  FROM pageRankInput;
4 INSERT OVERWRITE TABLE PageRankComputeTable
  SELECT named_struct('source', T1.pagerankCell.source,
  'pagerank', PageRank(T2.pagerank, $dpFactor, $noOfURLs),
  'outLinks', T1.pagerankCell.outLinks) AS cell
  FROM
  PageRankComputeTable T1
  LEFT OUTER JOIN
  (SELECT outlink,
  SUM(pagerankCell.pagerank/size(pagerankCell.outlinks))
  AS pagerank
  FROM PageRankComputeTable
  LATERAL VIEW
  explode(pagerankCell.outlinks) outLinkTable AS outlink
  Group by outlink) T2
  ON (T1.pagerankCell.source = T2.outlink);
```

FIGURE 2.12 Pig PageRank for a single iteration.

FIGURE 2.13 Hive PageRank for a single iteration.

the default Pig runtime optimizer creates extra mappers for the final STORE step when it calls the raw and prePgRank variables for CO-GROUP operators, which utilizes extra computing and memory resources.

Hive PageRank follows a similar logic as Pig PageRank, but the HiveQL script uses tables as data abstraction and nested queries for computation, as well as OUTER LEFT JOIN seen in Figure 2.13.

In *Pig+Harp PageRank* implementation, we provide a new data loader UDF to calculate the probabilities for each web page. For the first iteration, data is loaded in a graph data structure where vertices are partitioned across all worker nodes. Each vertex receives all in-edges information by calling re-groupEdges collective communication, and the number of out-edges is sent to all vertices by calling an AllMsgToAllVtx operation. The vertex and edge information is cached in memory for all iterations. Subsequently the PageRank values of each vertex are updated during every iteration and distributed by an AllGather communication until the program satisfies break conditions, e.g., the end of iterations. The script shown in Figure 2.14 is similar to that of Pig+Harp K-means.

```
1 pagerank = LOAD '$InputDir' USING
             HarpPageRank('$totalUrls',
             '$numMaps', '$itrs', '$jobID')
             AS (result);
2 STORE pagerank INTO '$output';
```

FIGURE 2.14 Pig+Harp PageRank.

2.6 BENCHMARKS

We have performed a set of extensive ad-hoc queries against Twitter's social network data using these high-level languages to illustrate their overheads and performance differences. We compare two scientific applications, K-means and PageRank, to evaluate the language expressiveness and performance in support of generic scientific algorithms in regard to high-level data abstractions, operations and execution flows. Currently we are not able to perform Spark SQL tests as the existing Spark SQL (latest version 1.3.1 as of April 2015) only supports a subset for HiveQL query and is best compatible with Hive 0.13.1. This limited compatibility causes our tests to fail. For example, when Spark SQL scans data from HBase, although the high-level abstraction StringType is used, Spark SQL in low level execution retrieves HBase's record as String instead of LazyString in Hive, which causes data loss to our ad-hoc queries test cases [3].

Our experiments run on MOE, a large-storage, large-memory and high-performance private cluster at Indiana University devoted to the Truthy project [30, 47, 21]. It consists of 3 login nodes and 10 compute nodes, where each login node is set up with two Intel(R) Xeon(R) CPU E5-2620 v2 CPUs, 64 GB memory, and each compute node has five Intel(R) Xeon(R) CPU E5-2660 v2 CPUs, 128 GB memory, 48TB HDD and 120GB SSD. All nodes are interconnected with a 10Gb Ethernet. Table 2.2 shows the specifications of MOE.

YARN Hadoop cluster on MOE is configured with a master on an independent login node. Meanwhile HBase uses another login as the master node and runs a ZooKeeper on each login node. YARN's NodeManager, HDFS's DataNode and HBase's RegionServer run on individual nodes and memory is shared among these processes. Table 2.3 specifies the software and runtime settings of MOE.

2.6.1 Performance of Ad-hoc Queries

We present the performance of running Truthy's queries on Twitter data using IndexedHBase in Figure 2.15. The query get-tweets-with-X initiates two steps; first it searches for tweet IDs from the related index table on HBase by

TABLE 2.2 HARDWARE SPECIFICATION OF MOE

	CPU	RAM	DISK	NETWORK
Login Node	2 x Intel(R) Xeon(R) CPU E5-2620 v2	64GB	120 SSD	10Gb Ethernet
Computer Node	5 x Intel(R) Xeon(R) CPU E5-2660 v2	128GB	48TB HDD + 120GB SSD	10Gb Ethernet

TABLE 2.3 RUNTIME SOFTWARE SPECIFICATION OF MOE

	Version	Memory	Disk
YARN	2.5.1	66GB per node	48TB per node
Pig	0.14.0	2GB per worker	Data on HDFS
Hive	1.0.0	2GB per worker	Data on HDFS
Pig+Harp	0.14, 0.1.0	2GB per worker	Data on HDFS
HBase	0.94.23	30GB per node	Data on HDFS
IndexedHBase	0.94 branch	2GB per worker	Data on HBase

TABLE 2.4 SIZE OF RECORDS OBTAINED BY "get-tweets-with-X"

	get-tweets-with-meme	get-tweets-with-text	get-tweets-with-userid
# of Records	1570261	202076	22

given keys such as meme, text or user ID under a specified time interval. The second step reuses the obtained tweet IDs to scan related tweets from the raw tweets table in HBase and stores the retrieved tweets on HDFS. The overall performance is dominated by the total amount of retrieved tweet IDs. Table 2.4 displays the number of records obtained from each query; we use hashtag "#ff" as meme, keyword "NBA" as text, and randomly choose a user ID to search tables in the December 2012 dataset.

The results in Figure 2.15 show that the IndexedHBase API command-line script outperforms the other solutions. This is because it calls an optimized Hadoop MapReduce job directly, and even the "search for tweet IDs" step is run as a local process. The Pig and Hive solutions execute these two steps in MapReduce jobs, therefore their performance is comparable. Hive requires more time for setting up the Table schema (including DROP and CREATE statements) in Metastore and Hive-related parameters in script for each query. As a result Hive performs the slowest in all of our tests. Table 2.5 lists the lines of code in script and the amount of submitted Hadoop jobs for each runtime based on query "get-tweets-with-X".

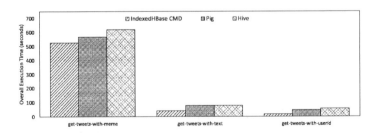

FIGURE 2.15 Truthy's get-tweets-with-X queries on Twitter data.

TABLE 2.5 SCRIPT AND EXECUTION COMPARISON OF "get-tweets-with-X"

get-tweets-with-X	IndexedHBase	Pig	Hive
Lines of code in script	1	11	17
Hadoop job(s)	1	2	2
Map(s)/Reduce(s)	24/0	1/0, 24/0	1/24, 24/0

2.6.2 Performance of Data Analysis

We use K-means and PageRank to evaluate the difference in performance for our solutions. Both algorithms are implemented in the same dataflow logic but using different syntax in Pig, Hive and Pig+Harp implementations.

The tests for K-means algorithm are shown in Table 2.6, where we compute 10 iterations for two data sets: a 100 million 3-dimensional data points against 500 centroids, and a 100 million 3-dimensional data points against 5000 centroids. The dataset is split into 128 partitions running 128 mappers and 8 reducers. Each mapper or reducer runs on 1 CPU core with 2GB memory.

Figure 2.16 illustrates the total execution time for the K-means algorithm with each runtime. Pig+Harp outperforms the other two runtimes due to in-memory objects cache for the loaded data points and centroids, fast network I/O for data aggregation, and reduced overheads of the job restart between iterations. In contrast, the Pig and Hive implementations have a huge cost due to reloading, at each iteration, of the intermediate data points and centroids from HDFS. The execution plans for Pig and Pig+Harp are similar. Pig K-means generates 1 Hadoop job per iteration and Pig+Harp K-means generates a single job for all iterations.

In the PageRank test, we compute 10 iterations for two data sets: 1 million numeric URLs and 2 million numeric URLs. The data is split into 64 partitions running 64 mappers and 64 reducers. Each mapper or reducer has 1 CPU core and 2GB memory.

Figure 2.17 presents the execution time of PageRank algorithm where Pig+Harp performs the best by storing the adjacency matrices as objects in memory, exchanging partial PageRank values via network I/O, and using long-running tasks.

As shown in Table 2.7, a maximum of 128 mappers (rather than our expected 64 mappers) are invoked for the partitions. This is due to the use of

TABLE 2.6 SCRIPT AND EXECUTION COMPARISON OF K-MEANS

K-means	Pig+Harp	Pig	Hive
Lines of code in script	3	11	13
Hadoop job(s) per iteration	1	1	1
Map(s)/Reduce(s)	128/0	128/8	128/8

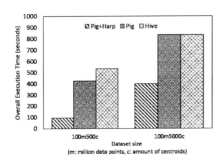

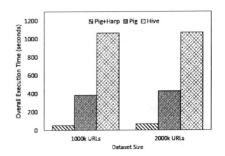

FIGURE 2.16 K-means result.   FIGURE 2.17 PageRank result.

TABLE 2.7 PAGERANK SCRIPT AND EXECUTION COMPARISON

K-means	Pig+Harp	Pig	Hive
Lines of code in script	3	8	16
Hadoop job(s) per iteration	1	1	4
Map(s)/Reduce(s)	64/0	128/64	64/64, 64/64, 128/64, 64/64

TABLE 2.8 CROSS COMPARISON FOR PIG, HIVE AND SPARK SQL

	Pig	Hive	Spark SQL
Target System	Dataflow	Data warehouse	Data warehouse, then data analytic applications
Syntax	Pig Latin	HiveQL (SQL-like)	HiveQL (SQL-like)
Script Parser	ANTLR	ANTLR	ANTLR
Logical Plan Compiler	Script → AST → Operator Trees	Script → AST → Operator Trees (DML DDL by tables)	Catalyst
Logical Plan Optimizer	Operators Trees (Rules based)	Operator Trees (Rules based)	Operator Trees (Rules based)
Physical / MR Compiler	Operators Trees → MR jobs	Operators Trees → MR jobs	Operators Trees → Spark jobs on YARN

TABLE 2.8 (CONTINUED) CROSS COMPARISON FOR PIG, HIVE AND SPARK SQL

Structured or Unstructured Data	Unstructured, structured, nested Structured raw data	Structured tabular data	Structured tabular data
Catalog Services	HCatalog (Optional)	Metastore and HCatalog	Metastore and HCatalog
Primitives Data Type	INT, LONG, FLOAT, DOUBLE, CHARARRAY, etc.	TINYINT, SMALLINT, INT, BIGINT, FLOAT, DOUBLE, etc.	ByteType, ShortType, IntegerType, LongType, FloatType, DoubleType , etc. And most of Hive's Primitives DataType
Non-Primitives Data Type	map, tuple, bag	maps, arrays, structs, union	ArrayType, MapType, StructType
Relational Statements	GROUP, DEFINE, FILTER, FOREACH, JOIN, UNION, ORDER BY, SAMPLE, etc.	SELECT, GROUP BY, ORDER BY, CLUSTER BY, DISTRIBUTE BY, JOIN, UNION, TABLESAMPLE, etc.	SELECT, GROUP BY, ORDER BY, CLUSTER BY, JOIN, UNION, TABLESAMPLE, etc.
Math Operators	ADDITION, SUBTRACTION, MULTIPLICATION, DIVISION, MODULO, etc.	ADDITION, SUBTRACTION, MULTIPLICATION, DIVISION, MODULO, etc.	ADDITION, SUBTRACTION, MULTIPLICATION, DIVISION, MODULO, etc.
Logical Operators	AND, OR, IN, NOT, EQUAL, NOT EQUAL, LESS THAN, GREATER THAN, PATTERN MATCHING	AND, OR, NOT, IN, EQUAL, NOT EQUAL, LESS THAN, GREATER THAN, PATTERN MATCHING, EXISTS, IF, COALESCE, CASE	AND, OR, NOT, IN, EQUAL, NOT EQUAL, LESS THAN, GREATER THAN, PATTERN MATCHING, EXISTS, IF, COALESCE, CASE
Collection and Aggregate Functions	AVG, SUM, COUNT, CONCAT, MAX, MIN, SIZE, SUBSTRACT, etc.	AVG, SUM, COUNT, CONCAT, MAX, MIN, SIZE, SUBSTRACT, etc.	AVG, SUM, COUNT, CONCAT, MAX, MIN, SIZE, SUBSTRACT, etc.

TABLE 2.8 (CONTINUED) CROSS COMPARISON FOR PIG, HIVE AND SPARK SQL

String Functions	Yes	Yes	Yes
DateTime Functions	Yes	Yes	Yes
UDF Support	Yes	Yes	Yes (partially Hive UDF)
JDBC/Thrift Support	Partial (No Thrift API)	Yes	Yes
Index Table	No	Yes	Yes
Storage Layer	Local Disk, HDFS, HBase	Local Disk, HDFS, HBase (Optional)	Local Disk, HDFS, HBase (Optional)
Applications	Data filtering, ETL, log analysis, general statistic applications, text processing	Ad-hoc queries, ODBC/JDBC applications, high-latency queries	Ad-hoc queries, ODBC/JDBC applications, low-latency queries

LEFT OUTER JOIN both in Pig and Hive implementation, and each partition is separately loaded in an extra mapper and prepared for the JOIN operations. In the case of Hive PageRank, although the HiveQL logic is the same as Pig's, Hive's physical plan executor generates a total of 4 Hadoop jobs per iteration, which results in a dramatic performance loss.

2.7 CONCLUSION

In this chapter, we investigated the Apache high-level languages and several runtimes of Hadoop ecosystems by conducting tests on real world applications with social media data. Terabytes of data streams are collected every day and stored on different large-scale storage systems such as HDFS and HBase. Pig, Hive, and Spark SQL have been widely adopted by developers and domain scientists for rapidly building their prototypes and performing daily analysis tasks on both new and historical data. Although Pig and Hive have provided desirable features and performance for ad-hoc queries, these high-level abstractions lack support for interactive applications that require in-memory caches and fast job restart between iterations for sophisticated post-query data analysis. This chapter compares different approaches of building high-level dataflow systems and ultimately demonstrates an integrated solution with Pig and Harp (called Pig+Harp) that outperforms both Pig and Hive by a factor of 2 to 10 in overall metrics. Our experimental results show that these high-level languages and their integrations make it easier for users to perform data analysis, and improve the flexibility of database systems through user-defined aggregations.

Bibliography

[1] Apache hadoop. http://hadoop.apache.org/core/.

[2] Apache spark sql. https://spark.apache.org/sql/.

[3] Test cases for scalable query and analysis for social networks. https://github.com/taklwu/apache-high-level-languages-survey.

[4] Hbase implementation of bigtable on hadoop file system. http://hbase.apache.org/, 2010.

[5] Pig programming tools. http://en.wikipedia.org/wiki/Pig_(programming _tool), 2014.

[6] Ablimit Aji, Xiling Sun, Hoang Vo, Qioaling Liu, Rubao Lee, Xiaodong Zhang, Joel Saltz, and Fusheng Wang. Demonstration of hadoop-gis: A spatial data warehousing system over mapreduce. In *Proceedings of the 21st ACM SIGSPATIAL International Conference on Advances in Geographic Information Systems*, pages 528–531. ACM, 2013.

[7] Yael Amsterdamer, Susan B Davidson, Daniel Deutch, Tova Milo, Julia Stoyanovich, and Val Tannen. Putting lipstick on pig: Enabling database-style workflow provenance. *Proceedings of the VLDB Endowment*, 5(4):346–357, 2011.

[8] Dhruba Borthakur, Jonathan Gray, Joydeep Sen Sarma, Kannan Muthukkaruppan, Nicolas Spiegelberg, Hairong Kuang, Karthik Ranganathan, Dmytro Molkov, Aravind Menon, Samuel Rash, et al. Apache hadoop goes realtime at facebook. In *Proceedings of the 2011 ACM SIGMOD International Conference on Management of data*, pages 1071–1080. ACM, 2011.

[9] Yingyi Bu, Bill Howe, Magdalena Balazinska, and Michael D Ernst. Haloop: efficient iterative data processing on large clusters. *Proceedings of the VLDB Endowment*, 3(1-2):285–296, 2010.

[10] Michael Conover, Jacob Ratkiewicz, Matthew Francisco, Bruno Gonffalves, Filippo Menczer, and Alessandro Flammini. Political polarization on twitter. In *ICWSM*, 2011.

[11] Michael D Conover, Clayton Davis, Emilio Ferrara, Karissa McKelvey, Filippo Menczer, and Alessandro Flammini. The geospatial characteristics of a social movement communication network. *PloS one*, 8(3):e55957, 2013.

[12] Michael D Conover, Emilio Ferrara, Filippo Menczer, and Alessandro Flammini. The digital evolution of occupy wall street. *PloS one*, 8(5):e64679, 2013.

[13] Michael D Conover, Bruno Gonffalves, Alessandro Flammini, and Filippo Menczer. Partisan asymmetries in online political activity. *EPJ Data Science*, 1(1):1–19, 2012.

[14] Joseph DiGrazia, Karissa McKelvey, Johan Bollen, and Fabio Rojas. More tweets, more votes: Social media as a quantitative indicator of political behavior. *PloS one*, 8(11):e79449, 2013.

[15] Jaliya Ekanayake, Hui Li, Bingjing Zhang, Thilina Gunarathne, Seung-Hee Bae, Judy Qiu, and Geoffrey Fox. Twister: a runtime for iterative mapreduce. In *Proceedings of the 19th ACM International Symposium on High Performance Distributed Computing*, pages 810–818. ACM, 2010.

[16] Emilio Ferrara, Onur Varol, Clayton Davis, Filippo Menczer, and Alessandro Flammini. The rise of social bots. *arXiv preprint arXiv:1407.5225*, 2014.

[17] Emilio Ferrara, Onur Varol, Filippo Menczer, and Alessandro Flammini. Traveling trends: social butterflies or frequent fliers? In *Proceedings of the first ACM conference on Online social networks*, pages 213–222. ACM, 2013.

[18] Xiaoming Gao, Emilio Ferrara, and Judy Qiu. Parallel clustering of high-dimensional social media data streams. *arXiv preprint arXiv:1502.00316*, 2015.

[19] Xiaoming Gao and Judy Qiu. Social media data analysis with indexed-hbase and iterative mapreduce. In *Proc. Workshop on Many-Task Computing on Clouds, Grids, and Supercomputers (MTAGS 2013) at Super Computing*, 2013.

[20] Xiaoming Gao and Judy Qiu. Supporting end-to-end social media data analysis with the indexedhbase platform. In *Invited talk at 6th Workshop on Many-Task Computing on Clouds, Grids, and Supercomputers (MTAGS) SC13*, 2013.

[21] Xiaoming Gao, Evan Roth, Karissa McKelvey, Clayton Davis, Andrew Younge, Emilio Ferrara, Filippo Menczer, and Judy Qiu. Supporting a social media observatory with customizable index structures: Architecture and performance. In *Cloud Computing for Data-Intensive Applications*, pages 401–427. Springer, 2014.

[22] Alan F Gates, Olga Natkovich, Shubham Chopra, Pradeep Kamath, Shravan M Narayanamurthy, Christopher Olston, Benjamin Reed, Santhosh Srinivasan, and Utkarsh Srivastava. Building a high-level dataflow system on top of map-reduce: the pig experience. *Proceedings of the VLDB Endowment*, 2(2):1414–1425, 2009.

[23] Tim Hegeman, Bogdan Ghit, Mihai Capota, Jan Hidders, Dick Epema, and Alexandru Iosup. The btworld use case for big data analytics: Description, mapreduce logical workflow, and empirical evaluation. In *Big Data, 2013 IEEE International Conference on*, pages 622–630. IEEE, 2013.

[24] CJ Hutto and Eric Gilbert. Vader: A parsimonious rule-based model for sentiment analysis of social media text. In *Eighth International AAAI Conference on Weblogs and Social Media*, 2014.

[25] Mohsen JafariAsbagh, Emilio Ferrara, Onur Varol, Filippo Menczer, and Alessandro Flammini. Clustering memes in social media streams. *Social Network Analysis and Mining*, 4(1):1–13, 2014.

[26] Yeonhee Lee and Youngseok Lee. Toward scalable internet traffic measurement and analysis with hadoop. *ACM SIGCOMM Computer Communication Review*, 43(1):5–13, 2013.

[27] Yunpeng Li, David J Crandall, and Daniel P Huttenlocher. Landmark classification in large-scale image collections. In *Computer Vision, 2009 IEEE 12th International Conference on*, pages 1957–1964. IEEE, 2009.

[28] David G Lowe. Distinctive image features from scale-invariant keypoints. *International Journal of Computer Vision*, 60(2):91–110, 2004.

[29] James MacQueen et al. Some methods for classification and analysis of multivariate observations. In *Proceedings of the Fifth Berkeley Symposium on Mathematical Statistics and Probability*, volume 1, pages 281–297. Oakland, CA, 1967.

[30] Karissa McKelvey and Filippo Menczer. Design and prototyping of a social media observatory. In *Proceedings of the 22nd International Conference on World Wide Web Companion*, pages 1351–1358. International World Wide Web Conferences Steering Committee, 2013.

[31] Mark EJ Newman. Finding community structure in networks using the eigenvectors of matrices. *Physical Review E*, 74(3):036104, 2006.

[32] Christopher Olston, Benjamin Reed, Utkarsh Srivastava, Ravi Kumar, and Andrew Tomkins. Pig latin: a not-so-foreign language for data processing. In *Proceedings of the 2008 ACM SIGMOD International Conference on Management of Data*, pages 1099–1110. ACM, 2008.

[33] Lawrence Page, Sergey Brin, Rajeev Motwani, and Terry Winograd. The pagerank citation ranking: Bringing order to the web. 1999.

[34] Terence J. Parr and Russell W. Quong. Antlr: A predicated-ll (k) parser generator. *Software: Practice and Experience*, 25(7):789–810, 1995.

[35] Judy Qiu and Bingjing Zhang. Mammoth data in the cloud: Clustering social images. *Clouds, Grids and Big Data*, 2013.

[36] Usha Nandini Raghavan, Reka Albert, and Soundar Kumara. Near linear time algorithm to detect community structures in large-scale networks. *Physical Review E*, 76(3):036106, 2007.

[37] Jacob Ratkiewicz, Michael Conover, Mark Meiss, Bruno Gonffalves, Alessandro Flammini, and Filippo Menczer. Detecting and tracking political abuse in social media. In *ICWSM*, 2011.

[38] Jacob Ratkiewicz, Michael Conover, Mark Meiss, Bruno Gonffalves, Snehal Patil, Alessandro Flammini, and Filippo Menczer. Truthy: mapping the spread of astroturf in microblog streams. In *Proceedings of the 20th International Conference Companion on World Wide Web*, pages 249–252. ACM, 2011.

[39] Konstantin Shvachko, Hairong Kuang, Sanjay Radia, and Robert Chansler. The hadoop distributed file system. In *Mass Storage Systems and Technologies (MSST), 2010 IEEE 26th Symposium on*, pages 1–10. IEEE, 2010.

[40] Ashish Thusoo, Joydeep Sen Sarma, Namit Jain, Zheng Shao, Prasad Chakka, Suresh Anthony, Hao Liu, Pete Wyckoff, and Raghotham Murthy. Hive: a warehousing solution over a map-reduce framework. *Proceedings of the VLDB Endowment*, 2(2):1626–1629, 2009.

[41] Onur Varol, Emilio Ferrara, Christine L Ogan, Filippo Menczer, and Alessandro Flammini. Evolution of online user behavior during a social upheaval. In *Proceedings of the 2014 ACM Conference on Web Science*, pages 81–90. ACM, 2014.

[42] Vinod Kumar Vavilapalli, Arun C Murthy, Chris Douglas, Sharad Agarwal, Mahadev Konar, Robert Evans, Thomas Graves, Jason Lowe, Hitesh Shah, Siddharth Seth, et al. Apache hadoop yarn: Yet another resource negotiator. In *Proceedings of the 4th Annual Symposium on Cloud Computing*, page 5. ACM, 2013.

[43] Tak-Lon Wu, Abhilash Koppula, and Judy Qiu. Integrating pig with harp to support iterative applications with fast cache and customized communication. In *Proceedings of the 5th International Workshop on Data-Intensive Computing in the Clouds*, pages 33–39. IEEE Press, 2014.

[44] Reynold S Xin, Josh Rosen, Matei Zaharia, Michael J Franklin, Scott Shenker, and Ion Stoica. Shark: Sql and rich analytics at scale. In *Proceedings of the 2013 ACM SIGMOD International Conference on Management of Data*, pages 13–24. ACM, 2013.

[45] Matei Zaharia, Mosharaf Chowdhury, Tathagata Das, Ankur Dave, Justin Ma, Murphy McCauley, Michael J Franklin, Scott Shenker, and Ion Stoica. Resilient distributed datasets: A fault-tolerant abstraction for in-memory cluster computing. In *Proceedings of the 9th USENIX Conference on Networked Systems Design and Implementation*, pages 2–2. USENIX Association, 2012.

[46] Matei Zaharia, Mosharaf Chowdhury, Michael J Franklin, Scott Shenker, and Ion Stoica. Spark: cluster computing with working sets. In *Proceedings of the 2nd USENIX Conference on Hot Topics in Cloud Computing*, pages 10–10, 2010.

[47] Bingjing Zhang, Yang Ruan, and Judy Qiu. Harp: Collective communication on hadoop. In *IEEE International Conference on Cloud Engineering (IC2E)*.

II

Big Data and Web Intelligence

CHAPTER 3

Predicting Content Popularity in Social Networks

Yan Yan, Ruibo Zhou, Xiaofeng Gao and Guihai Chen

CONTENTS

C ENTRALIZED with users being the creators and propagators, social networks tend to be an indispensable part of modern people's lives, in the era of Web 2.0. Massive amount of users' thoughts and friendships are implied in social networks, which becomes a promising source of big data. One of the most significant meanings for data mining is to analyze the underlined relations among data, and use it for the future. In a social network, the limitation of users' time and attention determines that users will only focus on what they are interested in and what is popular for the time being. Predicting what is popular in time will not only improve the utilization of users' time and attention, but also benefit social websites to offer better services to their users. In this chapter, we intend to research the popularity prediction of textual content, using big data in social networks. We focus on methods and models of prediction, which are well classified by elements the models consider, such as user behaviors, the life cycles of information, and the social network topology. We also reveal researchers' work on classifying social networks, evaluating metrics, as well as feature selection, and what remains to be done.

3.1 INTRODUCTION

Social networks such as Twitter, Facebook, Flickr and Instagram are well-known to people all over the world. People, especially the young, usually use more than one kind of social network service simultaneously in order to keep in touch with friends in different circles. Besides that, social networks also provide ordinary people with a fancy chance to keep a close eye on the life of celebrities, such as President Barack Obama, Taylor Swift, and Kobe Bryant. According to the Twitter Company Statistics, the total number of registered Twitter users is 645,750,000, and active users are 289,000,000. The total number of monthly active users in Facebook reaches 1,310,000,000. Via analyzing the large volume of data, we can know better what users need and what they like, so as to make more contributions to attract and keep more users in social network. Take Twitter as an example. Each Twitter user has a Homepage, from which we can view what is new of the person whom we are following. Moreover, on the left part of Homepage, there is a column called "trend". If the team of Twitter can predict accurately and instantaneously what is popular recently, and how long the trend will last, then they can put these popular contents on the trend, drawing more users' attention, which also benefits Twitter itself.

Social network has so many topics that we can dig deeper into, such as social group recognition and influential users discovery. Social group recognition is to divide social network users into groups by their hobbies, interests or occupations, so that organizers can recommend goods to each group easily. Discovering influential users is also important, in that these vital users may contribute a lot in topic spreading. Furthermore, big data in social network has the potential to solve cross-domain challenges, such as surveillance of public health. To keep pace with new developing technologies, social network is now combining with crowdsourcing, which is an up-to-date method to gather the wisdom of all people who take part in it. In addition to structural-hole theory, information-diffusion theory, the challenges in social network seem to have new ways to solve.

As our predicting basement is social network, we first give a brief introduction to the social network.

3.1.1 What is a Social Network?

A social network is a social structure made up of a set of social actors (such as individuals or organizations) and a set of the dyadic ties between these actors. The social network perspective provides a set of methods for analyzing the structure of the whole social entity as well as a variety of theories explaining the patterns observed in these structures [41]. Studies of these structures use social network analysis to identify local and global patterns, locate influential entities, and examine network dynamics.

3.1.2 Levels of Social Network

Social network is self-organized, emergent, and complex. Since there are so many aspects to analyze, we should firstly provide a partition for it. In general, social networks can be divided into three levels:[1] micro level (Figure 3.1(a)), meso level (Figure 3.1(b)), and macro level (Figure 3.1(c)). In the micro level, researchers focus on the individuals in the social network. Thus we dig deeper into users' behaviors in this level. In the meso level, the formation of groups draws our attention. Correspondingly, we find groups in social network, and try to pick out the leader of the group. In the macro level, we take the whole large-scale social network graph into account. At this moment, we are more interested in hierarchical structures.

3.1.3 The Long Tail

The long tail shape (shown in Figure 3.2) is a common shape to illustrate the 2-dimensional relationship in social network, such as the relationship between the number of users and their followers, or the number of users and things they post [25]. An example can be shown in Figure 3.2. From this figure we can observe users' relation shapes in the social network like Twitter. Users

---

[1] From Wikipedia: $https://en.wikipedia.org/wiki/Socialnetwork$

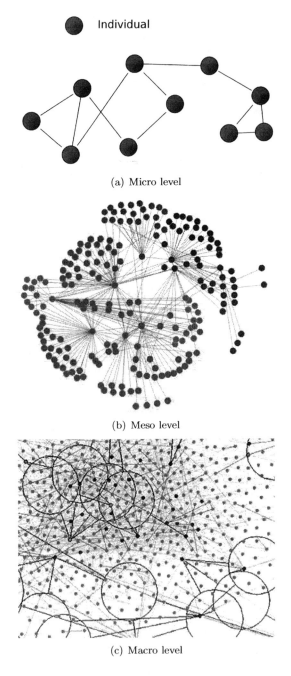

(a) Micro level

(b) Meso level

(c) Macro level

FIGURE 3.1 Different levels of social network (From: Wikipedia).

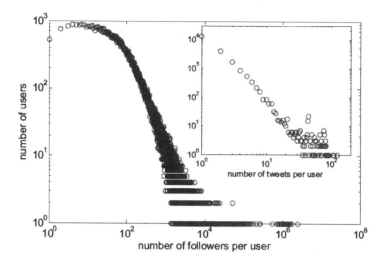

FIGURE 3.2 The long tail shape from Twitter data set [25].

who have a small number of followers are the majority, while it is rare to have a very large number of followers. So is the number of tweets [5]. Users who post less than 10 tweets are often to see, but those who post hundreds of tweets per day are rare.

3.2 CLASSIFICATION OF SOCIAL NETWORK

Now that we have taken a general look at what is a social network, let us learn more about the classification of social networks and the contents we are going to predict.

3.2.1 Narrow-Sensed Social Network

When it comes to social network, Facebook, Twitter, and Weibo are the most famous and frequently used ones [3]. These types can be referred to as narrow-sensed social network. The very characteristic of these social networks is the focus on communication. Users in these social networks share their own lives or interesting topics via fresh news, photos, videos, logs, etc. Their friends and followers read these textual contents and show their positive or negative opinions on them. In general, these social networks are widely used by people who are real-world friends or who are eager to understand more about celebrity news.

3.2.2 News-Based Social Network

News-based social network concerns news. News is packaged information about new events happening somewhere else. Nowadays, news is no longer

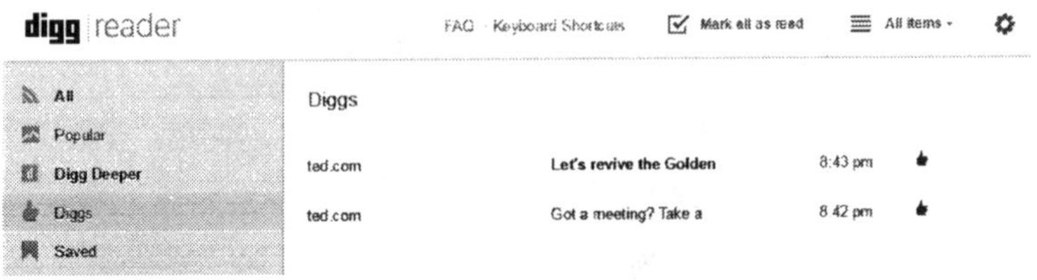

FIGURE 3.3 The user interface of Digg.

sold in the streets. They are in electronic versions, distributed to websites. Despite large amounts of news websites over the world, few of them can be called social networks.

Digg is a non-intuitive example (changes a lot in the past few years, the GUI is in Figure 3.3). Digg is a news aggregator with an editorially driven front page, aiming to select stories specifically for the Internet audience such as science, trending political issues, and viral Internet issues. News in Digg cannot only be created by professional journalists, but also by everyone who uses Digg by uploading news around them. This is why Digg can be defined as a social network. Users in Digg have friends (in specific, followings and followers). They can read news created by their friends, digg it (vote for it), and comment on it. That is where the interactions happen, which is an important standard to judge whether a news website can be identified as a social network. There are some studies carried out on Digg [25, 35, 40].

Reddit and Hacker News are other vivid examples of news-based social networks. Reddit is quite similar to Digg. Registered users of this website, usually referred to as "redditors", can vote "up" and "down" for the news and decide their positions on the site's page. Hacker news is a little bit different. We can easily tell from the name of Hacker that this social news website focuses on computer science and entrepreneurship. What is more, there is no option to down-vote the post which means users can only up-vote it or not vote on it. In general, content that can be submitted on Hacker News is defined as "anything that gratifies one's intellectual curiosity". No matter how distinct these websites are, the elements of interaction and communication make them the news-based social networks.

3.2.3 Major-Based Social Network

When it comes to major-based social networks, LinkedIn must be the most well-known one. LinkedIn (in Figure 3.4) is a business-oriented social network. The basic functionality of LinkedIn allows users to create profiles and establish relationships with each other in an online social network, mapping out real-world professional relationships. Compared with other social networks, the relationship in this special social network is more important in that users can seek jobs, people, and business opportunities recommended by someone

FIGURE 3.4 The user interface of LinkedIn.

in one's contact network. LinkedIn is called a major-based social network in that it works mainly for employers and job seekers. By using this social network, employers can list jobs and search for potential candidates by browsing candidates' profiles, which act like resumes in some way. Of course, job seekers should fill their profiles with their professional skills ahead of time and seek appropriate jobs.

Another kind of major-based social network is non-intuitive, which is used for single men and women to seek a mate. This kind of social network is really popular in China, such as Zhenai Net, Baihe Net, Shijijiayuan Net, etc.

Various kinds of social networks are used in research papers in experiment section. We give a statistic graph (Figure 3.5) after our survey on social networks used from year 2010 to 2013.

It should be mentioned that there are probably more than one social network used in one paper.

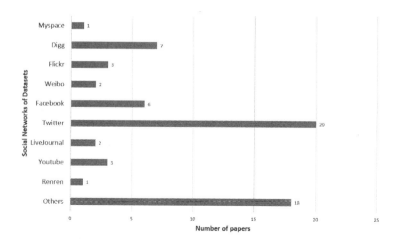

FIGURE 3.5 Social network used in research papers in recent years.

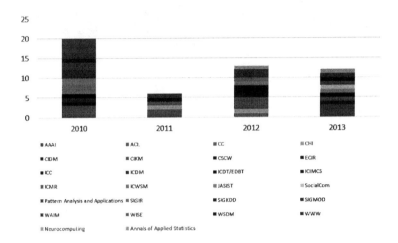

FIGURE 3.6 Number of papers in related conferences every years.

Furthermore, in Figure 3.6, we analyze the number of papers in conferences which pay attention to predict popularity of online contents every year.

3.3 PREDICTION MODEL

Our goal is to research the popularity prediction of textual content, so we shall investigate prediction models involved in this area. In this section, it first gives a brief description of the feature selection. After that three aspects worth considering in prediction models are followed.

3.3.1 Feature Selection

When establishing a prediction model, usually we need to find some elements or aspects based on which we can make a reliable prediction. We refer to these elements or aspects as features. There can be various features for prediction but not all of them contribute to the prediction result. Thus, selecting relevant and supporting features is crucial to the accuracy of prediction. Since the piece of datum in a social network usually contains many redundant or irrelevant features, we should implement some feature selection technique. At the very beginning, we may enumerate several features from different aspects. The most common features that we can think of in social network prediction includes length of a tweet, the number of words, etc. To filter useful features, different scenarios are proposed. We will explore them successively and conclude at the end of this subsection.

Before the overture, we should realize that feature selection technique is to be distinguished from feature extraction. Feature extraction creates new features from functions of the original features, whereas feature selection returns a subset of the features. The typical method that feature extraction applies would be Principal Components Analysis (PCA). Both selection and extraction are recommended, but we prefer selection because our features are mostly independent.

3.3.1.1 Mature Tool

We may first try some general methods to select features. Arunee Ratikan [33] uses Weka module to select attributes. Weka is a statistical tool that provides multiple functions. All of Weka's techniques are predicated on the assumption that the data is available as a single flat file or relation, where each data point is described by a fixed number of attributes. Weka builds an attribute selection function based on [4]. You can use it directly as a blackbox for its effectiveness and convenience.

3.3.1.2 Correlation-based Method

Other than mature tools, the most natural way to do feature reduction is correlation-based method. There are several evaluation measurements and the detailed processes are varied.

The main point of correlation is to score features via experiments. For instance, Marilyn A.Walker [29] calculates Pearson's correlation coefficients between Linguistic Inquiry and Word Count (LIWC) features and personality ratings. It can be acquired by Equation (3.1) given two variables X and Y as follows:

$$\rho = Cor(X, Y) = \frac{Cov(X, Y)}{\sigma_X \sigma_Y} \qquad (3.1)$$

where Cov is the covariance and σ_X is the standard deviation of X. The result falls between +1 and -1 inclusive, where 1 is total positive correlation, 0 is no correlation, and 1 is total negative correlation.

Besides the algorithm, we may employ some tactics for evaluation. The simple examples can be found in Rushi Bhatt's work [7]. Their models effectively combine user features and social features to predict adoption, which is better than using either user features or social features individually. A more complex instance is from Shoubin Kong's work [21]. It presents the evaluation method as F_1-score and gains the importance of features by dropping them one by one. The most influential one is obtained when the result is terrible without it.

3.3.1.3 Unique Method

It is also encouraged to cope with data differently under various circumstances. One intuitive case is Tim Paek's work [30], whose features are enormous. They reduced the number of features to the top $3K$ features in terms of log likelihood ratios as determined on the training set. A likelihood ratio test is based on the likelihood ratio, which expresses how many times more likely the data are under one model than the other. This likelihood ratio, or equivalently its logarithm, can then be used to compute a *p*-value. When it comes to the feature selection, Dunning first combined them together [11] and it has been widely used ever since.

Moreover, Hila Becker [6] involves an ensemble algorithm, which considers each feature as a weak indication of social media document similarity, and combines all features using a weighted similarity consensus function. Ensemble clustering is an approach that combines multiple clustering solutions for a document set. It enhances its ability to account for different similarity metrics.

Selecting features is not a necessary process, but it could improve the accuracy of the prediction result and reduce the computation complexity. When we encounter this problem, the suggested methods are mature tools and correlation-based method. Meanwhile, when we want to achieve some specific aims like choosing the most important feature, some special methods are also promising if designed properly. Also, several special cases illustrate the diversity of this issue.

3.3.2 Text Content

Before we turn to predicting models, there is a classification about the content we predict that should be clarified. Online contents that we would like to predict can be categorized into three main kinds: something, news, topics, events.

Something is a single message user post on social network. It's something new that a user wants to share with his social friends. *Something* can be either a tweet in Twitter, or a story in Digg.

News narrowly refers to news that is broadcast on TV or online newspapers.

Topics usually has some key words. And many *something* which all contain these key words consist of a topic. The contents of a topic could change from time to time. For example, we talked about the famous singer Taylor Swift yesterday because of her new song written to another ex-boyfriend, but we talk about her new song today because it wins a Grammy Award.

Event is defined as an activity or action with a clear, finite duration given a particular target entity which plays a key role in the duration [32].

3.3.3 Predicting Models

Predicting model is the soul of prediction. It is the most important element in this research area. A good model will not only emerge the inner characteristic of training data, but also predict what is popular in the future precisely and timely. The fundamental idea of constructing a model is to take possible and significant elements into account by combining them linearly with static or dynamic weights so that it can make the prediction with history information.

The difficult part of creating a prediction model comes when deciding what factors to include and how to represent them.

In this section, we are going to introduce several factors and methods of various models taken for prediction. We classify them into several types: user behaviors, life cycles of textual contents, and network topology. Notice that these methods are not totally independent. Actually you can find some of them together in one prediction model.

3.3.3.1 Prediction Based on User Behaviors

User behavior in social networks covers various activities that users can do online, including expressing new opinions, commenting, sharing, browsing and so on [18]. For instance, a typical user of Twitter may deliver a new tweet about the good weather, thumb's up a friend's tweet, share a funny story, and do not forget to update a new selfie. Every new update and every interaction with people in the social network makes up a series of user behaviors.

Notably, user behaviors, in different social networks, can be different. The most common behavior in Twitter is creating new tweets and retweeting others, but on other news and story websites like Digg and Flickr, page browsing, commenting, sharing, and other post-read actions [2] happen more often. User behaviors are dynamic. Users change their behaviors from time to time so user behaviors are usually represented in a function with time t as a variable because that is how these data are collected. For example, Kong et al. [21] monitored the time series of all hashtags and predicted the burst and popularity of them. We then introduce several examples to illustrate how to use user behaviors for prediction.

Box-Office Revenue Prediction: Asur and Huberman [4] tried to predict the box-office revenues by studying the tweets on Twitter. This study defines a Tweet-rate to reflect the user behavior of posting tweets of a movie prior its release. The definition of Tweet-rate is shown in Equation (3.2):

$$Tweet - rate(mov) = \frac{|tweets(mov)|}{|hours|} \qquad (3.2)$$

This definition means the number of tweets referring to a particular movie per hour. Then, the revenue is predicted based on the defined Tweet-rate in Equation (3.3).

$$Rev(mov) = \beta_0 + \sum_{i=1}^{7} \beta_i * Tweet\text{-}rate_i(mov) + \beta_{th} * thcnt, \qquad (3.3)$$

where *thcnt* means the number of theatres the movies are released in and β values represent the regression coefficients which is learned from historical records. Let us take a deeper look into this model. This model is a linear regression of tweet-rates in 7 days before the release of a particular movie. It collects tweets about a movie and views them as user behaviors on social network and uses them to predict the revenues. Different β_i are included so as to find out the different impacts tweet-rates on each day have on the result. This is one simple example of applying user behaviors on prediction.

News Popularity Prediction: Here is another example using the number of tweets to make the prediction for news popularity [5]. Bandari et al. chose 4 types of predictors to predict the popularity of news. They first defined a feature, named t-density, to represent the "popularity" of news per link using the number of tweets, as shown in Equation (3.4).

$$t\text{-}density = \frac{\texttt{Number of Tweets}}{\texttt{Number of Links}}, \tag{3.4}$$

where the "Number of Links" represents the links in a news category. The authors considered 4 types of predictors, *Category Score* represented by t-density of a category, *Subjectivity* obtained from an existing subjectivity classifier, *Name Entities* (a known place, person, or organization) obtained from an existing extraction tool, and *Source Score* represented by t-density of each source, to predict the popularity of the news with regression algorithms and the result using linear regression as shown in Equation (3.5):

$$ln(T) = 1.24ln(S) + 0.45ln(C) + 0.1Ent_{max} - 3 \tag{3.5}$$

where T represents the number of tweets, S represents the source t-density score, C represents the category t-density score, and Ent_{max} is the maximum t-density of all entities found in the paper.

User Behavior Prediction: The previous example takes advantage of user behaviors to make prediction of something outside of social network, while user behaviors can directly be used to predict user behaviors. Lee et al. [23] predicted total comments from early comments and Castillo et al. [9] predicted the visits from early visits, to name just a few.

Among numbers of researches, Huang et al. [15] is a typical example. They applied their model, the *Parameterized Social Activity Model* (PSAM), to predict the tendency of social activities (denoted as N_t). Here social activities can be something like becoming a member, posting a message, adding a comment, inviting a friend, etc., which just matches the user behaviors that we are discussing.

To predict the trend of the evolution of a social activity, this model uses a continuous-time stochastic process. The trend of N_t consists of two parts, one is the tendency of evolution, and the other is the random impact from the environment. The authors derived a parameterized stochastic process with a drift and diffusion as in Equation (3.6).

$$dN_t = \gamma(\vec{\lambda_t})N_t dt + \sigma(\vec{\lambda_t})N_t dW(t) \tag{3.6}$$

where t is the continuous time, $\overrightarrow{\lambda_t}$ is the time-involved activity features vector. The first part of Equation (3.6) indicates the growth or shrinkage of activities in a social network, while the second part is the random impact, which we emphasize here. In this part, the Wiener Process (WP, which is also called Brownian Motion) is used. WP has a good performance on predicting a near future using data from the present. (However, it cannot predict long time future because the expectation of the future is exactly the same as the expectation of the present. That is to say, WP has no tendency to increase or decrease in the future.)

Finally, for this model the authors evaluated three publicly available datasets: Facebook-wallpost dataset [39], Facebook friend-request dataset [39], and Citeseer co-authorship dataset [14]. The experimental result shows that the model has more than 0.8 accuracy which indicates the effectiveness of it.

Story Popularity Prediction: Apart from some easily recognized user behaviors, page browsing, as another kind of major user behavior in social news portal, can also be considered as part of the predicting model. According to [16], the distribution of the number of pages a user visits before leaving the web site can be modeled by a two-parameter inverse Gaussian distribution in Equation (3.7):

$$P(L) = \sqrt{\frac{\lambda}{2\pi L^3}} \exp\left[\frac{-\lambda(L-\mu)^2}{2\mu^2 L}\right] \tag{3.7}$$

where L is the random value of the number of links a user follows before the page value first reaches the stopping threshold. And mean $E(L) = \mu$, variance $Var(L) = \mu^3/\lambda$, where λ is a scale parameter.

Using this theorem, Lerman et al. [26] proposed a model of social dynamics to predict popularity of news based on the social network Digg. The standard for popularity is the number of votes a story in Digg gets. Moreover, the number of votes a story receives depends on the combination of its visibility and interest, with visibility coming from different parts of the Digg user interface (the friends interface $v_{friends}$, upcoming v_u, and front pages lists v_f) and the position within each list. Therefore, the Rate Equation for the number of votes a story gets N_{vote} is shown in Equation (3.8):

$$\frac{dN_{vote}(t)}{dt} = r(v_f(t) + v_u(t) + v_{friends}(t)) \tag{3.8}$$

where r is the probability a user seeing the story will vote on it. To represent v_f and v_u, we use the inverse Gaussian distribution in Equation (3.7), and get Equation (3.9):

$$v_f = v f_{page}(p(t))\Theta(N_{vote}(t) - h) \tag{3.9}$$

where f_{page} models user behaviors of browsing web pages, that is a decreasing visibility of stories on a page from upper to under, which refers to the inverse Gaussian distribution. And $p(t)$ is the position of a story in page p at time t.

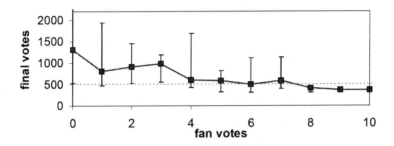

FIGURE 3.7 Number of fan votes within the first 10 votes VS final votes received by front page stories [26].

This model is extremely intuitive in sync with common sense. It derives human activity with precise mathematical models. Additionally, the result the model gets is similarly logical and reasonable. In another paper of Lerman's work [24], it derives that votes from fans of the submitter or previous voters ultimately go on to accumulate fewer votes than stories that initially receive few fan votes (Figure 3.7). That is because a story that is of interest to a narrow community will spread within that community only, while a generally interesting story will spread from many independent sites as users unconnected to previous voters discover it with some small probability and propagate it to their own fans.

3.3.3.2 Prediction Based on Life Cycles

Besides studying user behaviors alone, much research studies how one piece of information spreads in the social network, how it starts to be popular, and how soon it disappears. We describe the duration of a piece of information in the social network as life cycle. We believe that majority of social network users have such an experience: a topic suddenly appears out of nowhere and everyone talks about it immediately, but just two or three hours later, it has been forgotten and another new issue takes its place. In other words, some information spreading in social network bursts out suddenly and disappears quickly. If we can determine the pattern beforehand, we can distinguish among topics that will be popular and those that will not. By studying the life cycle, approximate prediction can be made. Combined with other factors like user behaviors, the prediction could be accurate.

Discussion on the Types of Life Cycles: Research on life cycles shows that different types of textual contents have every distinct life cycle pattern. In [9], the researches come up with a qualitative and quantitative analysis of the life cycle of online news stories. It probes into the Al Jazeera

English, a large international news network, finding out two life cycle patterns of two types of stories, News and In-Depth. The pattern for the News article can be roughly described by an "80:10:10" rule. To be specific, 78% of News articles decrease either at once or after a short delay when published. About 12% of News articles stay steadily or increase during the first 12 hours. The other 10% of the articles initially decline in visits per minute, until a special moment when the decline reverses. The authors called the phenomena *rebounding*. On the other hand, In-Depth articles sustain a level of visits during several hours and are not as time-sensitive as the News articles. Seeing the life cycle patterns, the authors designed a linear regression model using several social media features. The model can be represented as Equation (3.10) and Equation (3.11):

$$lm(vis7d \sim v) \tag{3.10}$$

$$lm(vis7d \sim (v + vr + vd + f + t + foll + ent + uni + unip + cp)^2) \tag{3.11}$$

where $vis7d$ means the predicted total visits after 7 days, and the features include number of visit (v), number of visits from link referrals (vr), email/IM (vd), shares on Facebook (f), Twitter (t), the mean number of followers of people sharing on Twitter ($foll$), the entropy of tweets (ent), the number and fraction of unique tweets (uni, $unip$), and the fraction of corporate retweets (cp). This model considers second-order interactions because some of the variables are interdependent.

Life Cycle with Influence Decay: Another work [20] focuses on the decay of information and uses the build novel model on it. It reranks the news from three datasets, Google News Archives (SES), dataset from web portals in China (WPS), and earlier data with the same resource as WPS (TS). The core idea is to include the influence decay factor so that the life cycle of the news can be considered into the model. Together with features from media focus and user attention, the authors used this model to rank the news again. They adopted a sigmoid function to simulate the influence decay, as shown in Equation (3.12):

$$f(x) = \begin{cases} \frac{\delta x}{1+\delta x}, & x > 0; \\ 0, & otherwise. \end{cases} \tag{3.12}$$

where δ is a smoothing parameter. The simplest model appears as:

$$I_d^\varepsilon = f(r_d^\varepsilon), \tag{3.13}$$

where I_d^ε represents the influence value of topic ε and r_d^ε is the report-frequency of topic ε during the dth day. Of course this model is too simple, so the authors modified it bit by bit. They remodeled it by calculating the accumulative effect of influence decay by adding continuous d days report-frequency together. What is more, they found that the decay itself can be dynamic from day to day so they tried to deride the influence decay factor from current situation and from Ebbinghaus Curve in Equation (3.14).

$$decay(d) = (1 - \beta_d^\varepsilon)^\lambda. \tag{3.14}$$

Equation (3.14) is a decay function where $decay(d)$ represents the decay function on the day d and β_d^ε is the decay rate which can be obtained from sigmoid function with report-frequencies of previous days, as shown in Equation (3.15):

$$s_d^\varepsilon = (\sum_{i=1}^{d-1} \alpha_e r_i^\varepsilon ln(\frac{\beta_e}{d-i}) + r_d^\varepsilon) \tag{3.15}$$

where the $ln(...)$ part is learned from the famous Ebbinghaus forgetting decline, just like memory loss.

Life Cycles for Hashtag: An Example. The study of life cycle proves to be very useful in predicting bursts and popularity. Hashtag is the very example that can be modeled upon the analysis of life cycle. Hashtags, "#" followed by a word [22], reflect the hidden trend of Twitter. If the next burst of Hashtag can be predicted beforehand, we can make good use of it. Kong et al. [21] studied exactly the burst, as well as the popularity of hashtags, by analyzing the life cycle of hashtags.

The authors of [21] provided formal definitions of four states in the life cycle of a bursting hashtag.

- **State 1, Active.** If all tweets containing the hashtag reach a threshold ϕ posted within four continuous time intervals after a time point t_a, it is defined that the hashtag becomes active since t_a.

- **State 2, Bursting.** Within 24 hours after a hashtag becomes active, if the number of tweets containing the hashtag during a time interval t becomes greater than the $\max(C_1 + \delta, 1.5C_1)$ where C_1 is the number of tweets containing the hashtag in the first time interval after the hashtag appears, it is defined that the hashtag bursts.

- **State 3, Off-Burst.** For the burst hashtags, if the number of tweets containing the hashtag drops bellow $\max(C_1 + \delta, 1.5C_1)$ in the following 24 hours after time interval t', it is defined that the hashtag becomes off-burst.

- **State 4, Inactive.** If the hashtag cannot trigger another active state, then it is defined as inactive. In [21] it was determined that among all hashtags, 95% burst within 6 hours since they become active; 96% become off-burst within 24 hours since active and about 98% are inactive within 48 hours since active.

With the findings of the life cycle of bursting hashtags, [21] makes attempts on five regression models including Linear Regression, Classification and Regression Tree, Gaussian Process Regression, Support Vector Regression, and Neural Network to make the prediction of whether a hashtag will burst and how long it will last if the hashtag bursts. Its result shows that Gaussian Process Regression appears to have the best performance and the correct prediction of bursting hashtags can be made 55 minutes on average earlier than the start of the burst.

The analysis of life cycle is fit to make predictions in social network because the message spreading in the network has its unique features which should be thought of when building the prediction model.

3.3.3.3 *Prediction Based on Network Topology*

The common way to solve problems within a network is to study its topology and the social network is not an exception. Indeed, the study of prediction based on network topology is traditional compared with user behaviors and life cycles of a piece of information because the analysis of network topology is widely used in other fields of study if a network is involved.

Another characteristic of network topology different from user behaviors and life cycle is the stableness. The topology is more static. The network has already been built before an event happens or a piece of news bursts, thus the topology features can be extracted using existing user profiles, following relationships or other hidden but existing qualities. First, let us take a look at the widely accepted formal concepts that work in the topology of social network and then view some examples.

The whole social network can be represented as a graph $G(V, E)$ with nodes V and edges E.

- **Node:** Every user in the social network is denoted as a single node. The number of nodes is usually denoted as $|V|$.

- **Edge:** If user A follows user B, there is a directed edge from user A pointing to user B. Since the following relationship is bidirectional, user B has an edge pointing to user A if user B follows user A back. The number of edges is usually denoted as $|E|$.

- **In-Degree:** The In-Degree of user i is the number of edges pointing from other users to user i. In other words, the number of users who follow user i.

- **Out-Degree:** The Out-Degree of user i is the number of edges pointing from user i to other users. In other words, the number of users who user i follows.

Discussion on Node Attribute. Among the topological attributes, the node attribute is the most frequently used in various models because of its generality and applicability. The In-Degree and Out-Degree can be straight-forwardly included into the qualities of nodes and the qualities of following relationships somehow can also be covered with the qualities of nodes with some ideas like density or similarity. What is more, the qualities of nodes can be applied in the establishment of models.

For example, Hu et al. [13] found out that celebrities have a great influence on spreading Osama Bin Laden's death in Twitter which helps explain that the qualities of some specific nodes can indeed be used in prediction and the life experience tells us that people are interested to read a tweet that is retweeted by President Obama.

Similarity between a user and a topic and user influence are concrete examples of using the qualities of nodes to make fine predictions in social network. We can see both qualities in Zhang's work [45].

Zhang et al. [45] provided a model, based on user influence and user's interest in a certain topic, to predict popularity of a burst event in Weibo, a Chinese social network. The volume of micro-blogs that discuss the event at time $t + 1$ is modeled as a linear function (3.16):

$$V_e(t+1) = \sum_{u \in In(t)} Sim(u, e) * F_u(t - t_u) + \chi_{t+1} H_e(t+1), \qquad (3.16)$$

where $Sim(u, e)$ represents the user u's interest in event e and $F_u(t - t_u)$ denotes user u's influence power after he is infected. The $Sim(u, e)$ is the underlying qualities that can be obtained from the network topology. In [45], the authors took advantage of Latent Dirichlet Allocation (LDA) model [8], an unsupervised machine learning technique to identify the topic information from a large set of documentation. In this example, the user u's history profiles and all collected tweets are about the event e. The LDA model produces a probability distribution over latent topics of the user and the distribution over each topic e. By taking the cosine similarity, the user's interest in each topic is reflected. The key point to Equation (3.16) is to train user influence so that it can be used to make prediction of the volume.

From all kinds of models we have discussed, we have a key observation that plenty of models are derived from search engines and blogs. It is reasonable, because social network is kind of evolved from these two branches. Whenever we long for innovation, never forget to look back for previous precious experience.

At the end of this section, we are able to summarize and category state-of-the-art papers into Table 3.1. This may give a general idea of predicting popular online content.

TABLE 3.1 State-of-the-art of predicting popular online content

Reference	Predict Model	Dataset	Content Class	Social Network Level	Details
[19]	User behavior	3500 stories with 2.1 million votes and 1.7 million social links in Digg	Something	Meso	Concentrate on user's attention
[10]	Life cycle	10G data from SNAP and Inforplease	Topic	Macro	Probabilistic prediction using Bayesian likelihood function
[13]	Life cycle	614,976 tweets containing string "laden"	News	Macro	Media people, mass media and celebrities help the propagation of news in Twitter
[32]	User behavior	104,713 celebrities from Twitter	Event	Macro	Use 3 models and gold standards for classification
[14]	User behavior	35,809 posts and their associated comments from Facebook	Something	Macro	Combine content specific features, author specific features and temporal activity features to predict
[28]	Life cycle	12 million Singapore Twitter users with 31 million tweets	Topic	Macro	Regards hashtag as a sort of classification problem and evaluates 7 content features as well as 11 contextual features
[43]	Life cycle	Through Twitter Search API	Something	Macro	Set up a Bayesian probabilistic model to analyze the trend of retweet
[44]	User behavior	16 million tweets, 2.6 million unique words and 148 popular events	Event	Micro	Detecting burst events and clustering burst words
[21]	Life cycle	Not known	Topic	Macro	Divides a hashtag into several statuses
[34]	User behavior	Over 3 million tweets from 250,000 in California, New York and Texas	News	Micro	Analyze the preference for news in different area in order to rerank the top 10 news
[26]	User behavior	510 stories on Digg	Something	Micro	A statistical model with probabilistic user online behavior

3.4 EVALUATION

3.4.1 The Importance of Evaluation

Once a novel prediction model is created, no one can guarantee that it will make the perfect prediction. Intuitively, we want to know whether the predicted result is correct, to what extent and whether it outperforms previous models if there exist some. At this moment, particular methods should be utilized to help scholars statistically analyze the effectiveness and performance of the model. This step is called evaluation. Without it, all the discussion about the model is impractical and not convincing. A good evaluation method reflects the abstract aspects of the model in concrete statistic figures and thus helps analyze it.

3.4.2 Evaluation Metrics

There does not exist one single evaluation metric applicable to all models but generally, some metrics are widely noticed in predictions in social network. Before we talk about specific evaluation metrics, we first distinguish three prediction goals:

1. Ranking prediction — predict the result in the form of a ranking list.

2. Classification prediction — predict the classification.

3. Numerical prediction — predict the exact value.

For each prediction goal, we sort out respective evaluation metrics that are widely used in predictions in social network.

3.4.2.1 Ranking Prediction

Some papers predict the influence or popularity in the form of ranking. [20], [37] and [34] predict the popularity of news events. [42] predicts the users who will be influenced by a focal user. To evaluate the quality of a ranking list, we can apply methods in information retrieval. $nDCG$ and AP are good choices.

Discounted Cumulative Gain (DCG): Discounted Cumulative Gain, abbreviated as DCG, is often used to measure the quality of web search engine algorithms but basically, it measures ranking quality.

Given a ranking list L, each item in L has a graded relevance which represents the true value of the item. Denote the graded relevance at position i in L as rel_i. The DCG at a particular position p is defined as:

$$DCG_p = rel_1 + \sum_{2}^{p} \frac{rel_i}{log_2(i)} \qquad (3.17)$$

The equation above takes into account the penalty of the higher graded relevance appearing in a lower position as a reduced graded relevance logarithmically proportional to its position.

An alternative formulation of DCG appears as:

$$DCG_p = \sum_1^p \frac{2^{rel_i} - 1}{log_2(i+1)} \tag{3.18}$$

$nDCG$, the normalized DCG, qualifies the measurement within 0 and 1 by comparing the DCG of predicted ranks with the DCG of the ideal one. It's defined as:

$$nDCG_p = \frac{DCG_p}{IDCG_p} \tag{3.19}$$

where $IDCG_p$ is the maximum DCG_p provided the graded relevance.

With $nDCG$, we can compare the ranking lists of different grading standards. When evaluating the ranking models, usually $nDCG$s at different positions are calculated so as to see the consistency and applicability of the model. For example, in [37], $nDCG@1(nDCG_1)$, $nDCG@5$, $nDCG@10$, $nDCG@20$, $nDCG@100$ are calculated and compared.

Average Precision (AP): Apart from DCG and $nDCG$, AP (average precision) is the other useful evaluation metric for rankings. For example, [32] uses AP to evaluate the ranking result of controversial events.

Before the presentation of AP, we first define the precision at position p.

$$Precision(k) = \frac{relevant\ documents\ in\ top\ k}{all\ documents\ in\ top\ k} \tag{3.20}$$

Then, AP can be defined as:

$$AP = \frac{\sum_k^n = 1(P(k) \times rel(k))}{number\ of\ relevant\ documents} \tag{3.21}$$

where $rel(k)$ is an indicator function equalling to 1 if the item at position k is relevant, zero otherwise.

AP evaluation metric is especially useful when ranking the extent of binary classification items like controversial events in [32] because it is quite difficult to give a concrete number to represent how controversial the event is.

3.4.2.2 Classification Prediction

There are some classification tasks in prediction in the field of social network like the binary classification problems of users' interest in news recommendation [17], and other classification of personality prediction [27]. The evaluation metrics used for classification is quite limited and confusion matrix is mostly seen.

TABLE 3.2 An example of confusion matrix

	Predicted class		
Actual class	A	B	C
A	5	3	0
B	1	6	0
C	1	2	5

Confusion Matrix. Confusion matrix divides the result for each class in the classification into four categories:

1. True positives(TP): correctly identified

2. False positives(FP): incorrectly identified

3. False negatives(FN): incorrectly rejected

4. True negatives(TN): correctly rejected

For example, we now have a classification result as Table 3.2. Samples are classified into three classes, A, B and C. We can calculate the TP, FP, FN and TN for each class. Take class A as an instance, the TP, FP, FN and TN for class A are: $TP = 5$ (A classified as A), $FP = 2$ ($\overline{A}$ classified as A), $FN = 3$ (A classified as $\overline{A}$) and $TN = 13$ ($\overline{A}$ classified as $\overline{A}$).

For each of the binary classification (like A and not $\overline{A}$), define the five frequently used indexes to evaluate the performance of classification prediction.

$$accuracy = \frac{TP + TF}{TP + TF + FP + FN} \tag{3.22}$$

$$precision = \frac{TP}{TP + FP} \tag{3.23}$$

$$sensitivity(recall) = \frac{TP}{TP + FN} \tag{3.24}$$

$$specificity = \frac{TN}{FP + TN} \tag{3.25}$$

$$F_1 = 2\frac{precision \cdot recall}{precision + recall} \tag{3.26}$$

Accuracy is used to express the percentage of correctly classified from all instances. Precision reflects the percentage of correctly classified from all positive instance. Precision has a significant effect when dealing with imbalanced classification where most of the instances belonging to the same class leads to high accuracy even without classification. Sensitivity, also called "recall", expresses the percentage of correctly identified actual positive. The F_1 score (also F-score or F-measure) is a measure of a test's accuracy using precision and recall. An F_1 score reaches its best value at 1 and worst score at 0. In [36], precision and F_1 score are both applied to test the prediction result of negative links in social media. Specificity shows the percentage of correctly identified actual negative. The application of confusion matrix and these five indexes are very classical in evaluating classification problems.

3.4.2.3 Numerical Prediction

Numerical prediction is mostly used compared to the other two because when predicting the popularity or influence in social network, a certain value is predicted to represent the popularity or influence, such as the box-office revenue [4], the number of votes for a piece of story [26] or scores for 5 aspects of personality [12]. Basically, the evaluation metrics for the numerical evaluation can be divided into two kinds: correlation-based method and error-based method.

Correlation-based Method: Correlation-based method tries to find the relationship between two arrays of variables.

1. The Pearson product-moment correlation coefficient

   For linear relation, the Pearson product-moment correlation coefficient is the most widely used.

   The Pearson product-moment correlation coefficient(r) measures the linear dependence between two variables X and Y. r ranges from -1 to 1, where 1 means positive correlation, 0 means no correlation and -1 means negative correlation. In practice, X can be the predicted value vector and Y can be the real value vector.

   The Pearson correlation coefficient is defined as:

   $$Corr(X, Y) = \frac{\sum_{i=1}^{n}(x_i - \bar{x})(y_i - \bar{y})}{\sqrt{\sum_{i=1}^{n}(x_i - \bar{x})^2 \sum_{i=1}^{n}(y_i - \bar{y})^2}} \qquad (3.27)$$

   where n means the total number of elements in X and Y, $\bar{x} = \frac{1}{n}\sum_{i=1}^{n} x_i$ and $\bar{y} = \frac{1}{n}\sum_{i=1}^{n} y_i$.

   For example, in [26], it uses the Pearson correlation to estimate the relations between predicted votes and the final actual votes for every piece of story. [12] and [15] are other examples using the Pearson correlation.

2. Coefficient of Determination

   More generally, the coefficient of determination, denoted as R^2 or r^2 when the model is simple linear regression, represents the percent of the data that is the closest to the line of best fit. R^2 ranges from 0 to 1, and the better values fit the model, the closer R^2 is to 1. [4] uses coefficient of determination to find out how the predicted box-office revenue fits the reality. [5] uses this to evaluate the performance of Linear Regression and SVM Regression in predicting the popularity of a piece of news. The R^2 is defined as follows:

$$R^2 = 1 - \frac{\sum (x_i - y_i)^2}{\sum (y_i - \overline{y})^2} \qquad (3.28)$$

where x_i can be the predicted value, and y_i is the real value.

Error-based Method: Error-based method evaluates the model by analyzing the error between predicted results and actual values statistically. The closer the calculated figures of error come to zero, the better the performance of the model is. The commonly used error-based metrics include:

$$RMSE = \sqrt{\frac{1}{n} \sum (x_i - y_i)^2} \qquad (3.29)$$

$$MAE = \frac{1}{n} \sum_{i=1}^{n} |x_i - y_i| \qquad (3.30)$$

RMSE indicates the root of the mean value of squared errors. MAE indicates the mean absolute error. In [38] MAE evaluates the performance of using the number of tweets mentioning a party as a predicator of the election result and other election polls and help prove the usability of using Twitter in election prediction.

3.5 LOOK FORWARD

The popularity prediction problem gets hot for a reason – making precise and accurate prediction brings us much good. Both inside the scope of social media and using similar methods in other fields, the problem proves its value in different scenarios. This chapter introduces several practical usages of the methods and proposes future outlooks that will bring advantages to different people.

Intuitively, we can optimize the web contents organization through predicting their future popularity, putting potential contents at conspicuous places. People love stuff online, while they can only cover a small part compared to all resources available. Nowadays, some websites hire web editors to help them dig up hot topics, events or articles daily from huge resource bonanzas, which usually contain millions of objects. However, this work takes time and money, with no guarantee for the chosen content to be popular in the future. With prediction techniques, websites can exempt themselves from all the expenses and refine the decision faster and better as well. Once the contents are set properly, sites' traffic will increase significantly. Here is a practical example. Agarwal et al. from Yahoo! Inc. succeeded in boosting the number of click counts for Yahoo! news by leveraging automatic selection algorithms which estimate users' interest in new articles [1].

Online marketing also benefits much from the prediction of web contents. We are now living in a society where companies spend around 30% of their budget to do online marketing. If a company pays money advertising proper items and stops those that are not promising in the future, it can then maximize its profit and save the budget. For instance, movies or shows can be studied and predicted, helping investors make a decision whether to put money in it or not. Netflix studied its big data pool and predicted that the show, House of Cards, would be a big hit. Therefore, the company invested in the show and promoted it, which has now proved to be a huge success. Moreover, predicting and scheduling can also be a real-time process. By monitoring the fluctuation along time, a company is able to dynamically change its strategy and adapt its decision according to the changing marketing environment, ensuring that it takes proper measures before the loophole is noticed and the damage is made.

Information predicted and gathered through social media even helps prevent potential social panic. Sometimes, false information permeates the social media and brings much trouble. Those pieces of rumors will be powerless unless they reach a certain amount of attention. If we can predict which event will burst, we hold the initiative. In April 23, 2013, Associated Press Twitter account was hacked by someone who sent the rumor that the president was injured due to explosions at the White House [21]. Though debunked later, the rumor became a widely spread hit topic shortly and thus fiercely shocked the stock market at that time. The Dow Jones Indice dropped by over 100 points, bringing irreversible damage to the market. However, if we had employed prediction skills, we would monitor the topics that were about to burst, and thus made timely measures to stop the false claims. Kong et al. wrote a paper on this topic, using different features to learn and predict whether a hashtag will burst in the future [21].

Prediction is capable of coming out of the virtual world and predicting a user's personality. The social networks provide us with abundant information about a person, from which we can predict a user's personality, with pretty good accuracy. We can thereby properly present different contents or services to different categories of people according to their personality, trying to make everyone happy. Furthermore, we can detect sociopath or psychopath using the same method [31]. These people often show anomalies during personality prediction tests, allowing us to find them by several criteria. By detecting them beforehand, we may prevent the potential hazard they will bring and make our cyberspace a safer place.

The predicting techniques can also extend to other fields. The data amount we are dealing with is simply unprecedented. In order to handle this situation, some methods are utilized to improve the performance of data retrieval and management, including CDN (Content Delivery Network), cache, etc. The current strategy usually prefetches or duplicates data that stood out in the history, say, prioritizing the items with most clicks either in history or in recent times [31]. However, the intention of these cache-like methods is to reduce the future traffic overload, not the past. If we can predict the future hot contents and prioritize them, the miss rate reduces and the delay time decreases, improving the system performance and the user experience.

The advance of predicting technique may help develop a better search engine. Although the state-of-the-art search engines provide a relatively satisfactory result, like Google or Bing search, we still find room to improve. Some people have found that those engines fail to retrieve the latest web contents. They argue that more percentage of new elements shall be brought into the users' horizon. By integrating the predicting algorithm into the previous ones, we then prioritize future potential popular items over the obsolete ones and thus provide the users with the results that will arouse their interests. This prediction can be made according to the overall data or, more precisely but costly, according to each person's historical data.

Considering all the merits that the popularity prediction could bring us, both the academics and the industry shall do further study and research in order to perfect the relevant ideas and techniques. We can either polish the algorithm to improve the accuracy of the prediction, or bring the method to a broader stage where the prediction can provide benefits.

Bibliography

[1] Deepak Agarwal, Bee-Chung Chen, Pradheep Elango, Nitin Motgi, Seung-Taek Park, Raghu Ramakrishnan, Scott Roy, and Joe Zachariah. Online models for content optimization. In *Annual Conference on Neural Information Processing Systems (NIPS)*, pages 17–24, 2008.

[2] Deepak Agarwal, Bee-Chung Chen, and Xuanhui Wang. Multi-faceted ranking of news articles using post-read actions. In *ACM International Conference on Information and Knowledge Management (CIKM)*, pages 694–703, 2012.

[3] Anne Archambault and Jonathan Grudin. A longitudinal study of facebook, linkedin, & twitter use. In *ACM Conference on Human Factors in Computing Systems (CHI)*, pages 2741–2750, 2012.

[4] Sitaram Asur and Bernardo A Huberman. Predicting the future with social media. In *IEEE/WIC/ACM International Conference on Web Intelligence (WI)*, pages 492–499, 2010.

[5] Roja Bandari, Sitaram Asur, and Bernardo A Huberman. The pulse of news in social media: Forecasting popularity. In *International Conference on Weblogs and Social Media (ICWSM)*, pages 26–33, 2012.

[6] Hila Becker, Mor Naaman, and Luis Gravano. Learning similarity metrics for event identification in social media. In *ACM International Conference on Web Search and Data Mining (WSDM)*, pages 291–300, 2010.

[7] Rushi Bhatt, Vineet Chaoji, and Rajesh Parekh. Predicting product adoption in large-scale social networks. In *ACM International Conference on Information and Knowledge Management (CIKM)*, pages 1039–1048, 2010.

[8] David M Blei, Andrew Y Ng, and Michael I Jordan. Latent dirichlet allocation. *Journal of Machine Learning Research*, 3:993–1022, 2003.

[9] Carlos Castillo, Mohammed El-Haddad, Jürgen Pfeffer, and Matt Stempeck. Characterizing the life cycle of online news stories using social media reactions. In *ACM Conference on Computer Supported Cooperative Work and Social Computing (CSCW)*, pages 211–223, 2014.

[10] Zhi-Hong Deng, Xiuwen Gong, Frank Jiang, and Ivor W Tsang. Effectively predicting whether and when a topic will become prevalent in a social network. *AAAI Conference on Artificial Intelligence*, pages 210–216, 2015.

[11] Ted Dunning. Accurate methods for the statistics of surprise and coincidence. *Computational Linguistics*, 19(1):61–74, 1993.

[12] Jennifer Golbeck, Cristina Robles, and Karen Turner. Predicting personality with social media. In *CHI Extended Abstracts on Human Factors in Computing Systems*, pages 253–262. ACM, 2011.

[13] Mengdie Hu, Shixia Liu, Furu Wei, Yingcai Wu, John Stasko, and Kwan-Liu Ma. Breaking news on twitter. In *ACM Conference on Human Factors in Computing Systems (CHI)*, pages 2751–2754, 2012.

[14] Jian Huang, Ziming Zhuang, Jia Li, and C Lee Giles. Collaboration over time: Characterizing and modeling network evolution. In *ACM International Conference on Web Search and Data Mining (WSDM)*, pages 107–116, 2008.

[15] Shu Huang, Min Chen, Bo Luo, and Dongwon Lee. Predicting aggregate social activities using continuous-time stochastic process. In *ACM International Conference on Information and Knowledge Management (CIKM)*, pages 982–991, 2012.

[16] Bernardo A Huberman, Peter LT Pirolli, James E Pitkow, and Rajan M Lukose. Strong regularities in world wide web surfing. *AAAS Science*, 280(5360):95–97, 1998.

[17] Wouter IJntema, Frank Goossen, Flavius Frasincar, and Frederik Hogenboom. Ontology-based news recommendation. In *International Conference on Extending Database Technology (EDBT)/International Conference on Database Theory (ICDT) Workshops*, page 16, 2010.

[18] Long Jin, Yang Chen, Tianyi Wang, Pan Hui, and Athanasios V Vasi-lakos. Understanding user behavior in online social networks: A survey. *IEEE Communications Magazine*, 51(9):144–150, 2013.

[19] Jeon-Hyung Kang and Kristina Lerman. La-ctr: A limited attention collaborative topic regression for social media. *arXiv preprint arXiv:1311.1247*, 2013.

[20] Liang Kong, Shan Jiang, Rui Yan, Shize Xu, and Yan Zhang. Ranking news events by influence decay and information fusion for media and users. In *ACM International Conference on Information and Knowledge Management (CIKM)*, pages 1849–1853, 2012.

[21] Shoubin Kong, Qiaozhu Mei, Ling Feng, Fei Ye, and Zhe Zhao. Predicting bursts and popularity of hashtags in real-time. In *ACM International Conference on Research on Development in Information Retrieval (SIGIR)*, pages 927–930, 2014.

[22] Haewoon Kwak, Changhyun Lee, Hosung Park, and Sue Moon. What is twitter, a social network or a news media? In *ACM International Conference on World Wide Web (WWW)*, pages 591–600, 2010.

[23] Jong Gun Lee, Sue Moon, and Kave Salamatian. An approach to model and predict the popularity of online contents with explanatory factors. In *IEEE/WIC/ACM International Conference on Web Intelligence and Intelligent Agent Technology (WI-IAT), 2010*, volume 1, pages 623–630, 2010.

[24] Kristina Lerman and Aram Galstyan. Analysis of social voting patterns on digg. In *ACM Workshop on Online Social Networks (WOSN)*, pages 7–12, 2008.

[25] Kristina Lerman and Rumi Ghosh. Information contagion: An empirical study of the spread of news on digg and twitter social networks. In *AAAI International Conference on Weblogs and Social Media (ICWSM)*, volume 10, pages 90–97, 2010.

[26] Kristina Lerman and Tad Hogg. Using a model of social dynamics to predict popularity of news. In *ACM International Conference on World Wide Web (WWW)*, pages 621–630, 2010.

[27] Ana Carolina ES Lima and Leandro Nunes De Castro. A multi-label, semi-supervised classification approach applied to personality prediction in social media. *Neural Networks*, 58:122–130, 2014.

[28] Zongyang Ma, Aixin Sun, and Gao Cong. On predicting the popularity of newly emerging hashtags in twitter. *Journal of the American Society for Information Science and Technology (JASIST)*, 64(7):1399–1410, 2013.

[29] Franffois Mairesse, Marilyn A Walker, Matthias R Mehl, and Roger K Moore. Using linguistic cues for the automatic recognition of personality in conversation and text. *Journal of Artificial Intelligence Research (JAIR)*, 30:457–500, 2007.

[30] Tim Paek, Michael Gamon, Scott Counts, David Maxwell Chickering, and Aman Dhesi. Predicting the importance of newsfeed posts and social network friends. In *AAAI Conference on Artificial Intelligence (AAAI)*, volume 10, pages 1419–1424, 2010.

[31] Stefan Podlipnig and Laszlo Bszrmenyi. A survey of web cache replacement strategies. *ACM Computing Surveys (CSUR)*, 35(4):374–398, 2003.

[32] Ana-Maria Popescu and Marco Pennacchiotti. Detecting controversial events from twitter. In *ACM International Conference on Information and Knowledge Management (CIKM)*, pages 1873–1876, 2010.

[33] Arunee Ratikan and Mikifumi Shikida. Feature selection based on audience's behavior for information filtering in online social networks. In *IEEE International Conference on Knowledge, Information and Creativity Support Systems (KICSS)*, pages 81–88, 2012.

[34] Xin Shuai, Xiaozhong Liu, and Johan Bollen. Improving news ranking by community tweets. In *International Conference Companion on World Wide Web Companion Volume (WWW)*, pages 1227–1232. ACM, 2012.

[35] Gabor Szabo and Bernardo A Huberman. Predicting the popularity of online content. *Communications of the ACM (CACM)*, 53(8):80–88, 2010.

[36] Jiliang Tang, Shiyu Chang, Charu Aggarwal, and Huan Liu. Negative link prediction in social media. In *ACM International Conference on Web Search and Data Mining (WSDM)*, pages 87–96, 2015.

[37] Alexandru Tatar, Panayotis Antoniadis, Marcelo Dias De Amorim, and Serge Fdida. From popularity prediction to ranking online news. *Social Network Analysis and Mining*, 4(1):1–12, 2014.

[38] Andranik Tumasjan, Timm Oliver Sprenger, Philipp G Sandner, and Isabell M Welpe. Predicting elections with twitter: What 140 characters reveal about political sentiment. In *International Conference on Weblogs and Social Media (ICWSM)*, volume 10, pages 178–185, 2010.

[39] Bimal Viswanath, Alan Mislove, Meeyoung Cha, and Krishna P Gummadi. On the evolution of user interaction in facebook. In *ACM Workshop on Online Social Networks (WOSN)*, pages 37–42, 2009.

[40] Chunyan Wang, Mao Ye, and Bernardo A Huberman. From user comments to on-line conversations. In *ACM SIGKDD International Conference on Knowledge Discovery and Data Mining (KDD)*, pages 244–252, 2012.

[41] Stanley Wasserman. *Social Network Analysis: Methods and Applications.*, volume 8. Cambridge University Press, 1994.

[42] Shanchan Wu and Louiqa Raschid. Prediction in a microblog hybrid network using bonacich potential. In *ACM International Conference on Web Search and Data Mining (WSDM)*, pages 383–392, 2014.

[43] Tauhid Zaman, Emily B Fox, Eric T Bradlow, et al. A bayesian approach for predicting the popularity of tweets. *The Annals of Applied Statistics*, 8(3):1583–1611, 2014.

[44] Xiaoming Zhang, Xiaoming Chen, Yan Chen, Senzhang Wang, Zhoujun Li, and Jiali Xia. Event detection and popularity prediction in microblogging. *Neurocomputing*, 149:1469–1480, 2015.

[45] Xiaoming Zhang, Zhoujun Li, Wenhan Chao, and Jiali Xia. Popularity prediction of burst event in microblogging. In *International Conference on Web Age Information Management (WAIM)*, pages 484–487. Springer, 2014.

CHAPTER 4

Mining User Behaviors in Large Social Networks

Meng Jiang and Peng Cui

CONTENTS

GIVEN large social networks that have recorded millions of users and items (e.g., messages on Facebook/Twitter, articles on Shashdot/Digg), billions of item adoption behaviors and millions of user connection behaviors, what is the underlying behavioral mechanism of the social network user? Can we accurately predict the most probable items that the user will adopt? Can we recommend to them what they really want? How can we alleviate the challenging problem of high sparsity of the behavioral data? The general philosophy underlying these applications is a deep understanding of the multi-aspect nature of users' behavioral intention.

This chapter will answer the above questions by introducing a series of work on mining user behaviors in three different thrusts: (1) uncovering the behavioral mechanism of social network users; (2) modeling context-aware behavior for recommendation and prediction; (3) mining cross-domain behavior in social networks to address the sparsity and cold-start issues.

4.1 MINING BEHAVIORAL MECHANISM FOR SOCIAL RECOMMENDATION

Social network users generate large volumes of information such as blogs, articles and tweets. Exponential growth of information generated by online social networks demands effective and scalable recommender systems to give useful results. A widely used definition of social recommendation is any recommendation with online social relations as an additional input, i.e., augmenting an existing recommendation engine with additional social signals [28]. Social relations can be trust relations, friendships, memberships or following relations [12, 9]. Besides the social relations, the social networks usually contain four types of contextual information: (1) user-user interaction, (2) social relation, (3) user-item interaction, and (4) item content, as show in Figure 4.1.

When receiving a new item (e.g., message, article), users typically examine item content and information on senders [1, 25]. For example, in Twitter, when a user receives a tweet that is posted by one of his friends (the sender), she usually reads its content to see whether the item is interesting. Her preference considers both item content and user-item interaction information [24]. At

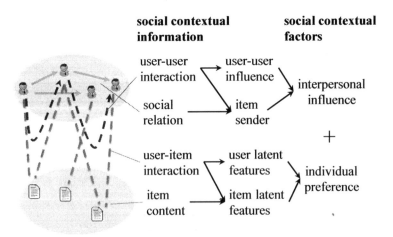

FIGURE 4.1 Contextual information in social networks.

the same time, the user cares about who the sender is and whether the sender is a close friend or authoritative [21, 7, 20]. If more than one friend sends her the same tweet, she may read it more attentively. Influence from her friends considers both social relation and user-user interaction information [19, 4, 3, 2, 5]. Both of these aspects are important for the user whether to adopt the item (e.g., sharing, retweeting). The contextual information can be summarized as two contextual factors: (1) *individual preference* and (2) *interpersonal influence*. This section will study the social contextual factors derived from the rich information, and integrate them into a unified social recommendation framework [10, 13].

4.1.1 Social Contextual Factor Analysis

Statistical analysis results demonstrate the effect of social contextual factors (i.e., individual preference and interpersonal influence) on users' decisions in social networks (i.e., adopting or rejecting the received item). Two real-world social network datasets used in this section enable quantification of the factors. They are *Renren*, a Facebook-style social website in China, and *Tencent Weibo* one of the largest Twitter-style microblogging platforms in China.

Given an item, individual preference describes how much a user likes it, in other words, how much the topics/semantics of this item match the user's preferred topic distribution. Existing probabilistic graphical models such as advanced variants of the LDA model can extract topic-level distributions of the items. A straightforward preference measurement for how much user u likes item a is defined as

$$P_u(a) = T_a \cdot \left(\frac{1}{|A(u,a)|} \sum_{a' \in A(u,a)} T_{a'}\right), \tag{4.1}$$

where $A(u, a)$ is the set of items adopted by user u excluding a, and T_a is the topic distribution of item a.

Interpersonal influence describes whether the user has close relationships with the item senders (e.g., followees who post the tweet in Twitter) from the perspective of user-user interactions on social web. It can be defined as the percentage of recommended items adopted by u from u's friends or followees who send the item a:

$$I_u(a) = \frac{1}{|V(u,a)|} \sum_{v \in V(u,a)} \frac{|\mathcal{S}(u,v) \cap \mathcal{A}(u)|}{|\mathcal{S}(u,v)|}, \tag{4.2}$$

where $V(u, a)$ is the set of senders who send item a to user u, $\mathcal{S}(u, v)$ is the set of items sent from v to u, and $\mathcal{A}(u)$ is the set of items that u adopts.

A user-item pair (u, a) can be labeled as either *adopted* or *rejected*. Figure 4.2 plots the pairs as points (red for adopted items and blue for rejected items; see color ebook) by individual preference $P_u(a)$ versus interpersonal influence $I_u(a)$: Renren dataset on the left-hand and Tencent Weibo dataset on the

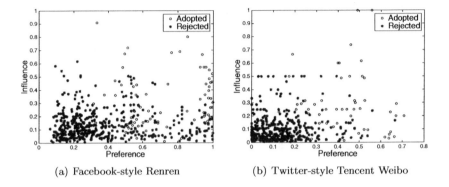

(a) Facebook-style Renren　　　　(b) Twitter-style Tencent Weibo

FIGURE 4.2 Contextual factors of users' decisions: individual preference and interpersonal influence.

right-hand. It is easy to observe that the red points are located at the top and right corner of both the figures, indicating that users intend to adopt items with higher preference scores and from higher influential friends or followees in social networks.

4.1.2 Social Contextual Modeling for Recommendation

The goal is to address social recommendation problem by answering how to model social contextual information as contextual factors and integrate them into a framework.

Framework design. Figure 4.3 shows the social recommendation framework based on probabilistic matrix factorization to incorporate individual

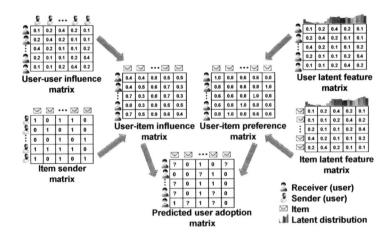

FIGURE 4.3 Social contextual recommendation framework.

preference and interpersonal influence [16, 18, 30]. Specifically, it factorizes the user-item interaction matrix into two intermediated latent matrices including the user-item influence matrix and user-item preference matrix, which are generated from three objective latent matrices: user latent feature matrix, item latent feature matrix, and user-user influence matrix. Moreover, it regularizes the three latent matrices with observed context-aware data including items' semantic similarity and users' interaction frequency.

The details of this framework are introduced as below. Suppose that there are M users with the i-th user denoted as u_i, and N items with the j-th item denoted as p_j. The information adoption matrix is denoted by $\mathbf{R} \in \{0,1\}^{M \times N}$, with its (i, j)-th entry as

$$R_{ij} = \begin{cases} 1 & \text{if } u_i \text{ adopted } p_j; \\ 0 & \text{otherwise.} \end{cases} \tag{4.3}$$

Then the social recommendation problem is converted to predict the unobserved entries in the information adoption matrix $\mathbf{R}$ based on the observed entries and other factors.

In social scenarios, whether a user adopts an item on social networks is determined by three aspects: (1) item content: what the item tells about, (2) user-item interaction: what items the user likes, and (3) social relation and user-user interaction: who the senders are. Let $\mathbf{U} \in \mathbb{R}^{k \times M}$ be the latent user feature matrix, and let $\mathbf{V} \in \mathbb{R}^{k \times N}$ be the latent item feature matrix. $\mathbf{S} \in \mathbb{R}^{M \times M}$ is the interpersonal influence matrix with each entry S_{ij} representing the value of influence user u_i has on user u_j. The value $S_{ij} > 0$ if and only if u_i is the friend of u_j in social networks such as Facebook and Renren, or is followed by u_j in microblogging services such as Twitter and Tencent Weibo. $\mathbf{G} \in \mathbb{R}^{N \times M}$ is the item sender matrix with entry $G_{ij} = 1$ meaning that u_j sends the item p_i and vice versa. Based on these denotations and the assumption that users can only receive items from their friends as social networks usually do ($G_{ii} = 0$), the social recommendation problem is to find out $\mathbf{U}$, $\mathbf{V}$ and $\mathbf{S}$ so that $((\mathbf{SG}^\top) \odot (\mathbf{U}^\top \mathbf{V}))$ can well approximate the observed entries in $\mathbf{R}$ without over-fitting, where $\odot$ is the Hadamard Product.

From the observed social network data, regularizations can be derived to improve learning of $\mathbf{U}$, $\mathbf{V}$ and $\mathbf{S}$. The following formulas compute user-user preference similarity matrix $\mathbf{W} \in \mathbb{R}^{M \times M}$, item-item content similarity matrix $\mathbf{C} \in \mathbb{R}^{N \times N}$, and user-user interaction matrix $\mathbf{F} \in \mathbb{R}^{M \times M}$:

$$W_{i,j} = \frac{\sum\limits_{a \in \mathcal{A}(u_i)} P_{u_i}(a)}{|\mathcal{A}(u_i)|} \cdot \frac{\sum\limits_{a' \in \mathcal{A}(u_j)} P_{u_j}(a')}{|\mathcal{A}(u_j)|}, \tag{4.4}$$

$$C_{i,j} = T_{a_i} \cdot T_{a_j}, \tag{4.5}$$

$$F_{i,j} = \frac{|\mathcal{S}(u_i, u_j) \cap \mathcal{A}(u_i)|}{|\mathcal{S}(u_i, u_j)|}. \tag{4.6}$$

The heuristic for choosing regularizations on the three latent factors with the observed matrices are listed as follows: (1) the users that are similar in user latent space $\mathbf{U}$ have similar preferences (derived from preference similarity matrix $\mathbf{W}$); (2) the items that are similar in item latent space $\mathbf{V}$ have similar descriptive contents (derived from content similarity matrix $\mathbf{C}$); (3) high interpersonal influence in the influence latent space $\mathbf{S}$ generates frequent interpersonal interactions $\mathbf{F}$; (4) the product of user latent space $\mathbf{U}$ and item latent space $\mathbf{V}$ corresponds to the users' individual preference on the items; (5) the Hadamard product of interpersonal influence and individual preference is proportional to the probability of item adoptions.

By adopting a probabilistic model with Gaussian observation noise, the conditional distribution over the observed entries in $\mathbf{R}$ can be defined as

$$P(\mathbf{R}|\mathbf{S},\mathbf{U},\mathbf{V},\sigma_R^2) = \prod_{i=1}^{M}\prod_{j=1}^{N} \mathcal{N}(\mathbf{R}_{ij}|\mathbf{S}_i\mathbf{G}_j^\top \odot \mathbf{U}_i^\top\mathbf{V}_j, \sigma_R^2). \qquad (4.7)$$

Incorporating the social contextual factors, we define the posterior distribution as

$$
\begin{aligned}
P(\mathbf{S},\mathbf{U},\mathbf{V}|\mathbf{R},\mathbf{G},\mathbf{W},\mathbf{C},\mathbf{F}) &= \tfrac{P(\mathbf{R},\mathbf{G},\mathbf{W},\mathbf{C},\mathbf{F}|\mathbf{S},\mathbf{U},\mathbf{V})P(\mathbf{S},\mathbf{U},\mathbf{V})}{P(\mathbf{R},\mathbf{G},\mathbf{W},\mathbf{C},\mathbf{F})} \\
&\propto P(\mathbf{R}|\mathbf{S},\mathbf{U},\mathbf{V})P(\mathbf{W}|\mathbf{U})P(\mathbf{C}|\mathbf{V})P(\mathbf{F}|\mathbf{S})P(\mathbf{S})P(\mathbf{U})P(\mathbf{V}) \\
&= \prod_{i,j}\mathcal{N}(R_{ij}|\mathbf{S}_i\mathbf{G}_j^\top \odot \mathbf{U}_i^\top\mathbf{V}_j,\sigma_R^2) \\
&\quad \prod_{p,q}\mathcal{N}(W_{pq}|\mathbf{U}_p^\top\mathbf{U}_q,\sigma_W^2)\prod_{m,n}\mathcal{N}(C_{mn}|\mathbf{V}_m^\top\mathbf{V}_n,\sigma_C^2)\prod_{s,t}\mathcal{N}(F_{st}|S_{st},\sigma_F^2) \\
&\quad \prod_{x}\mathcal{N}(\mathbf{S}_x|0,\sigma_S^2)\prod_{y}\mathcal{N}(\mathbf{U}_y|0,\sigma_U^2)\prod_{z}\mathcal{N}(\mathbf{V}_z|0,\sigma_V^2),
\end{aligned}
\qquad (4.8)
$$

where $\sigma_{(.)}$ denotes that zero-mean spherical Gaussian priors are placed on latent feature vectors and observed matrices. Then the logarithm of the above probability is

$$
\begin{aligned}
\ln P(\mathbf{S},\mathbf{U},\mathbf{V}|\mathbf{R},\mathbf{G},\mathbf{M},\mathbf{C},\mathbf{F}) \\
\propto -\tfrac{1}{2\sigma_R^2}\sum_{i,j}(R_{ij}-\mathbf{S}_i\mathbf{G}_j^\top \odot \mathbf{U}_i^\top\mathbf{V}_j)^2 - \tfrac{1}{2\sigma_W^2}\sum_{p,q}(W_{pq}-\mathbf{U}_p^\top\mathbf{U}_q)^2 \\
-\tfrac{1}{2\sigma_C^2}\sum_{m,n}(C_{mn}-\mathbf{V}_m^\top\mathbf{V}_n)^2 - \tfrac{1}{2\sigma_F^2}\sum_{s,t}(F_{st}-S_{st})^2 - \tfrac{1}{2\sigma_S^2}\sum_{x}\mathbf{S}_x^\top\mathbf{S}_x \\
-\tfrac{1}{2\sigma_U^2}\sum_{y}\mathbf{U}_y^\top\mathbf{U}_y - \tfrac{1}{2\sigma_V^2}\sum_{z}\mathbf{V}_z^\top\mathbf{V}_z.
\end{aligned}
\qquad (4.9)
$$

Maximizing the posterior distribution is equivalent to minimizing the sum-of-squared errors function with hybrid quadratic regularization terms:

$$
\begin{aligned}
\mathcal{J}(\mathbf{S},\mathbf{U},\mathbf{V}) &= ||\mathbf{R}-\mathbf{S}\mathbf{G}^\top \odot \mathbf{U}^\top\mathbf{V}||_F^2 + \alpha||\mathbf{W}-\mathbf{U}^\top\mathbf{U}||_F^2 + \beta||\mathbf{C}-\mathbf{V}^\top\mathbf{V}||_F^2 \\
&\quad + \gamma||\mathbf{F}-\mathbf{S}||_F^2 + \delta||\mathbf{S}||_F^2 + \eta||\mathbf{U}||_F^2 + \lambda||\mathbf{V}||_F^2,
\end{aligned}
\qquad (4.10)
$$

where $\alpha = \frac{\sigma_R^2}{\sigma_W^2}, \beta = \frac{\sigma_R^2}{\sigma_C^2}, \gamma = \frac{\sigma_R^2}{\sigma_F^2}, \delta = \frac{\sigma_R^2}{\sigma_S^2}, \eta = \frac{\sigma_R^2}{\sigma_U^2}, \lambda = \frac{\sigma_R^2}{\sigma_V^2}$, and $||.||_F$ is the Frobenius norm.

To minimize the above objective function, the framework adopts a block coordinate descent scheme to solve the problem. That is, starting from random initialization on $\mathbf{S}, \mathbf{U}, \mathbf{V}$, it optimizes each of them alternatively with the other two matrices fixed and proceed step by step until convergence. As the objective is obviously lower bounded by 0 and the alternating gradient search procedure will reduce it monotonically, the algorithm is guaranteed to be convergent. Using a gradient search method, the gradients of the objective with respect to the variables are

$$\frac{\partial \mathcal{J}}{\partial \mathbf{S}} = -2(\mathbf{R} - \mathbf{S}\mathbf{G}^\top \odot \mathbf{U}^\top \mathbf{V})\mathbf{G} - 2\gamma(\mathbf{F} - \mathbf{S}) + 2\delta\mathbf{S}, \tag{4.11}$$

$$\frac{\partial \mathcal{J}}{\partial \mathbf{U}} = -2\mathbf{V}(\mathbf{R} - \mathbf{S}\mathbf{G}^\top \odot \mathbf{U}^\top \mathbf{V})^\top - 4\alpha\mathbf{U}(\mathbf{W} - \mathbf{U}^\top \mathbf{U}) + 2\eta\mathbf{U}, \tag{4.12}$$

$$\frac{\partial \mathcal{J}}{\partial \mathbf{V}} = -2\mathbf{U}(\mathbf{R} - \mathbf{S}\mathbf{G}^\top \odot \mathbf{U}^\top \mathbf{V}) - 4\beta\mathbf{V}(\mathbf{C} - \mathbf{V}^\top \mathbf{V}) + 2\lambda\mathbf{V}. \tag{4.13}$$

$\mathcal{J}$ decreases the fastest in the direction of gradients during each iteration and the sequence $\mathcal{J}^{(t)}$ converges to the desired minimum.

4.1.3 Conclusions

This section introduced a social recommendation model utilizing social contextual factors, i.e., individual preference and interpersonal influence. The extensive experiments showed that social contextual information can greatly boost the performance of recommendation on social network datasets.

4.2 MINING CONTEXTUAL BEHAVIOR FOR PREDICTION

Scientists study human behavior from a variety of cultural, political, and psychological perspectives, looking for consistent patterns of individual and social behavior and for scientific explanations on those patterns. The discovered patterns can be used in many real world applications such as web search, recommender system and advertisement targeting. It is well accepted that human behavior is the product of a multitude of interrelated factors. The factors such as physical environment, social interaction, and social identity affect how the behavior takes place with our personalities and interests. As an example, if a researcher changes his affiliation, he will start to collaborate with new friends, join in new projects and eventually study new topics. Given the complexity of multi-faceted factors influencing human behaviors, it is difficult to concisely summarize what they are and how they interact. Moreover, psychological studies demonstrate that human behaviors naturally evolve with the changing of both endogenous factors (e.g., personality) and exogenous factors (e.g., environment), resulting in different dynamic (temporal) behavioral patterns over time [17, 23, 22]. For example, in the early 1990s, many researchers focused on database systems and query processing. In the late 1990s, with various data collective methods emerging and scales of unlabeled data increasing, they turned to work on clustering and pattern mining problems. In the 2000s, people started to focus on social networks and communities since Facebook and Twitter become popular. Consequently, the patterns of human behaviors differ from place to place, era to era and across environments, depending on *spatio-temporal contexts*. These characteristics cause severe data sparsity and computational complexity problems: they pose great challenges to understanding and predicting human behaviors. Behavioral modeling with spatio-temporal contexts requires multi-faceted and temporal information [11]. This section will introduce how to model the multi-faceted dynamic behaviors, and how to develop fast algorithms for behavior prediction with advanced flexible evolutionary multi-faceted analysis (FEMA).

4.2.1 Modeling Multi-Faceted Dynamic Behaviors

Problem definition. Let the Facebook dataset be an example of this problem: we focus on finding temporal patterns of web posting behavior. The dataset can be denoted by a list of tuples (u, g, w, t): a Facebook user u at a geo-location g posts a message about a word w at time t ($t = 1, \dots, T$). The data is thus represented with a 3-order tensor sequence [26, 27, 15, 14] $\mathcal{X}_t \in \mathbb{R}^{n^{(u)} \times n^{(g)} \times n^{(w)}}$, where $n^{(u)}$ is the number of users, $n^{(g)}$ is the number of geo-locations, and $n^{(w)}$ is the number of words. $\mathcal{X}_t(u, g, w)$ has a value of the number of existing tuples (u, g, w, t') ($t' \le t$). The goal is to factorize the tensor sequence

$$\mathcal{X}_t \approx \mathcal{Y}_t \times_{(u)} \mathbf{U}_t \times_{(g)} \mathbf{G}_t \times_{(w)} \mathbf{W}_t \tag{4.14}$$

where
1. $\mathcal{Y}_t \in \mathbb{R}^{r^{(u)} \times r^{(g)} \times r^{(w)}}$ is the core tensor sequence, which encodes the temporal behavioral patterns, i.e., the relationship among user, geo-location and word groups. $\mathcal{Y}_t(j^{(u)}, j^{(g)}, j^{(w)})$ indicates the probability of the behavior before time t if the $j^{(u)}$-th user group in the $j^{(g)}$-th geo-location group posts about the $j^{(w)}$-th word group.
2. $\mathbf{U}_t \in \mathbb{R}^{n^{(u)} \times r^{(u)}}$ is the users' projection matrix before time t. $\mathbf{U}(i^{(u)}, j^{(u)})$ represents the probability that the $i^{(u)}$-th user belongs to the $j^{(u)}$-th group before time t.
3. $\mathbf{G}_t \in \mathbb{R}^{n^{(g)} \times r^{(g)}}$ is the geo-locations' projection matrix before time t. $\mathbf{G}_t(i^{(g)}, j^{(g)})$ represents the probability that the $i^{(g)}$-th geo-location belongs to the $j^{(g)}$-th group before time t.
4. $\mathbf{W}_t \in \mathbb{R}^{n^{(w)} \times r^{(w)}}$ is the words' projection matrix before time t. $\mathbf{W}_t(i^{(w)}, j^{(w)})$ represents the probability that the $i^{(w)}$-th word belongs to the $j^{(w)}$-th group before time t.

Figure 4.4 describes how to model a time-evolving dataset — using tensor sequence. The key to solving the sparsity problem in *tensor sequence* decompositions is to learn the *flexible regularizers* such as the users' social relations, the geo-locations' geographical distance and the words' semantic information.

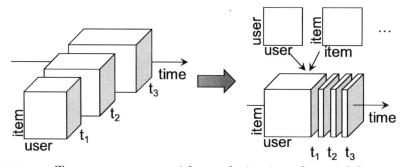

FIGURE 4.4 Tensor sequences with regularizations for modeling multi-faceted dynamic behaviors.

The regularizers can be encoded as Laplacian matrices $\mathbf{L}^{(\mathbf{u})}$, $\mathbf{L}^{(\mathbf{g})}$, $\mathbf{L}^{(\mathbf{w})}$, where the (i, j)-th element represents the similarity between the i-th and j-th entities (users, geo-locations, words). Examples of possible similarity functions are the frequency of user communication and the proximity of geographic locations.

The problem is now how to compute the factorizations for the core tensor sequence and projection matrices, given the tensor sequence and constraints. Note that the scale of the tensors are large but the changes are very small. We denote by $\Delta\mathcal{X}_\mathbf{t}$ the increment at time t, which is very sparse: for any $1 \le t < T$, $\Delta\mathcal{X}_\mathbf{t} = \mathcal{X}_{\mathbf{t+1}} - \mathcal{X}_\mathbf{t}$. The problem can be summarized into two steps:

1. **Given** the first tensor $\mathcal{X}_\mathbf{1}$ and the constraints $\mathbf{L}^{(\mathbf{u})}$, $\mathbf{L}^{(\mathbf{g})}$, $\mathbf{L}^{(\mathbf{w})}$, **find** the projection $\mathbf{U}_\mathbf{1}$, $\mathbf{G}_\mathbf{1}$, $\mathbf{W}_\mathbf{1}$, and the first core tensor $\mathcal{Y}_\mathbf{1}$.

2. At time t $(1 \le t < T)$, **given** the tensor $\mathcal{X}_\mathbf{t}$, the increment $\Delta\mathcal{X}_\mathbf{t}$, the old projection matrices $\mathbf{U}_\mathbf{t}$, $\mathbf{G}_\mathbf{t}$, $\mathbf{W}_\mathbf{t}$, and the constraints $\mathbf{L}^{(\mathbf{u})}$, $\mathbf{L}^{(\mathbf{g})}$, $\mathbf{L}^{(\mathbf{w})}$, **find** the new projection matrices $\mathbf{U}_{\mathbf{t+1}}$, $\mathbf{G}_{\mathbf{t+1}}$, $\mathbf{W}_{\mathbf{t+1}}$, and the new core tensor $\mathcal{Y}_{\mathbf{t+1}}$.

A general problem definition. It is easy to extend the formulation from 3 to M dimensions and give a general definition.

Definition 4.1 (Flexible Evolutionary Multi-faceted Analysis)
Initialization: *Given the first M-way tensor $\mathcal{X}_\mathbf{1} \in \mathbb{R}^{n^{(1)} \times \dots \times n^{(M)}}$ and the constraints $\mathbf{L}^{(\mathbf{m})}|_{m=1}^{M} \in \mathbb{R}^{n^{(m)} \times n^{(m)}}$, find the first projection matrices $\mathbf{A}_\mathbf{1}^{(\mathbf{m})}|_{m=1}^{M} \in \mathbb{R}^{n^{(m)} \times r^{(m)}}$ and the first core tensor $\mathcal{Y}_\mathbf{1} \in \mathbb{R}^{r^{(1)} \times \dots \times r^{(M)}}$.* **Evolutionary analysis:** *At time t $(1 \le t < T)$, given the tensor $\mathcal{X}_\mathbf{t} \in \mathbb{R}^{n^{(1)} \times \dots \times n^{(M)}}$, the increment $\Delta\mathcal{X}_\mathbf{t}$, the old projection matrices $\mathbf{A}_\mathbf{t}^{(\mathbf{m})}|_{m=1}^{M}$, and the constraints $\mathbf{L}^{(\mathbf{m})}|_{m=1}^{M}$, find the new projection matrices $\mathbf{A}_{\mathbf{t+1}}^{(\mathbf{m})}|_{m=1}^{M}$ and the new core tensor $\mathcal{Y}_{\mathbf{t+1}}$.*

Challenges. The first challenge is **high sparsity**. Multi-faceted data in real applications is often very sparse. In user-location-word case, for example, users cannot appear in many geo-locations or all the words in the dataset. The problem is even disastrous when adding temporal dimension to the multi-faceted behavioral information. The second one is **high complexity**. Considering the dynamic characteristic, new multi-faceted human behaviors continuously appear over time. The continuously generated data of high volume, high dimension and high sparsity pose great challenges for modeling and analysis due to high computational complexity. The issue of fast processing increments is still critical for modeling and predicting human behavior.

4.2.2 Flexible Evolutionary Multi-Faceted Analysis

Framework design. Flexible evolutionary multi-faceted analysis (FEMA) is designed based on a dynamic scheme of tensor factorization for temporal multi-faceted behavior pattern mining and prediction (see Figure 4.5). First, flexible regularizers are imposed to alleviate the problems brought by high sparsity. Second, in order to efficiently decompose high-order tensor sequences, instead of re-decomposing the updated matricized tensor, it uses approximation algorithms to factorize the new tensor with sparse increments, where the bound of approximation loss is theoretically proved.

Initialization. We denote by $\mu^{(m)}$ the weight of the mode-m Laplacian matrix $\mathbf{L}^{(\mathbf{m})}$. The covariance matrix of the m-th mode at time $t = 1$ is

$$\mathbf{C}_1^{(\mathbf{m})} = \mathbf{X}_1^{(\mathbf{m})}\mathbf{X}_1^{(\mathbf{m})\mathbf{T}} + \mu^{(m)}\mathbf{L}^{(\mathbf{m})} \qquad (4.15)$$

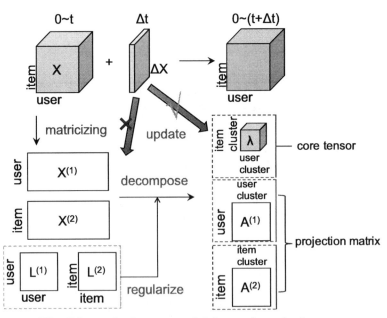

FIGURE 4.5 Flexible evolutionary multi-faceted analysis.

where $\mathbf{X}_1^{(\mathbf{m})} \in \mathbb{R}^{n^{(m)} \times \prod_{i \neq m} n^{(i)}}$ is the mode-m matricizing of the tensor $\mathcal{X}_1$. The projection matrices $\mathbf{A}_1^{(\mathbf{m})}|_{m=1}^M$ can be computed by diagonalization: they are the top $r^{(m)}$ eigenvectors of the covariance matrix $\mathbf{C}_1^{(m)}|_{m=1}^M$.

Evolutionary analysis. Next we introduce an efficient technique based on tensor perturbation to adjust the projection matrices according to changes of the tensor. We denote by $\mathbf{X}_t^{(\mathbf{m})} \in \mathbb{R}^{n^{(m)} \times \prod_{i \neq m} n^{(i)}}$ the mode-m matricizing of the tensor $\mathcal{X}_t$. We define the covariance matrix $\mathbf{C}_t^{(m)} = \mathbf{X}_t^{(\mathbf{m})} \mathbf{X}_t^{(\mathbf{m})\top} + \mu^{(m)} \mathbf{L}^{(m)}$ and define $(\lambda_{t,i}^{(m)}, \mathbf{a}_{t,i}^{(\mathbf{m})})$ as one eigenvalue-eigenvector pair of the matrix $\mathbf{C}_t^{(m)}$. The vector $\mathbf{a}_{t,i}^{(\mathbf{m})}$ is exactly the i-th column of the projection matrix $\mathbf{A}_t^{(\mathbf{m})}$. Then we can rewrite $(\lambda_{t+1,i}^{(m)}, \mathbf{a}_{t+1,i}^{(\mathbf{m})})$ as

$$\lambda_{t+1,i}^{(m)} = \lambda_{t,i}^{(m)} + \Delta\lambda_{t,i}^{(m)} \tag{4.16}$$

$$\mathbf{a}_{t+1,i}^{(\mathbf{m})} = \mathbf{a}_{t,i}^{(\mathbf{m})} + \Delta\mathbf{a}_{t,i}^{(\mathbf{m})} \tag{4.17}$$

To simplify the denotions, we omit "t" in the terms and equations when it is unnecessary. Thus we can obtain

$$[(\mathbf{X}^{(\mathbf{m})} + \Delta\mathbf{X}^{(\mathbf{m})})(\mathbf{X}^{(\mathbf{m})} + \Delta\mathbf{X}^{(\mathbf{m})})^\top + \mu^{(m)}\mathbf{L}^{(m)}] \cdot (\mathbf{a}_i^{(\mathbf{m})} + \Delta\mathbf{a}_i^{(\mathbf{m})})$$
$$= (\lambda_i^{(m)} + \Delta\lambda_i^{(m)})(\mathbf{a}_i^{(\mathbf{m})} + \Delta\mathbf{a}_i^{(\mathbf{m})}) \tag{4.18}$$

Now the key questions are how to compute changes to the eigenvalue $\Delta\lambda_i^{(m)}$ and eigenvector $\Delta\mathbf{a}_i^{(\mathbf{m})}$, respectively.

If we concentrate on first-order approximation when expanding Equation (4.18), we assume all high order perturbation terms are negligible. By further using the fact that $(\mathbf{X}^{(\mathbf{m})}\mathbf{X}^{(\mathbf{m})\top} + \mu^{(m)}\mathbf{L}^{(m)})\mathbf{a}_i^{(\mathbf{m})} = \lambda_i^{(m)}\mathbf{a}_i^{(\mathbf{m})}$, we can obtain

$$\mathbf{X}^{(\mathbf{m})}\mathbf{X}^{(\mathbf{m})\top}\Delta\mathbf{a}_i^{(\mathbf{m})} + (\mathbf{X}^{(\mathbf{m})}\Delta\mathbf{X}^{(\mathbf{m})\top} + \Delta\mathbf{X}^{(\mathbf{m})}\mathbf{X}^{(\mathbf{m})\top})\mathbf{a}_i^{(\mathbf{m})} + \mu^{(m)}\mathbf{L}^{(m)}\Delta\mathbf{a}_i^{(\mathbf{m})}$$
$$= \lambda_i^{(m)}\Delta\mathbf{a}_i^{(\mathbf{m})} + \Delta\lambda_i^{(m)}\mathbf{a}_i^{(\mathbf{m})} \tag{4.19}$$

Now multiplying both sides of Equation (4.19) with $\mathbf{a}_i^{(\mathbf{m})\top}$ and because of the symmetry of $\mathbf{X}^{(\mathbf{m})}\mathbf{X}^{(\mathbf{m})\top}$ and $\mathbf{L}^{(m)}$, we get

$$\Delta\lambda_i^{(m)} = \mathbf{a}_i^{(\mathbf{m})\top}(\mathbf{X}^{(\mathbf{m})}\Delta\mathbf{X}^{(\mathbf{m})\top} + \Delta\mathbf{X}^{(\mathbf{m})}\mathbf{X}^{(\mathbf{m})\top})\mathbf{a}_i^{(\mathbf{m})} \tag{4.20}$$

Since the eigenvectors are orthogonal to each other, we assume that the change of the eigenvector $\Delta\mathbf{a}_i^{(\mathbf{m})}$ is in the subspace spanned by those original eigenvectors, i.e.,

$$\Delta\mathbf{a}_i^{(\mathbf{m})} \approx \sum_{j=1}^{r^{(m)}} \alpha_{ij}\mathbf{a}_j^{(\mathbf{m})} \tag{4.21}$$

where $\{\alpha_{ij}\}$ are small constants to be determined. Bringing Equation (4.21) into Equation (4.19), we obtain

$$(\mathbf{X^{(m)}X^{(m)}}^\top + \mu^{(m)}\mathbf{L^{(m)}}) \sum_{j=1}^{r^{(m)}} \alpha_{ij}\mathbf{a_j^{(m)}} + (\mathbf{X^{(m)}\Delta X^{(m)}}^\top + \mathbf{\Delta X^{(m)}X^{(m)}}^\top)\mathbf{a_i^{(m)}}$$
$$= \lambda_i^{(m)} \sum_{j=1}^{r^{(m)}} \alpha_{ij}\mathbf{a_j^{(m)}} + \Delta\lambda_i^{(m)}\mathbf{a_i^{(m)}} \tag{4.22}$$

which is equivalent to

$$\sum_{j=1}^{r^{(m)}} \lambda_j^{(m)}\alpha_{ij}\mathbf{a_j^{(m)}} + \mathbf{X^{(m)}\Delta X^{(m)}}^\top\mathbf{a_i^{(m)}} + \mathbf{\Delta X^{(m)}X^{(m)}}^\top\mathbf{a_i^{(m)}}$$
$$= \lambda_i^{(m)} \sum_{j=1}^{r^{(m)}} \alpha_{ij}\mathbf{a_j^{(m)}} + \Delta\lambda_i^{(m)}\mathbf{a_i^{(m)}} \tag{4.23}$$

Multiplying $\mathbf{a_k^{(m)}}^\top$ ($k \neq i$) on both sides of the above equation, we get

$$\lambda_k^{(m)}\alpha_{ik} + \mathbf{a_k^{(m)}}^\top\mathbf{X^{(m)}\Delta X^{(m)}}^\top\mathbf{a_i^{(m)}} + \mathbf{a_k^{(m)}}^\top\mathbf{\Delta X^{(m)}X^{(m)}}^\top\mathbf{a_i^{(m)}} = \lambda_i^{(m)}\alpha_{ik} \tag{4.24}$$

Therefore,

$$\alpha_{ik} = \frac{\mathbf{a_k^{(m)}}^\top(\mathbf{X^{(m)}\Delta X^{(m)}}^\top + \mathbf{\Delta X^{(m)}X^{(m)}}^\top)\mathbf{a_i^{(m)}}}{\lambda_i^{(m)} - \lambda_k^{(m)}} \tag{4.25}$$

To get α_{ii}, we use the fact that

$$(\mathbf{a_i^{(m)}} + \Delta\mathbf{a_i^{(m)}})^\top(\mathbf{a_i^{(m)}} + \Delta\mathbf{a_i^{(m)}}) = 1 \Longleftrightarrow 1 + 2\mathbf{a_i^{(m)}}^\top\Delta\mathbf{a_i^{(m)}} + O(\|\Delta\mathbf{a_i^{(m)}}\|^2) = 1 \tag{4.26}$$

Discarding the high order term, and bringing in Equation (4.21), we get $\alpha_{ii} = 0$. Therefore,

$$\Delta\mathbf{a_i^{(m)}} = \sum_{j\neq i} \frac{\mathbf{a_j^{(m)}}^\top(\mathbf{X^{(m)}\Delta X^{(m)}}^\top + \mathbf{\Delta X^{(m)}X^{(m)}}^\top)\mathbf{a_i^{(m)}}}{\lambda_i^{(m)} - \lambda_j^{(m)}}\mathbf{a_j^{(m)}} \tag{4.27}$$

Note that the constraints $\mathbf{L^{(m)}}$ do not appear in the eigenvalue and eigenvector updating functions Equation (4.20) and Equation (4.27). Note that the constraints have to be learned only *once*.

Computational complexity. For the m-th mode, we define $D^{(m)}$ as the number of features of each point on the m-th dimension. Since the tensors are usually extremely sparse, we know $D^{(m)} \leq E \ll \prod_{m'\neq m} n^{(m')}$, where E is the number of non-zero entries in the tensors. In order to compute the increment on the eigenvalue and eigenvector using Equation (4.20) and Equation (4.27) for the m-th mode, we need to compute $\mathbf{v_i^{(m)}}$, which requires $O(n^{(m)}D^{(m)})$ time. As $\Delta\mathbf{X^{(m)}}$ is very sparse, $\Delta\mathbf{X^{(m)}}\mathbf{v_i^{(m)}}$

only requires constant time $O(D^{(m)})$. Therefore, for computing $\Delta\lambda_i^{(m)}$ and $\Delta\mathbf{a_i^{(m)}}$, we need $O(r^{(m)}n^{(m)}D^{(m)} + r^{(m)}D^{(m)})$ time, and updating eigenvalues and eigenvectors for T times requires $O(T\sum_{m=1}^{M} r^{(m)}(n^{(m)} + 1)D^{(m)})$ time. In comparison, if we redo the eigenvalue decomposition on $\mathcal{X}_{\mathbf{t+1}}$, it costs $O(T\sum_{m=1}^{M}(D^{(m)}(n^{(m)})^2 + (n^{(m)})^3))$ time, which is much higher.

Approximation quality. We now present two theorems that bound the magnitude of $\Delta\lambda_i^{(m)}$ and $\Delta\mathbf{a_i^{(m)}}$. Both theorems confirm our intuition that the magnitude of $\Delta\lambda_i^{(m)}$ and $\Delta\mathbf{a_i^{(m)}}$ is directly related to the norm of $\Delta\mathbf{X^{(m)}}$. Also since the higher order terms are ignored in the approximation, FEMA only works when those terms are relatively small.

Theorem 4.1 *The magnitude of the variation on the eigenvalue, i.e.,* $|\Delta\lambda_i^{(m)}|$, $(\forall i = 1,\ldots,r^{(m)})$, *satisfies the following inequality*

$$|\Delta\lambda_i^{(m)}| \leq 2(\lambda_{\mathbf{X^{(m)}}^\top\mathbf{X^{(m)}}}^{\max})^{\frac{1}{2}} \left\|\Delta\mathbf{X^{(m)}}\right\|_2 \qquad (4.28)$$

where $\lambda_{\mathbf{X^{(m)}}^\top\mathbf{X^{(m)}}}^{\max}$ *is the maximum eigenvalue of the data inner product matrix* $\mathbf{X^{(m)}}^\top\mathbf{X^{(m)}}$, $\left\|\Delta\mathbf{X^{(m)}}\right\|_2$ *is the 2-norm of* $\Delta\mathbf{X^{(m)}}$.

Proof: See the solution to Exercise 1.2.

Theorem 4.2 *The magnitude of the variation on the eigenvector, i.e.,* $|\Delta\mathbf{a_i^{(m)}}|$, $(\forall i = 1,\ldots,r^{(m)})$, *satisfies the following inequality*

$$|\Delta\mathbf{a_i^{(m)}}| \leq 2\left\|\Delta\mathbf{X^{(m)}}\right\|_2 \sum_{j\neq i} \frac{(\lambda_{\mathbf{X^{(m)}}^\top\mathbf{X^{(m)}}}^{\max})^{\frac{1}{2}}}{|\lambda_i^{(m)} - \lambda_j^{(m)}|} \qquad (4.29)$$

where $\lambda_{\mathbf{X^{(m)}}^\top\mathbf{X^{(m)}}}^{\max}$ *is the maximum eigenvalue of the data inner product matrix* $\mathbf{X^{(m)}}^\top\mathbf{X^{(m)}}$, $\left\|\Delta\mathbf{X^{(m)}}\right\|_2$ *is the 2-norm of* $\Delta\mathbf{X^{(m)}}$.

Proof: See the solution to Exercise 1.2.

4.2.3 Conclusions

This section introduced a tensor factorization based framework for temporal multi-faceted behavior prediction and behavioral pattern mining. The model used flexible regularizers to alleviate the sparsity problem and gave approximation algorithms to efficiently process the increments with a theoretical guarantee. Extensive experiments performed on real world datasets demonstrate that the framework was effective and efficient in behavior prediction tasks.

4.3 MINING CROSS-DOMAIN BEHAVIOR FOR KNOWLEDGE TRANSFER

Social networks allow users to create and adopt different types of items — not only web posts but also user labels, images and videos. Traditional web post recommendation approaches suffer from data sparsity (i.e., limited interaction between users and web posts) and the issue of cold start (i.e., giving recommendations to new users who have not yet created any web posts). The social connections and multiple item domains provide an unprecedented opportunity to alleviate these issues in real applications. This section will introduce a general framework for cross-domain behavior modeling [12, 9].

4.3.1 Cross-Domain Behavior Modeling

Users' characteristics relate both to social connections and to different user-item interactions. For example, users read web posts created by their community and may adopt similar user labels to their friends. Therefore, an effective social recommendation approach should acknowledge (1) social tie strength (henceforth, tie strength) between users and (2) different user-item interactions. How to incorporate a social domain and auxiliary item domains (e.g., user labels and images) into a unified framework?

Note that multiple item domains reflect users' intrinsic preferences and tend to be tightly connected among a massive number of users. Figure 4.6 shows a new representation of social networks and proposes a star-structured graph, where the social domain is at the center and is connected to the surrounding item domains.

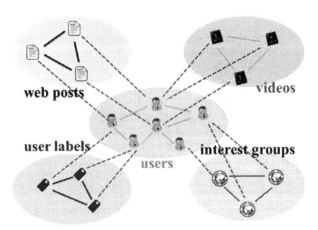

FIGURE 4.6 Star-structured graph for cross-domain behavior modeling.

The value of the *cross-domain link*[1] weight represents how often a given user adopts a given item, while the value of the *within-domain link*[2] weight in the social domain represents the tie strength between users. Users are more likely to have stronger ties if they share similar characteristics. Cross-domain links reflect users' characteristics in different ways. For example, a cross-domain link from a user to a web post about iPhones shows his or her short-term interest in iPhones, and a cross-domain link from him or her to a label "iPhone Fan" implies his or her long-term interest in iPhones. A basic assumption is that the more auxiliary knowledge we have, the more we know about the users, thereby enabling more accurate estimates of tie strength. When a user and his or her friend have many common user labels, we assume a greater tie strength and expect them to be more similar in terms of their web post adoption behaviors. Even if the web post domain is extremely sparse, we may still produce effective recommendations by transferring auxiliary knowledge from other item domains through the social domain.

General idea. The Hybrid Random Walk (HRW) method can transfer knowledge from auxiliary item domains according to a star-structured configuration to improve social recommendations in a target domain. HRW estimates weights for (1) links between user nodes within the social domain, and (2) links between user nodes in the social domain and item nodes in the item domain. The weights respectively represent (1) tie strength between users and (2) the probability of a user adopting or rejecting an item. HRW integrates knowledge from multiple relational domains and alleviates sparsity and cold-start issues.

4.3.2 Hybrid Random Walk Algorithm

A real-world example of a second-order hybrid star-structured graph is presented in Figure 4.7. It differs from traditional star-structured graphs that do not include entity relationships within each domain. This hybrid graph considers both within-domain and cross-domain entity relationships. Table 4.1 summarizes the symbols used in this section to denote the five subgraphs in Figure 4.7:

1. $\mathcal{G}^{(\mathcal{U})} = \{\mathcal{U}, \mathcal{E}^{(\mathcal{U})}\}$, where $\mathcal{E}^{(\mathcal{U})}$ represents the edge set linking the nodes in $\mathcal{U}$;
2. $\mathcal{G}^{(\mathcal{P})} = \{\mathcal{P}, \mathcal{E}^{(\mathcal{P})}\}$, where $\mathcal{E}^{(\mathcal{P})}$ represents the edge set linking the nodes in $\mathcal{P}$;
3. $\mathcal{G}^{(\mathcal{T})} = \{\mathcal{T}, \mathcal{E}^{(\mathcal{T})}\}$, where $\mathcal{E}^{(\mathcal{T})}$ represents the edge set linking the nodes in $\mathcal{T}$;

---

[1] Cross-domain links are user-item links (item adoptions), i.e., links between the social domain and the item domains.

[2] Within-domain links are user-user links in the social domain (social connections) and the item-item links in each item domain.

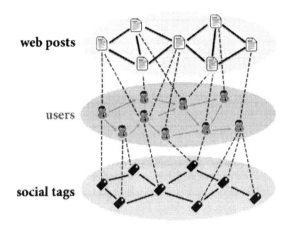

web posts

users

social tags

FIGURE 4.7 Hybrid random walk on a second-order star-structured graph.

4. $\mathcal{G}^{(\mathcal{UP})} = \{\mathcal{U} \bigcup \mathcal{P}, \mathcal{E}^{(\mathcal{UP})}\}$, where $\mathcal{E}^{(\mathcal{UP})}$ represents the edges linking the nodes in $\mathcal{U}$ and $\mathcal{P}$;

5. $\mathcal{G}^{(\mathcal{UT})} = \{\mathcal{U} \bigcup \mathcal{T}, \mathcal{E}^{(\mathcal{UT})}\}$, where $\mathcal{E}^{(\mathcal{UT})}$ represents the edges linking the nodes in $\mathcal{U}$ and $\mathcal{T}$.

To conceptualize user relationships in $\mathcal{G}^{(\mathcal{U})}$, consider the relevance from user u_i to u_j as

$$w_{ij}^{(\mathcal{U})} = \begin{cases} 1 & \text{if user } u_i \text{ is a friend of } u_j, \\ 0 & \text{otherwise.} \end{cases} \qquad (4.30)$$

To compute web-post relationships in $\mathcal{P}$, HRW uses a Term Frequency-Inverse Document Frequency (TF-IDF) representation vector for each post $b_i = [b_{i1}, \cdots, b_{ik}, \cdots, b_{iK}]^\top$ in matrix $\mathbf{B}$ (where K is the size of vocabulary),

TABLE 4.1 Symbols for hybrid random walk algorithm

Symbol	Description
u_i	The i-th user
$\mathcal{U} = \{u_1, u_2, \cdots, u_m\}$	The set of users
p_i	The i-th web post
$\mathcal{P} = \{p_1, p_2, \cdots, p_n\}$	The set of web posts
t_i	The i-th user label
$\mathcal{T} = \{t_1, t_2, \cdots, t_l\}$	The set of user labels
d_{ij}	The j-th item in the i-th domain
$\mathcal{D}_i = \{d_{i1}, d_{i2}, \cdots, d_{i|\mathcal{D}_i|}\}$	The set of items in the i-th domain
$\mathcal{D} = \{\mathcal{D}_1, \mathcal{D}_2, \cdots, \mathcal{D}_N\}$	The set of item domains

and then measure the semantic similarity between post b_i and b_j as

$$w_{ij}^{(\mathcal{P})} = \frac{\sum_k b_{ik} b_{jk}}{\sqrt{\sum_k b_{ik}^2}\sqrt{\sum_k b_{jk}^2}}. \tag{4.31}$$

For user labels, HRW measures their similarity using the Jaccard similarity. Assume that labels t_i and t_j appear in c_i and c_j tweets as a word, and co-appear in c_{ij} tweets. Then the semantic relationship is computed as

$$w_{ij}^{(\mathcal{T})} = \frac{c_{ij}}{c_i + c_j - c_{ij}}. \tag{4.32}$$

Thus, three similarity matrices $\mathbf{W}^{(\mathcal{U})} = \{w_{ij}^{(\mathcal{U})}\}$, $\mathbf{W}^{(\mathcal{P})} = \{w_{ij}^{(\mathcal{P})}\}$ and $\mathbf{W}^{(\mathcal{T})} = \{w_{ij}^{(\mathcal{T})}\}$ have been constructed to encode edge weights for three within-domain subgraphs.

Further, we have two cross-domain subgraphs $\mathcal{G}^{(\mathcal{UP})}$ and $\mathcal{G}^{(\mathcal{UT})}$, whose edge weights need to be estimated. Since web posts can be adopted or rejected but user labels are edited by users, both positive and negative user-post links exist, but only positive user-label links exist. These links are presented as undirected edges $e_{ij}^{(\mathcal{UP})}$ and $e_{ij}^{(\mathcal{UT})}$. Their weights are determined as follows.

$$w_{ij}^{(\mathcal{UP})^+} = \begin{cases} 1 & \text{if user } u_i \text{ adopts web post } \rho_j, \\ 0 & \text{otherwise;} \end{cases} \tag{4.33}$$

$$w_{ij}^{(\mathcal{UP})^-} = \begin{cases} 1 & \text{if user } u_i \text{ rejects web post } \rho_j, \\ 0 & \text{otherwise;} \end{cases} \tag{4.34}$$

$$w_{ij}^{(\mathcal{UT})^+} = \begin{cases} 1 & \text{if user } u_i \text{ adopts web post } t_j, \\ 0 & \text{otherwise.} \end{cases} \tag{4.35}$$

Thus, we obtain the three weight matrices $\mathbf{W}^{(\mathcal{UP})^+} = \{w_{ij}^{(\mathcal{UP})^+}\}$, $\mathbf{W}^{(\mathcal{UP})^-} = \{w_{ij}^{(\mathcal{UP})^-}\}$ and $\mathbf{W}^{(\mathcal{UT})^+} = \{w_{ij}^{(\mathcal{UT})^+}\}$.

Now we can derive a random walk algorithm [29, 6, 8] to predict missing links on $\mathcal{G}^{(\mathcal{UP})}$ and $\mathcal{G}^{(\mathcal{UT})}$, which includes both within-domain and cross-domain random walks. For $\mathcal{G}^{(\mathcal{U})}$, $\mathcal{G}^{(\mathcal{P})}$ and $\mathcal{G}^{(\mathcal{T})}$, we derive steady-state distributions, indicating the intrinsic relevance among users, posts and labels. For a standard random walk model, a walker starts from the i-th vertex and iteratively jumps to other vertices with transition probabilities $\mathbf{p}_i = \{p_{i1}, \cdots, p_{in}\}$. After reaching the steady state, the probability of the walker staying at the j-th vertex corresponds to the relevance score of vertex j to i. Specifically, the transition probability matrices are computed as the row-normalized weight matrices:

$$
\begin{aligned}
\mathbf{P}^{(\mathcal{U})} &= (\mathbf{D}^{(\mathcal{U})})^{-1}\mathbf{W}^{(\mathcal{U})}, & (4.36) \\
\mathbf{P}^{(\mathcal{P})} &= (\mathbf{D}^{(\mathcal{P})})^{-1}\mathbf{W}^{(\mathcal{P})}, & (4.37) \\
\mathbf{P}^{(\mathcal{T})} &= (\mathbf{D}^{(\mathcal{T})})^{-1}\mathbf{W}^{(\mathcal{T})}, & (4.38)
\end{aligned}
$$

where we denote the degree matrices of cross-domain links by $\mathbf{D}^{(\mathcal{UP})^{+}}$, $\mathbf{D}^{(\mathcal{UP})^{-}}$, and $\mathbf{D}^{(\mathcal{UT})^{+}}$. The final steady-state probability matrices can be obtained by iterating the following updates:

$$
\begin{aligned}
\mathbf{R}^{(\mathcal{U})}(t+1) &= \alpha\mathbf{P}^{(\mathcal{U})}\mathbf{R}^{(\mathcal{U})}(t) + (1-\alpha)\mathbf{I}, & (4.39) \\
\mathbf{R}^{(\mathcal{P})}(t+1) &= \beta\mathbf{P}^{(\mathcal{P})}\mathbf{R}^{(\mathcal{P})}(t) + (1-\beta)\mathbf{I}, & (4.40) \\
\mathbf{R}^{(\mathcal{T})}(t+1) &= \gamma\mathbf{P}^{(\mathcal{T})}\mathbf{R}^{(\mathcal{T})}(t) + (1-\gamma)\mathbf{I}, & (4.41)
\end{aligned}
$$

where $\mathbf{R}^{(\mathcal{U})}(t)$, $\mathbf{R}^{(\mathcal{P})}(t)$, $\mathbf{R}^{(\mathcal{T})}(t)$, $\mathbf{R}^{(\mathcal{U})}(t+1)$, $\mathbf{R}^{(\mathcal{P})}(t+1)$ and $\mathbf{R}^{(\mathcal{T})}(t+1)$ are the state probability matrices at time t and $t+1$; and $0 \le \alpha, \beta, \gamma \le 1$ are the prior probabilities that the random walker will leave its current state. It can be easily shown that the above iterations will finally converge to the steady state matrices when $t \to \infty$:

$$
\begin{aligned}
\mathbf{R}^{(\mathcal{U})} &= (1-\alpha)(\mathbf{I} - \alpha\mathbf{P}^{(\mathcal{U})})^{-1}, & (4.42) \\
\mathbf{R}^{(\mathcal{P})} &= (1-\beta)(\mathbf{I} - \beta\mathbf{P}^{(\mathcal{P})})^{-1}, & (4.43) \\
\mathbf{R}^{(\mathcal{T})} &= (1-\gamma)(\mathbf{I} - \gamma\mathbf{P}^{(\mathcal{T})})^{-1}. & (4.44)
\end{aligned}
$$

For cross-domain links, we compute the transition probability matrices as

$$
\begin{aligned}
\mathbf{P}^{(\mathcal{UP})^{+}} &= (\mathbf{D}^{(\mathcal{UP})^{+}})^{-1}\mathbf{W}^{(\mathcal{UP})^{+}}, & (4.45) \\
\mathbf{P}^{(\mathcal{UP})^{-}} &= (\mathbf{D}^{(\mathcal{UP})^{-}})^{-1}\mathbf{W}^{(\mathcal{UP})^{-}}, & (4.46) \\
\mathbf{P}^{(\mathcal{UT})^{+}} &= (\mathbf{D}^{(\mathcal{UT})^{+}})^{-1}\mathbf{W}^{(\mathcal{UT})^{+}}, & (4.47)
\end{aligned}
$$

where elements $p_{ij}^{(\mathcal{UP})^{+}}$ and $p_{ij}^{(\mathcal{UP})^{-}}$ represent the transition probability that user u_i will adopt/ignore post p_j; and $p_{ij}^{(\mathcal{UT})^{+}}$ represents the transition probability that user u_i will adopt label t_j. Now, we simultaneously determine relevance scores $\mathbf{R}^{(\mathcal{U})} = \{r_{ij}^{(\mathcal{U})}\}$ between each pair of users, which finally reflects the tie strength on the real user graph. Element $r_{ij}^{(\mathcal{U})}$ represents the probability that a random walker jumps from user u_i to u_j.

Now, we consider the above transition paths and estimate the transition probabilities $p_{ij}^{(\mathcal{UP})^+}$, $p_{ij}^{(\mathcal{UP})^-}$, $p_{ij}^{(\mathcal{UT})^+}$, and $r_{ij}^{(\mathcal{U})}$ of one step random walk over $\mathcal{G}^{(\mathcal{UP})}$, $\mathcal{G}^{(\mathcal{UT})}$, and $\mathcal{G}^{(\mathcal{U})}$ as

$$p_{ij}^{(\mathcal{UP})^+} = \delta \sum_{u_k \in \mathcal{U}} r_{ik}^{(\mathcal{U})} p_{kj}^{(\mathcal{UP})^+} + (1-\delta) \sum_{p_k \in \mathcal{P}} p_{ik}^{(\mathcal{UP})^+} r_{kj}^{(\mathcal{P})}, \qquad (4.48)$$

$$p_{ij}^{(\mathcal{UP})^-} = \delta \sum_{u_k \in \mathcal{U}} r_{ik}^{(\mathcal{U})} p_{kj}^{(\mathcal{UP})^-} + (1-\delta) \sum_{p_k \in \mathcal{P}} p_{ik}^{(\mathcal{UP})^-} r_{kj}^{(\mathcal{P})}, \qquad (4.49)$$

$$p_{ij}^{(\mathcal{UT})^+} = \eta \sum_{u_k \in \mathcal{U}} r_{ik}^{(\mathcal{U})} p_{kj}^{(\mathcal{UT})^+} + (1-\eta) \sum_{t_k \in \mathcal{T}} p_{ik}^{(\mathcal{UT})^+} r_{kj}^{(\mathcal{T})}, \qquad (4.50)$$

$$r_{ij}^{(\mathcal{U})} = \tau^{(\mathcal{P})} (\mu \sum_{p_k \in \mathcal{P}} p_{ik}^{(\mathcal{UP})^+} p_{jk}^{(\mathcal{UP})^+} + (1-\mu) \sum_{p_k \in \mathcal{P}} p_{ik}^{(\mathcal{UP})^-} p_{jk}^{(\mathcal{UP})^-})$$

$$+ \tau^{(\mathcal{T})} \sum_{t_k \in \mathcal{T}} p_{ik}^{(\mathcal{UT})^+} p_{jk}^{(\mathcal{UT})^+} + \tau^{(\mathcal{U})} \sum_{u_k \in \mathcal{U}} r_{ik}^{(\mathcal{U})} r_{kj}^{(\mathcal{U})}, \qquad (4.51)$$

where $0 \leq \delta, \eta, \mu, \tau^{(\mathcal{P})}, \tau^{(\mathcal{T})}, \tau^{(\mathcal{U})} \leq 1$ are the parameters for trading off different transition routes. Note that for the update of cross-domain transition probability matrices (Equation (4.48) to Equation (4.50)), we consider two types of routes shown in Figure 4.8. HRW also assumes that the update of the cross-domain probability matrices will affect the within-domain probability matrix of the user subgraph.

On the other hand, the update of cross-domain transition probability affects only the within-domain transition probabilities of the user graph, because the user tie strength is influenced by (1) common posts, (2) common labels, and (3) social relationships. The cross-domain links (adoption behaviors) do not affect the within-domain transition probability of other item domains. The rationale is that the transition probability of items (posts, labels, videos, etc.) should be derived by their semantic similarity, which would not be changed by the users who adopt them. Therefore, the HRW method updates cross-domain links between the user and all types of items as well as within-domain links

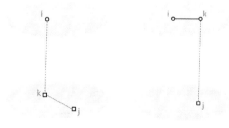

FIGURE 4.8 Transition routes we consider when updating cross-domain transition probability matrix.

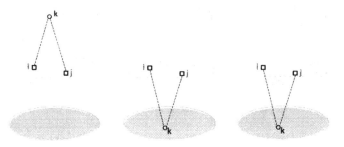

FIGURE 4.9 Transition routes when updating within-domain transition probability matrix on the user subgraph.

between users (not items). The updating rule Equation (4.51) considers three routes shown in Figure 4.9.

We can further give matrix formulations for the update of transition probability from time t to $t+1$.

$$\mathbf{P}^{(\mathcal{UP})^+}(t+1) = \delta \mathbf{R}^{(\mathcal{U})}(t)\mathbf{P}^{(\mathcal{UP})^+}(t) + (1-\delta)\mathbf{P}^{(\mathcal{UP})^+}(t)\mathbf{R}^{(\mathcal{P})}, \quad (4.52)$$

$$\mathbf{P}^{(\mathcal{UP})^-}(t+1) = \delta \mathbf{R}^{(\mathcal{U})}(t)\mathbf{P}^{(\mathcal{UP})^-}(t) + (1-\delta)\mathbf{P}^{(\mathcal{UP})^-}(t)\mathbf{R}^{(\mathcal{P})}, \quad (4.53)$$

$$\mathbf{P}^{(\mathcal{UT})^+}(t+1) = \eta \mathbf{R}^{(\mathcal{U})}(t)\mathbf{P}^{(\mathcal{UT})^+}(t) + (1-\eta)\mathbf{P}^{(\mathcal{UT})^+}(t)\mathbf{R}^{(\mathcal{T})}, \quad (4.54)$$

$$\mathbf{R}^{(\mathcal{U})}(t+1) = \tau^{(\mathcal{P})}(\mu \mathbf{P}^{(\mathcal{UP})^+}(t)\mathbf{P}^{(\mathcal{UP})^+}(t)^T$$
$$+ (1-\mu)\mathbf{P}^{(\mathcal{UP})^-}(t)\mathbf{P}^{(\mathcal{UP})^-}(t)^T)$$
$$+ \tau^{(\mathcal{T})}\mathbf{P}^{(\mathcal{UT})^+}(t)\mathbf{P}^{(\mathcal{UT})^+}(t)^T$$
$$+ \tau^{(\mathcal{U})}\mathbf{R}^{(\mathcal{U})}(t)\mathbf{R}^{(\mathcal{U})}(t)^T. \quad (4.55)$$

With graphs $\mathcal{G}^{(\mathcal{U})}$, $\mathcal{G}^{(\mathcal{UP})}$, and $\mathcal{G}^{(\mathcal{UT})}$, the corresponding transition matrices $\mathbf{R}^{(\mathcal{U})}$, $\mathbf{P}^{(\mathcal{UP})^+}$, $\mathbf{P}^{(\mathcal{UP})^-}$, and $\mathbf{P}^{(\mathcal{UT})^+}$ are computed for the next random walk step.

Complexity. The space complexity of the HRW algorithm is $O(m^2 + n^2 + l^2 + 2m(n+l))$, and the time complexity is $O((m^2 + 4m(n+l) + 2(n^2 + l^2))mT)$, where m, n, and l are the number of users, posts, and labels, respectively, and T is the number of iterations. Since the matrices are usually sparse and $m, n \gg l$, the space complexity is $O((m+n)^2)$ and the time complexity is $O((m+n)ET)$, where E is the number of links between users and posts.

4.3.3 Conclusions

This section addressed the problems of data sparsity and cold start in social recommendation. It reconsidered the problem from the transfer learning perspective and alleviated the data sparsity problem in a target domain by transferring knowledge from other auxiliary social relational domains. By considering the special structures of multiple relational domains in social networks, an innovative random walk method has been derived on a star-structured graph, which is a general method to incorporate complex and heterogeneous link structures. Extensive experiments on a large real-world social network dataset showed that this method greatly boosts the social recommendation performance. In particular, it gained improvement in web-post recommendation by transferring knowledge from the user-label domain for the user tie strength updating process, compared with the recommendation methods, which only use information from the web-post domain. In addition, by using only 27.6% of the available information in the target domain, the method achieved comparable performance with methods that use all available information in the target domain without transfer learning. The proposed method and insightful experiments indicate a promising and general way to solve the data sparsity problem.

4.4   SUMMARY

This chapter introduces novel techniques of mining user behaviors for three social applications: (1) uncovering the behavioral mechanism in social networks and modeling the social contexts for social recommendation, (2) modeling spatio-temporal contexts for behavior prediction, and (3) mining cross-domain behavior to address the sparsity challenge. Section 4.1 demonstrates the important roles of preference and influence in users' behavioral intention of information adoption and rejection. The next section proposes a framework of flexible evolutionary multi-faceted analysis to model the multi-aspect and dynamic behavioral patterns. The third section proposes a hybrid random walk method that uses the social relationship as a bridge to connect multiple domains in social networks. The procedure of knowledge transfer can alleviate the data sparsity issue in a single domain. We sincerely hope these three parts of work would shed insights on mining and modeling large behavioral data in social networks.

EXERCISES

4.1   In Section 4.1, use statistical measures to prove there is NOT a close relationship between scores on the two contextual factors: *individual preference* and *interpersonal influence*.

Solution:

We can calculate the correlation between the two factors in recommendation cases. If we use P and I for each user to denote preference and influence of her adopted items. The Pearson correlation is defined as

$$\rho_{P,I} = \frac{cov(P, I)}{\sigma_P \sigma_I} = \frac{E[(P - \mu_P)(I - \mu_I)]}{\sigma_P \sigma_I}, \qquad (P4.1)$$

where μ. is the mean value, σ. denotes the standard deviation and $cov(.,.)$ denotes the covariance. The correlation is 1 or -1 in the case of perfect positive or negative linear relationship, and zero if preference and influence are uncorrelated. We can demonstrate the existence and significance of the two factors when the absolute correlation value is small.

4.2 In Section 4.2, prove Theorem 4.1 and Theorem 4.2 for the guarantee of FEMA's effectiveness.

Solution :

(1) Proof for Theorem 4.1: According to Equation (4.20), we have

$$|\Delta\lambda_i^{(m)}| = |\mathbf{a}_i^{(m)\top}(\mathbf{X}^{(m)}\Delta\mathbf{X}^{(m)\top} + \Delta\mathbf{X}^{(m)}\mathbf{X}^{(m)\top})\mathbf{a}_i^{(m)}|. \quad (P4.2)$$

By Cauchy-Schwarz inequality,

$$
\begin{aligned}
&|\mathbf{a}_i^{(m)\top}(\mathbf{X}^{(m)}\Delta\mathbf{X}^{(m)\top} + \Delta\mathbf{X}^{(m)}\mathbf{X}^{(m)\top})\mathbf{a}_i^{(m)}| \\
&\leq 2\left\|\Delta\mathbf{X}^{(m)}\mathbf{X}^{(m)\top}\mathbf{a}_i^{(m)}\right\|_2 \left\|\mathbf{a}_i^{(m)}\right\|_2 \\
&= 2\left\|\Delta\mathbf{X}^{(m)}\mathbf{X}^{(m)\top}\mathbf{a}_i^{(m)}\right\|_2, \quad (P4.3)
\end{aligned}
$$

where in the first step we use the symmetry of $\mathbf{X}^{(m)}\Delta\mathbf{X}^{(m)\top} + \Delta\mathbf{X}^{(m)}\mathbf{X}^{(m)\top}$ and in the second step we use the fact that $\left\|\mathbf{a}_i^{(m)}\right\| = 1$. By the definition of matrix 2-norm, we have that

$$\left\|\Delta\mathbf{X}^{(m)}\mathbf{X}^{(m)\top}\right\|_2 = \sup_{\|\mathbf{w}\|_2=1}\left\|\Delta\mathbf{X}^{(m)}\mathbf{X}^{(m)\top}\mathbf{w}\right\|_2. \quad (P4.4)$$

Therefore

$$
\begin{aligned}
&|\mathbf{a}_i^{(m)\top}(\mathbf{X}^{(m)}\Delta\mathbf{X}^{(m)\top} + \Delta\mathbf{X}^{(m)}\mathbf{X}^{(m)\top})\mathbf{a}_i^{(m)}| \\
&\leq 2\left\|\Delta\mathbf{X}^{(m)}\mathbf{X}^{(m)\top}\right\|_2 \leq 2\left\|\mathbf{X}^{(m)}\right\|_2\left\|\Delta\mathbf{X}^{(m)}\right\|_2 \\
&= 2(\lambda_{\mathbf{X}^{(m)\top}\mathbf{X}^{(m)}}^{\max})^{\frac{1}{2}}\left\|\Delta\mathbf{X}^{(m)}\right\|_2 \quad (P4.5)
\end{aligned}
$$

(2) Proof for Theorem 4.2: From Equation (4.27), we have that

$$
\begin{aligned}
|\Delta\mathbf{a}_i^{(m)}| &= 2\left|\sum_{j\neq i}\frac{\mathbf{a}_j^{(m)\top}\Delta\mathbf{X}^{(m)}\mathbf{X}^{(m)\top}\mathbf{a}_i^{(m)}}{\lambda_i^{(m)} - \lambda_j^{(m)}}\mathbf{a}_j^{(m)}\right| \\
&\leq 2\sum_{j\neq i}\left\|\frac{\mathbf{a}_j^{(m)\top}\Delta\mathbf{X}^{(m)}\mathbf{X}^{(m)\top}\mathbf{a}_i^{(m)}}{\lambda_i^{(m)} - \lambda_j^{(m)}}\mathbf{a}_j^{(m)}\right\| \\
&\leq 2\sum_{j\neq i}\frac{\left\|\mathbf{a}_j^{(m)}\right\|}{|\lambda_i^{(m)} - \lambda_j^{(m)}|}\left\|\mathbf{a}_j^{(m)\top}\Delta\mathbf{X}^{(m)}\mathbf{X}^{(m)\top}\mathbf{a}_i^{(m)}\right\| \\
&\leq 2\left\|\Delta\mathbf{X}^{(m)}\right\|_2\sum_{j\neq i}\frac{(\lambda_{\mathbf{X}^{(m)\top}\mathbf{X}^{(m)}}^{\max})^{\frac{1}{2}}}{|\lambda_i^{(m)} - \lambda_j^{(m)}|}. \quad (P4.6)
\end{aligned}
$$

4.3 In Section 4.3, we used two types of item domains, web post and user label. However, social networks have multiple types of User-Generated Content (UGC), e.g., posts, labels, music, and movies. Therefore, the second-order graph is insufficient. How can the random walk strategy be extended to higher-order cases?

Solution :

We represent the following subgraphs contained in the high-order hybrid graph:

- $\mathcal{G}^{(\mathcal{U})} = \{\mathcal{U}, \mathcal{E}^{(\mathcal{U})}\}$, where $\mathcal{E}^{(\mathcal{U})}$ represents the edge set linking the nodes in $\mathcal{U}$;
- $\mathcal{G}^{(\mathcal{D}_i)} = \{\mathcal{D}_i, \mathcal{E}^{(\mathcal{D}_i)}\}$, where $\mathcal{E}^{(\mathcal{D}_i)}$ represents the edge set linking the nodes in $\mathcal{D}_i$, $i = 1, \cdots, N$;
- $\mathcal{G}^{(\mathcal{U}\mathcal{D}_i)} = \{\mathcal{U}\bigcup\mathcal{D}_i, \mathcal{E}^{(\mathcal{U}\mathcal{D}_i)}\}$, where $\mathcal{E}^{(\mathcal{U}\mathcal{D}_i)}$ represents the edges linking the nodes in $\mathcal{U}$ and $\mathcal{D}_i$, $i = 1, \cdots, N$.

With respect to $\mathcal{G}^{(\mathcal{U})}$ and $\{\mathcal{G}^{(\mathcal{D}_i)}\}_{i=1}^{N}$, we construct their corresponding edge weight matrices $\mathbf{W}^{(\mathcal{U})}$ and $\{\mathbf{W}^{(\mathcal{D}_i)}\}_{i=1}^{N}$. Thus, the within-domain transition probability matrices can be obtained by $(i = 1, \cdots, N)$

$$\mathbf{P}^{(\mathcal{U})} = (\mathbf{D}^{(\mathcal{U})})^{-1}\mathbf{W}^{(\mathcal{U})}, \tag{P4.7}$$

$$\mathbf{P}^{(\mathcal{D}_i)} = (\mathbf{D}^{(\mathcal{D}_i)})^{-1}\mathbf{W}^{(\mathcal{D}_i)}, \tag{P4.8}$$

where $\mathbf{D}^{(\mathcal{U})}$ and $\{\mathbf{D}^{(\mathcal{D}_i)}\}_{i=1}^{N}$ are the degree matrices induced by $\mathbf{W}^{(\mathcal{U})}$ and $\{\mathbf{W}^{(\mathcal{D}_i)}\}_{i=1}^{N}$. The final steady-state probability matrices can be iteratively calculated by

$$\mathbf{R}^{(\mathcal{U})}(t+1) = \alpha\mathbf{P}^{(\mathcal{U})}\mathbf{R}^{(\mathcal{U})}(t) + (1-\alpha)\mathbf{I}, \tag{P4.9}$$

$$\mathbf{R}^{(\mathcal{D}_i)}(t+1) = \beta_i\mathbf{P}^{(\mathcal{D}_i)}\mathbf{R}^{(\mathcal{D}_i)}(t) + (1-\beta_i)\mathbf{I}, \tag{P4.10}$$

where $i = 1, 2, \cdots, N$, $0 \le \alpha, \beta_1, \cdots, \beta_N \le 1$. For the cross-domain subgraphs $\{\mathcal{G}^{(\mathcal{U}\mathcal{D}_i)}\}_{i=1}^{N}$, we compute the edge weight matrices $\{\mathbf{W}^{(\mathcal{U}\mathcal{D}_i)}\}_{i=1}^{N}$ based on the user interactions with other item domains $\{\mathcal{D}_i\}_{i=1}^{N}$. Thus, the cross-domain transition probability matrices can be computed as

$$\mathbf{P}^{(\mathcal{U}\mathcal{D}_i)+} = (\mathbf{D}^{(\mathcal{U}\mathcal{D}_i)+})^{-1}\mathbf{W}^{(\mathcal{U}\mathcal{D}_i)+}, \tag{P4.11}$$

$$\mathbf{P}^{(\mathcal{U}\mathcal{D}_i)-} = (\mathbf{D}^{(\mathcal{U}\mathcal{D}_i)-})^{-1}\mathbf{W}^{(\mathcal{U}\mathcal{D}_i)-}, \tag{P4.12}$$

where $i = 1, \cdots, N$. The cross-domain transition probability matrices can be updated using the following rules:

$$
\begin{aligned}
\mathbf{P}^{(\mathcal{U}\mathcal{D}_i)^+}(t+1) &= \delta_i \mathbf{R}^{(\mathcal{U})}(t)\mathbf{P}^{(\mathcal{U}\mathcal{D}_i)^+}(t) \\
&\quad +(1-\delta_i)\mathbf{P}^{(\mathcal{U}\mathcal{D}_i)^+}(t)\mathbf{R}^{(\mathcal{D}_i)}, \quad\quad\quad (\text{P4.13}) \\
\mathbf{P}^{(\mathcal{U}\mathcal{D}_i)^-}(t+1) &= \delta_i \mathbf{R}^{(\mathcal{U})}(t)\mathbf{P}^{(\mathcal{U}\mathcal{D}_i)^-}(t) \\
&\quad +(1-\delta_i)\mathbf{P}^{(\mathcal{U}\mathcal{D}_i)^-}(t)\mathbf{R}^{(\mathcal{D}_i)}, \quad\quad\quad (\text{P4.14}) \\
\mathbf{R}^{(\mathcal{U})}(t+1) &= \sum_{\mathcal{D}_i \in \mathcal{D}} \tau_i \mu_i \mathbf{P}^{(\mathcal{U}\mathcal{D}_i)^+}(t)\mathbf{P}^{(\mathcal{U}\mathcal{D}_i)^+}(t)^T \\
&\quad + \sum_{\mathcal{D}_i \in \mathcal{D}} \tau_i (1-\mu_i) \mathbf{P}^{(\mathcal{U}\mathcal{D}_i)^-}(t)\mathbf{P}^{(\mathcal{U}\mathcal{D}_i)^-}(t)^T \\
&\quad + \tau^{(\mathcal{U})}\mathbf{R}^{(\mathcal{U})}(t)\mathbf{R}^{(\mathcal{U})}(t)^T, \quad\quad\quad (\text{P4.15})
\end{aligned}
$$

where $0 \le \delta_i, \mu_i, \tau_i \le 1$ are the trade-off parameters and $i = 1, 2, \cdots, N$. For a domain $\mathcal{D}_i$ without negative user-item links, we set $\mu_i = 1$ to update $\mathbf{R}^{(\mathcal{U})}$. The space complexity of this algorithm is $O(m^2 + 2m \sum |\mathcal{D}_i| + \sum |\mathcal{D}_i|^2)$ and the time complexity is $O((m^2 + 4m \sum |\mathcal{D}_i| + 2 \sum |\mathcal{D}_i|^2)mT)$, where T is the number of iterations

Bibliography

[1] Marko Balabanovic and Yoav Shoham. Fab: content-based, collaborative recommendation. *Communications of the ACM*, 40(3):66–72, 1997.

[2] Peng Cui, Shifei Jin, Linyun Yu, Fei Wang, Wenwu Zhu, and Shiqiang Yang. Cascading outbreak prediction in networks: a data-driven approach. In *Proceedings of the 19th ACM SIGKDD International Conference on Knowledge Discovery and Data Mining*, pages 901–909. ACM, 2013.

[3] Peng Cui, Fei Wang, Shaowei Liu, Mingdong Ou, Shiqiang Yang, and Lifeng Sun. Who should share what?: item-level social influence prediction for users and posts ranking. In *Proceedings of the 34th International ACM SIGIR Conference on Research and Development in Information Retrieval*, pages 185–194. ACM, 2011.

[4] Peng Cui, Fei Wang, Shiqiang Yang, and Lifeng Sun. Item-level social influence prediction with probabilistic hybrid factor matrix factorization. In *Twenty-Fifth AAAI Conference on Artificial Intelligence*, 2011.

[5] Peng Cui, Tianyang Zhang, Fei Wang, and Peng He. Perceiving group themes from collective social and behavioral information. In *Twenty-Ninth AAAI Conference on Artificial Intelligence*, 2015.

[6] Marco Gori, Augusto Pucci, V Roma, and I Siena. Itemrank: A random-walk based scoring algorithm for recommender engines. In *IJCAI*, volume 7, pages 2766–2771, 2007.

[7] Junming Huang, Xueqi Cheng, Jiafeng Guo, Huawei Shen, and Kun Yang. Social recommendation with interpersonal influence. In *ECAI*, volume 10, pages 601–606, 2010.

[8] Mohsen Jamali and Martin Ester. Trustwalker: a random walk model for combining trust-based and item-based recommendation. In *Proceedings of the 15th ACM SIGKDD International Conference on Knowledge Discovery and Data Mining*, pages 397–406. ACM, 2009.

[9] Meng Jiang, Peng Cui, Xumin Chen, Fei Wang, Wenwu Zhu, and Shiqiang Yang. Social recommendation with cross-domain transferable knowledge. *Knowledge and Data Engineering, IEEE Transactions on (TKDE)*, 2015.

[10] Meng Jiang, Peng Cui, Rui Liu, Qiang Yang, Fei Wang, Wenwu Zhu, and Shiqiang Yang. Social contextual recommendation. In *Proceedings of the 21st ACM International Conference on Information and Knowledge Management (CIKM)*, pages 45–54. ACM, 2012.

[11] Meng Jiang, Peng Cui, Fei Wang, Xinran Xu, Wenwu Zhu, and Shiqiang Yang. Fema: flexible evolutionary multi-faceted analysis for dynamic behavioral pattern discovery. In *Proceedings of the 20th ACM SIGKDD International Conference on Knowledge Discovery and Data Mining (SIGKDD)*, pages 1186–1195. ACM, 2014.

[12] Meng Jiang, Peng Cui, Fei Wang, Qiang Yang, Wenwu Zhu, and Shiqiang Yang. Social recommendation across multiple relational domains. In *Proceedings of the 21st ACM International Conference on Information and Knowledge Management (CIKM)*, pages 1422–1431. ACM, 2012.

[13] Meng Jiang, Peng Cui, Fei Wang, Wenwu Zhu, and Shiqiang Yang. Scalable recommendation with social contextual information. *Knowledge and Data Engineering, IEEE Transactions on (TKDE)*, 26(11):2789–2802, 2014.

[14] Tamara G Kolda and Brett W Bader. Tensor decompositions and applications. *SIAM Review*, 51(3):455–500, 2009.

[15] Tamara G Kolda and Jimeng Sun. Scalable tensor decompositions for multi-aspect data mining. In *Data Mining, 2008. ICDM'08. Eighth IEEE International Conference on*, pages 363–372. IEEE, 2008.

[16] Yehuda Koren. Factorization meets the neighborhood: a multifaceted collaborative filtering model. In *Proceedings of the 14th ACM SIGKDD International Conference on Knowledge Discovery and Data Mining*, pages 426–434. ACM, 2008.

[17] Yehuda Koren. Collaborative filtering with temporal dynamics. *Communications of the ACM*, 53(4):89–97, 2010.

[18] Yehuda Koren, Robert Bell, and Chris Volinsky. Matrix factorization techniques for recommender systems. *Computer*, (8):30–37, 2009.

[19] Jure Leskovec, Ajit Singh, and Jon Kleinberg. Patterns of influence in a recommendation network. In *Advances in Knowledge Discovery and Data Mining*, pages 380–389. Springer, 2006.

[20] Lu Liu, Jie Tang, Jiawei Han, Meng Jiang, and Shiqiang Yang. Mining topic-level influence in heterogeneous networks. In *Proceedings of the 19th ACM International Conference on Information and Knowledge Management*, pages 199–208. ACM, 2010.

[21] Hao Ma, Irwin King, and Michael R Lyu. Learning to recommend with explicit and implicit social relations. *ACM Transactions on Intelligent Systems and Technology (TIST)*, 2(3):29, 2011.

[22] Kanika Narang, Seema Nagar, Sameep Mehta, L Venkata Subramaniam, and Kuntal Dey. Discovery and analysis of evolving topical social discussions on unstructured microblogs. In *Advances in Information Retrieval*, pages 545–556. Springer, 2013.

[23] Kira Radinsky, Krysta Svore, Susan Dumais, Jaime Teevan, Alex Bocharov, and Eric Horvitz. Modeling and predicting behavioral dynamics on the web. In *Proceedings of the 21st International Conference on World Wide Web*, pages 599–608. ACM, 2012.

[24] Badrul Sarwar, George Karypis, Joseph Konstan, and John Riedl. Item-based collaborative filtering recommendation algorithms. In *Proceedings of the 10th International Conference on World Wide Web*, pages 285–295. ACM, 2001.

[25] Luo Si and Rong Jin. Unified filtering by combining collaborative filtering and content-based filtering via mixture model and exponential model. In *Proceedings of the Thirteenth ACM International Conference on Information and Knowledge Management*, pages 156–157. ACM, 2004.

[26] Jimeng Sun, Dacheng Tao, and Christos Faloutsos. Beyond streams and graphs: dynamic tensor analysis. In *Proceedings of the 12th ACM SIGKDD International Conference on Knowledge Discovery and Data Mining*, pages 374–383. ACM, 2006.

[27] Jimeng Sun, Dacheng Tao, Spiros Papadimitriou, Philip S Yu, and Christos Faloutsos. Incremental tensor analysis: Theory and applications. *ACM Transactions on Knowledge Discovery from Data (TKDD)*, 2(3):11, 2008.

[28] Jiliang Tang, Xia Hu, and Huan Liu. Social recommendation: a review. *Social Network Analysis and Mining*, 3(4):1113–1133, 2013.

[29] Hanghang Tong, Christos Faloutsos, and Jia-Yu Pan. Fast random walk with restart and its applications. 2006.

[30] Fei Wang, Hanghang Tong, and Ching-Yung Lin. Towards evolutionary nonnegative matrix factorization. In *AAAI*, volume 11, pages 501–506, 2011.

III

Security and Privacy Issues of Social Networks

CHAPTER 5

Mining Misinformation in Social Media

Liang Wu, Fred Morstatter, Xia Hu and Huan Liu

CONTENTS

A RAPID INCREASE of social media services in recent years has enabled people to share and seek information effectively. The openness, however, also makes them one of the most effective channels for misinformation. Given the speed of information diffusion on social networks coupled with the widespread propagation of fake news [55], phishing URLs [24], and inaccurate information [37], misinformation escalates and can significantly impact users with undesirable consequences and wreak havoc instantaneously. In this chapter, we discuss the generation and diffusion of misinformation in social media, and introduce challenges of identification, intervention, and prevention methods. We use examples to illustrate how to mine misinformation in social media, and also suggest possible future work.

5.1 INTRODUCTION

Social media has changed the way we communicate. More and more people use such platforms to read, release and spread either breaking news [45] or their updates to their friends [52] [20]. The openness of social network platforms enables and motivates them to communicate freely online, but it also brings new problems. Without careful proofreading and fact-checking, fake news and inaccurate information will unintentionally be spread widely by well-meaning users. Such misinformation and disinformation could be devastating in social media, as it corrupts the trustworthiness.

Misinformation is fake or inaccurate information which is unintentionally spread, while disinformation is intentionally false and deliberately spread. In this work, we generally focus on inaccurate information in social media which misleads people, so we refer to them as misinformation. Misinformation causes distress and various kinds of destructive effect among social network users, especially when timely intervention is absent. As mentioned in several news,[1] misinformation has helped unnecessary fears and conspiracies spread through social media. One such example is Ebola. As some potential cases are found in Miami and Washington D.C., some tweets sounded as if Ebola were rampant and some kept tweeting even after government issued a statement to dispel the rumor [38]. In this work, we survey recent related research results and provide a thorough analysis of misinformation in social media.

Definition of Misinformation in Social Networks

Toward better investigating misinformation in social media websites, we organize it according to the intention of user spreading misinformation:

Unintentionally Spread Misinformation:
Some misinformation is created and forwarded spontaneously. People tend to help spread such information due to their trust of their friends and influencers in a social network, and want to inform their friends of the underlying issue.

Intentionally Spread Misinformation:
Some rumors and fake news are created and spread intentionally by malicious users to cause public anxiety, mislead people and deceive social network users for improper profit. This kind of misinformation is also called disinformation. In this work we use both words interchangeably.

The suggested categories cover most social media misinformation. But in the real world, misinformation is often more complex and may meet both

---

[1] http://time.com/3479254/ebola-social-media/

criteria. For example, some rumors are created by malicious users and people are tricked into amplifying it [40, 49].

Misinformation such as fake news, rumors and inaccurate information can cause ripple effects in the real world. In 2013, a rumor said that explosions at the White House happened and the president was injured.[2] The rumor sent a shudder through the stock market. Misinformation not only triggers financial panic, it also causes public anxiety [48], and ends careers [35]. In the 2013 World Economic Forum,[3] the issue of "misinformation spread" has been voted as one of the top ten globally significant issues of the year [56]. In order to cope with misinformation in social networks, researchers launch crowdsourcing systems to verify social media information[4] [53]; police arrest users who spread specific rumors to reduce the destructive effects [48]. However, since the spread is faster and wider than ever thanks to social networks, the damage is often beyond control.

Although crowdsourcing helps identify misinformation for journalists, the high velocity of online social media data generation makes it nearly impossible for them to keep up. Traditional penalties toward malicious information spreaders are still useful for shocking them, but observations from the financial panic [56] and the mass shooting at Sandy Hook Elementary School [48] reveal that misinformation keeps spreading and infecting users even after they are claimed to be false officially. Thus, an effective misinformation intervention method is in need for combating diffusion in social networks. In order to cope with the misinformation issue, we first introduce misinformation diffusion, its detection and intervention:

- Misinformation Diffusion: In order to know why misinformation is spread wider and faster than ever, we provide readers with a general understanding of information diffusion models. The distinct aspects of misinformation are then discussed. Interesting observations are given about the relationship between misinformation and network structures.

- Misinformation Detection: To cope with the high velocity and volume of social media data, we introduce several learning algorithms that detect malicious information or its spreaders.

- Misinformation Intervention: We introduce several methods about limiting misinformation spread in an early age or after it is diffused, so as to remove or reduce its impact.

5.2 MISINFORMATION MODELING

Misinformation can be widely spread in a very short time. As denoted in the "financial panic" case, the rumor was forwarded over 3000 times before Twitter blocked it. To explain how the information is diffused in a networked

---

[2]http://www.cnn.com/2013/04/23/tech/social-media/tweet-ripple-effect/
[3]http://reports.weforum.org/outlook-14/top-ten-trends-category-page/
[4]https://veri.ly/

environment, we first introduce several diffusion models. In addition, we discuss the distinct aspects of misinformation diffusion and provide readers with several findings between misinformation spread and network structure.

5.2.1 Information Diffusion in Social Networks

Information diffusion in social networks can be viewed as a process by which the news, events and different kinds of information are posted, forwarded and received by social network users. By representing each user as a node and the friendship between users as edges, social networks are transformed into a graph $G = (V, E)$, where V is the set of nodes and E is the set of edges between nodes. Then the information diffusion process can be viewed as some signal or label being propagated in the network. A formal definition can be found in [8].

There are various models which are designed to abstract the pattern of information diffusion. Here we introduce four diffusion models, i.e., *SIR Model* [29], *Tipping Model* [7], *Independent Cascade Model* [28] and *Linear Threshold Model* [28].

As discussed in [58], there are three essential roles for diffusion: **Senders** who initiate the diffusion process, **Spreaders** who forward such information to their followers, and **Receivers** who receive information being diffused in the social media websites, which are the largest group of people in the whole process and sometimes overlap with spreaders: if people choose to forward news they receive, they become receivers.

The key distinguishing points of different diffusion models are twofold: (1) method of information being diffused between senders, spreaders and receivers; (2) and evolution of individual roles during the process of diffusion. In the following parts, we will describe these aspects of different information and misinformation diffusion models.

SIR Model

The SIR model describes the information diffusion process in network as an infectious disease spread in a community. So the nodes are generally classified into three categories: **S** — the susceptible to be infected, **I** — the infected individuals who are active to infect others, **R** — the recovered individuals who recovered and are vaccinated against the disease. In the context of information diffusion in a social network, infected nodes can be regarded as those who were already informed of certain news or events, and are ready to pass them to neighbors; recovered nodes are those who have been informed, but are not passing the information to neighbors; susceptible nodes are the users who are not informed, but may be informed by others.

According to the user categorization, the information exchange happens between infectious nodes and susceptible nodes. In order to model the process, a global parameter is introduced as the probability that a susceptible user will be activated if it has an infected friend called β, in addition, a global parameter is also introduced to represent the probability of infected nodes

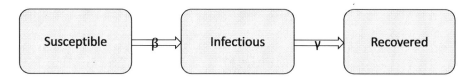

FIGURE 5.1 Different user roles and their relationships in SIR model.

getting recovered called γ. Figure 5.1 depicts the structure of the SIR model. In the SIR model, if a user has multiple linked infectious neighbors, the links are all independent with each other and the user can be infected by at most one neighbor. The infection process is modeled as Equation 5.1:

$$I_\beta(a) = \mathbf{1}\left(\sum_{\substack{(b,a)\in\mathbf{E}, \\ b\in\mathbf{V}\cap\mathbf{I}}} \mathbf{1}(f^{rand} \geq \beta) > 0\right), \tag{5.1}$$

where $I_\beta(a)$ represents the infection status of a susceptible node a in the next time stamp given β, and $\mathbf{1}(\cdot)$ is a function which equals one when its component is true and equals zero otherwise. $\mathbf{E}$ and $\mathbf{V}$ are the set of edges and nodes, respectively, and $\mathbf{I}$ is the infectious node set. We use (b, a) to denote the directed/indirected link between two nodes and use f^{rand} to denote the random probability generation function. Thus, node b is a's infectious neighbor and a will be activated if any of its neighbor actives it.

Tipping Model

As implied by "The Power of Context" [16], human behavior is strongly influenced by its environment. Similar intuition has been adopted by the tipping point model. In the tipping model, there are two kinds of users: people who adopted the behavior and people who did not, where spreaders and senders are not explicitly distinguished. Since the adoption process is irreversible, information diffusion only happens between the second class of users and their active neighbors.

As depicted in Figure 5.2, a node will be influenced by its friends about adopting a certain behavior. The behavior can be buying a new cell phone or wearing a specific brand of clothes. In order to model the diffusion process, a threshold probability θ is introduced to judge whether the behavior reaches the "tipping point": If the ratio of a user's friends adopting a certain behavior reaches the tipping point probability θ, the user will also adopt the behavior. The infection process is modeled as Equation 5.2:

$$I_0(a) = \mathbf{1}\left(\sum_{\substack{(b,a)\in\mathbf{E}, \\ b\in\mathbf{V}\cap\mathbf{I}}} f(b, a) \geq \theta\right), \tag{5.2}$$

where $f(b, a)$ is the activation probability between b and a, and a will be activated when influence from all infectious neighbors exceeds the threshold θ.

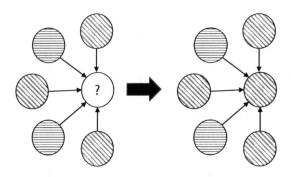

FIGURE 5.2 An illustrative example of the Tipping model, where the bar's height indicates extent of belief.

Independent Cascade Model

The SIR model and the Tipping model have different definitions of information being diffused, but they all assume a global parameter should work for the whole network. This strong assumption reduces the computational complexity, but it fails to handle the complex situations in the real world. More generalized models with variable parameters are proposed to handle such cases. The Independent Cascade (IC) model is the generalized form of the SIR model. Similarly, it formulates the diffusion process as a disease epidemic, but the infectious probability is associated with different edges. The infection process is modeled as Equation 5.3:

$$I_\beta(a) = \mathbf{1}(\sum_{\substack{(b,a)\in\mathbf{E},\\b\in\mathbf{V}\cap\mathbf{I}}} \mathbf{1}(f(b,a) \ge \beta) > 0). \tag{5.3}$$

The probability $f(b,a)$ can be achieved based on different applications such as the interaction frequency, geographic proximity and so on. Thus, the IC model is able to embed more contextual information.

Linear Threshold Model

The Linear Threshold (LT) model is a generalized form of the Tipping model. Instead of setting a global threshold θ for every edge between users, LT defines a probability distribution over all edges. The infection process is modeled as Equation 5.4:

$$I_\theta(a) = \mathbf{1}(\sum_{\substack{(b,a)\in\mathbf{E},\\b\in\mathbf{V}\cap\mathbf{I}}} f(b,a) \ge \theta_{(b,a)}). \tag{5.4}$$

Tipping thus can be viewed as a special form of the LT model, which employs a uniform distribution. By replacing the deterministic threshold θ with probabilistic thresholds, the LT model is more capable of predicting the outcome of a diffusion given the seed set users. A problem of the LT is the computational complexity. The probabilistic diffusion process makes the outcome calculation a #P-Hard problem, which cannot be efficiently computed in polynomial time as the Tipping model. In order to solve the problem, some more scalable methods have been introduced to reduce simulation runs.

One efficient method is called SIMPATH [17]. Normally, the social network linkage structure is complex and contains numerous edges with various probability. When information diffusion starts from the seed set users and goes to the rest of the individuals, some paths are more influential than the rest. SIMPATH reduces the computational time through filtering out paths without enough confidence. A similar method called Maximum Influence Arborescence (MIA) [9] was also proposed to accelerate the computation of the IC model. Various other acceleration algorithms are also available [41] [18].

5.2.2 Misinformation Diffusion

In this section, we introduce the diffusion model of misinformation. The diffusion of misinformation is more related to the trust and belief in social networks. The epidemic models, including SIR and IC, assume the infection occurs between an infectious user and a susceptible user with a predefined probability. As mentioned earlier, the probability may increase with more interactions or other contextual conditions. Although the links of a user are independent, a user who has more infectious friends is more likely to be infected. The Tipping and LT models also contain a parameter to estimate probability of a user being infected based on the number of activated friends. Generally, given infinite time and an optimal seed set of senders, they assume all users will be infected.

However, the diffusion outcome of misinformation is often the global recovery or immunity. Such phenomena reveal that, no matter how widespread a piece of misinformation is diffused, some nodes will not be affected and will keep intervening such diffusion. In order to model such a process, the existing approach categorizes people into two genres: regular individuals and forceful individuals [1].

The information diffusion process is reformulated as belief exchange. A parameter $\theta \in \mathbb{R}$ is introduced to represent the probability of learning or accepting some information. Misinformation diffusion process is then defined as the exchange of belief between two nodes.

As depicted in Figure 5.3, the exchange between different users is different. When a regular user interacts with another regular user, they are simultaneously affecting each other. A consensus belief will be achieved by averaging their beliefs. But when a regular node interacts with its forceful counterpart, only the regular node will be affected and the forceful individual will keep the original belief.

Regular Users

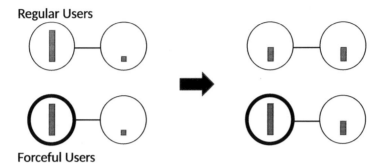

Forceful Users

FIGURE 5.3 An example of belief exchange of misinformation, where the heights of the bars in circles represent extent of belief.

In the beginning of misinformation diffusion, all regular nodes are assumed to have a belief probability taken from a certain probability distribution, and forceful individuals may hold some specific scores against the regular. Through iterations of belief exchange, the belief converges to a consensus among all individuals. The higher the consensus belief is, the more widespread misinformation is diffused over the network. More formally, the process is modeled as:

$$x_i(0) = \epsilon_i x_i(0) + (1 - \epsilon_i)x_j(0). \tag{5.5}$$

Here, we assume the social network has n agents. $x(0) \in \mathbb{R}^n$ records the belief level of users at time 0. Equation 5.5 shows how belief exchange takes place between two nodes i and j, where θ measures the belief and ϵ_i measures the extent user i will stick to his original belief. If both user i and j are regular users, then $\epsilon_i = 0.5$ and such change happens to j's belief score ($\epsilon_j = 0.5$). If only user i is regular but user j is a forceful individual, then $\epsilon < 0.5$ and user j is not significantly affected by the exchange ($\epsilon_j \approx 1$). When user i is a forceful user, then $\epsilon \approx 1$ and user j will be affected only if he is regular.

Various models have been proposed to predict the extent of misinformation diffusion given different network topology and user roles [1]. Authors provide an efficient algorithm to estimate the upper bound of potential for misinformation in a social network. They study properties of different network structures. Three interesting observations are found, which will be described in the following paragraph.

If the nodes in a graph are connected to various forceful nodes as well as connected to many regular nodes, as shown in Figure 5.4(a), misinformation diffusion will be attenuated by a large scale of social networks, i.e., the larger the graph is, the smaller the diffusion will be. On the contrary, if the social network is not well connected, as shown in Figure 5.4(b), consisting of disconnected communities, the extent of misinformation diffusion will be strengthened. If a forceful node is connected to both the separate communi-

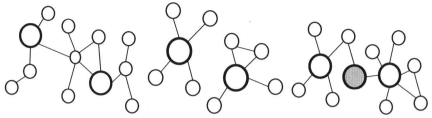

(a) A graph where force-ful nodes may be affected by other forceful nodes and communities.

(b) A graph with two dis-connected communities and forceful nodes have infinite impact.

(c) A graph with two sepa-rate communities which are bridged by a forceful node.

FIGURE 5.4 Examples of network structures.

ties, which serves like a bridge as shown in Figure 5.4(c), the potential extent of misinformation belief will be affected by the bridge: no matter whether being connected to the bridge or not, members in a same community tend to share a common belief level.

The three observations can be explained by some real world examples. When there are enough people and authorities in a social network, negative effects of misinformation will be reduced after thorough public scrutiny. When nodes in a social network are not well connected and many disconnected sub-graphs exist, information aggregation takes place mainly at the intra-group level. The belief level can be easily biased by the local leaders in different com-munities. Thus the underlying topology is prone to attack of misinformation. The third structure, where a forceful individual bridges different disconnected communities, approximates situations where political leaders obtain different information from different groups of individuals. Thus the intra-group belief level converges to the consensus.

Note that the key difference of diffusion models between misinformation and information is the adoption of trust. The information spread can be mod-eled as an epidemic process, where being contacted increases the probabil-ity of infection. On the other hand, being informed of misinformation only changes the extent of trust instead of literally infecting the node. Since dif-fusion models aim to find the optimal seed set for spreading information, nodes with high centrality scores are better focused. In misinformation diffu-sion processes, globally influential nodes prove to be less effective than local influencers in gaining trust of their followers. These research results indicate the importance of locally influential nodes of controlling misinformation.

Different models have been proposed to study behavioral features of peo-ple. Rumor spreading has also been regarded as a dynamics model, where social actors are categorized as susceptible, infected and refractory. Karlova et al. categorize users into two genres [27], diffusers and receivers. When re-ceivers receive some information from diffusers, they judge whether to trust and further pass the information based on contextual features. A unified model which jointly considers information and misinformation was also proposed [2].

5.3 MISINFORMATION IDENTIFICATION

In order to provide a brief introduction of misinformation identification techniques, we examine several representative works from two aspects: directly identifying misinformation itself and detecting misinformation through exposing its spreaders. In fact, detecting misinformation from online information flow has a long history, and has been studied extensively since the last decade when the email system was entangled with a huge amount of junk mail. Traditionally, the content and network structure are two key factors of telling spam from regular information. Here, content means the information in the email. Since spam is designed to advertise certain websites or products, content is a useful clue for detecting such information. Network structure refers to the graph built by the routes of email transmission. If a user/server has an abnormal pattern of sending emails, such as sending numerous similar emails to a lot of strangers, we can probably predict it is suspicious. Similarly, misinformation and disinformation in a social network also have both features. So we will focus on content and network structure of the two kinds of methods.

5.3.1 Misinformation Detection

Algorithm 1 illustrates the learning framework of misinformation detection algorithms.

Algorithm 1 Misinformation Detection in Social Networks

Input: The raw content $X \in \mathbb{R}^{m \times n}$, the identity label vector $y \in \mathbb{R}^m$,
Output: The optimal misinformation estimator f.
   Generate compact representation $X' \in \mathbb{R}^{m \times k}$ based on X;
   Obtain the label vector y
   Repeat
   Update f to reduce loss $\sum_{i=1}^{m} \mathcal{L}(f(x_i), y_i)$;
   until Convergence or Maximum Iterations

Identifying misinformation has been studied in psychology [3] [4] [11] [10]. They refer to misinformation as rumors and study the exhibition of rumors and the psychological reasons of spreading rumors. Several detection methods are introduced based on human behaviors. Recent research also reveals how rumor is differently diffused online in microblogging platforms.

More scalable algorithms have been proposed to study the spread of memes and misinformation on the web. Some algorithms directly use the raw features to model the patterns of misinformation. In [47], Ratkiewicz et al. built up a "Truthy" system to automatically identify misleading political memes on

Twitter. They directly extract raw features, such as hashtags, links and mentions in their system. By selecting such features, a compact representation could be generated. Then different kinds of bayesian classifiers are trained and used to classify misinformation.

Although merely using hashtags and links directly leads to a compact representation, the vast information hidden in user text may be ignored. In order to reduce the dimensionality of raw tweet content, Gao et al. [14] propose to cluster tweet content in an unsupervised manner. They try to quantify and characterize campaigns on Facebook by analyzing wall messages spreading between Facebook users. An initial solution is provided [14]. Empirical analysis is employed to test their proposed model based on real data. The characteristics, impact and sources of malicious accounts are also studied based on their model and empirical analysis. In addition, some third-party tools are also employed for validation.

Another similar intuition of compacting social content is to focus on the topics instead of words. When users tweet online, each word can be seen as generating from a certain topic. Then the corresponding tweet can be reduced to a probability distribution over multiple topics. Since the number of topics is normally far smaller than that of words, another low dimensional representation can then be achieved. Existing work has proven the effectiveness of employing LDA to detect deceptive information in a social network [50].

Misinformation detection algorithms normally model the prediction as a discriminant learning problem: directly optimizing the prediction based on training data. Since both the clusters and topics can be viewed as a subset of words, the underlying assumption of such models is that information consisting of similar words or topics tend to have the same labels. But this may not hold in the real world applications.

Since content on social media platforms, like Twitter, is shorter, sometimes a single word, a hashtag and even some marks may reverse the whole meaning of a sentence. Misinformation mining focuses on inaccurate and wrong information, which requires a fine-grained analysis of social media. Qazvinian et al. propose to solve the detection problem through Natural Language Processing techniques [46]. They include three kinds of features in their system, including Content-based features, Network-based features and Twitter-based features. Content-based features are taken from the text of Twitter. They extract the words to represent the lexical features, and label all words with their Part-Of-Speech (POS) tags to get the POS features. In order to increase the descriptive power, they also incorporate bigrams of content-based features. Twitter-based features include hashtags and URLs of a tweet. They further extract features from users for each tweet as Network-based features. This is reasonable since the author is a property of his tweets and articles. The tweets, however, are more oftentimes regarded as a feature of its author in fact. When we concentrate on users instead of tweets, misinformation detection problem is transformed to detecting spreaders of misinformation. Since it is common that online reviews influence customers' decisions on purchase, spreading misinformation has been used for advertising a product or damaging the others' reputation. Jindal and Liu propose to solve this problem based on textual features, user behaviors [25] and review opinions [26]. Links between accounts and reviews are further exploited for collective inference. Mukherjee et al. propose to detect spammer groups through analyzing the textual similarity between reviewers. Li et al. links reviewers based on their prior IP address history [36].

5.3.2 Spreader Detection

Identifying spreaders of misinformation is another way to detect misinformation. As discussed in Section 5.2.2, although some users have the intent to spread rumors, many regular users may be persuaded to believe or respread misinformation according to their belief levels. Normally, the majority of information of a regular user is accurate. Thus identifying spreaders who are with intent to mislead people is the main focus of spreader detection.

Since information on social media sites is spread from node to node, the spreader of a specific piece of misinformation can be trivially found if provenance paths are known in advance. For example, if roots of a provenance path are found, they are likely to be sources of misinformation. Finding such sources is not only useful for preventing misinformation from being further spread, but is also useful for analyzing truthfulness of rumors. However, since provenance paths are often unknown, Gundecha et al. propose to solve this problem through finding a node subset with maximum utility [19]. Here, utility represents the number of nodes that are ultimately affected, which depends on certain information propagation models.

Since content of misinformation spreaders are different from that of regular users, detecting them can also be reduced to a binomial classification problem. The estimator is trained to predict whether a user is a misinformation spreader based on his social media content and/or his social behaviors. More formally, here we formulated the optimization objective in Equation 5.6:

$$\min_f \sum_{i=1}^{m} \mathcal{L}(f(\boldsymbol{x}_i, \boldsymbol{A}), y_i). \tag{5.6}$$

Equation 5.6 requires a data matrix $\boldsymbol{X} \in \mathbb{R}^{m \times n}$ as input, where $\boldsymbol{X} = \boldsymbol{x}_1, \boldsymbol{x}_2 \dots \boldsymbol{x}_m$. Here, m is the number of all users instead of tweets. Since the number of users is normally much smaller than that of tweets, focusing on user-level helps to reduce the computational cost. n is the number of features. y denotes the identity label vector of users. A learning method f is needed to predict the identity label of a user based on the content. The second argument of f is the adjacency matrix $A \in \mathbb{R}^{m \times m}$, where $A_{i,j} = 1$ means there is an edge between user i and j. Since social network users connect to their friends and follow people they are interested in, then it may be difficult for intentional misinformation spreaders to connect with others as regular users. Thus the linkage structure is useful for identifying such spreaders. Algorithm 2 depicts the learning framework of misinformation spreader detection.

Two specific kinds of misinformation spreaders have attracted a great deal of attention in recent years, i.e., spammers and bots. Social spammers generally refer to those accounts who tweet spam, which refers to unwanted information such as malicious content, fraudulent reviews, profanity and political astroturf. Since a large portion of spammers are automatic programs instead of real people, as Italian security researchers Andrea Stroppa and Carlo De Micheli pointed, as many as 9% of the monthly active users in Twitter are bots [13]. These bots are controlled by human beings and can send information according to some commands and predefined programs.

Although it is easy to distinguish between regular users and bots from their definitions, it is almost impossible to accurately tell whether a spammer is a bot. Fortunately, bots controlled by the same party behave similarly with each other and differently from regular users. Research on exposing bots focuses on retrieving similar anomalies based on content and graph structure.

Algorithm 2 Misinformation Spreader Detection in a Social Network

---

Input: The raw content $X \in \mathbb{R}^{m \times n}$, the identity label vector $y \in \mathbb{R}^m$,
Output: The optimal misinformation estimator f.
    Generate compact representation $X' \in \mathbb{R}^{m \times k}$ based on X;
    Obtain the label vector y
    Repeat
    Update f to reduce loss $\sum_{i=1}^{m} \mathcal{L}(f(x_i, A), y_i)$;
    until Convergence

Existing work builds up discriminative models directly based on user generated content [39]. Useful features include social tags, advertisements, and URLs in social media content. They try to leverage the content through measuring the similarity between different users' text, i.e., plagiarism. This indirect method avoids the model to be entangled with high dimensional data.

In order to directly cope with the content information, a more advanced framework has been proposed. A unified framework Online Social Spammer Detection (OSSD) is put forward by Hu et al., which jointly considers content and structural information [23]. Figure 5.5 displays the framework of dimensionality reduction algorithm.

The general aim of all dimension reduction algorithms is to map the raw data onto a low dimensional space. In order to smooth the mapping, OSSD defines two constraints: (1) If two users' social media contents are similar in the raw feature space, their projections on the reduced low dimension should keep the similarity; (2) if two users are connected, their similarity should be high after being mapped into the latent space. The first constraint focuses on

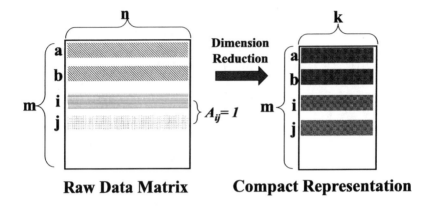

Raw Data Matrix   **Compact Representation**

FIGURE 5.5 The dimension reduction framework of OSSD.

the content and is widely accepted by dimension reduction algorithms, while the second one incorporates the social graph structure.

$$\mathcal{R} = \frac{1}{2} \sum_{i,j:\boldsymbol{A}_{ij}=1} \boldsymbol{\pi}(i)\boldsymbol{P}(i,j)\|\boldsymbol{H}_{i*} - \boldsymbol{H}_{j*}\|. \tag{5.7}$$

The social graph constraint is formulated as in Equation 5.7. Since in the training dataset, links exist not only between regular users, but also between spammers. Spammers pretend to be regular users through following numerous other people. Thus the links that spammers follow regular users are taken out from the adjacency matrix. Links created by regular users are reserved. Since the relationship between spammers may indicate they have similar intentions, such links are also reserved.

Due to the different levels of activeness, some users may follow many people while some others may follow very few. In order to normalize the impact of different links, a probability matrix $\boldsymbol{P} \in \mathbb{R}^{m \times m}$ is introduced. The correlation between two users i and j are denoted as $\boldsymbol{P}_{ij} = \boldsymbol{A}_{ij}/\boldsymbol{d}_i^{out}$, where $\boldsymbol{d}^{out}$ is a vector that contains out degree of all nodes. Since users have different global impacts, Hu et al. introduces a random walk model to measure it. $\boldsymbol{\pi}$ is the stationary distribution of the transition matrix $\boldsymbol{P}$. Then $\boldsymbol{\pi}_i$ represents the influence of the corresponding node. Due to the explosive increase of users, efficient and incremental update of such models is also a key concern for real applications. Authors also present an algorithm for incremental optimization.

Various variants have been proposed to solve the problem from different perspectives. Hu et al. study how sentiment information can be leveraged to expose spammers from social media [22]. Their experimental results show that significant differences exist between sentiment posed by spammers and regular users. In order to cope with the huge amounts of social media users, Zhao et al. propose a distributed learning system which is able to detect anomalies

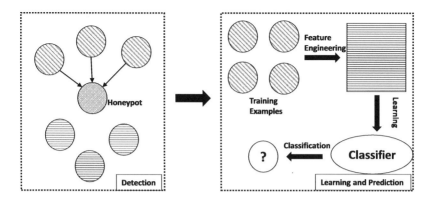

FIGURE 5.6 Misinformation spreader detection framework based on social honeypot.

from graph based on the linkage structure [60]. Nguyen et al. proposed to find the sources of certain diffusions to detect malicious users [43].

A problem of most existing spammer and bot detection algorithms is their dependency on third-party data. In order to enable scalable analysis, they often leverage the labels released by either independent third parties or service providers, e.g., Twitter suspends a lot of accounts and such accounts are often considered to be malicious users. In [32], Lee et al. propose a passive way to wait for social network anomalies to "label" themselves. Figure 5.6 illustrates their proposed framework. They first create several social honeypots, which are social network accounts with legitimate profiles. Once the honeypot detects suspicious behaviors, such as sending deceptive information and malicious links, such users are labeled as a spammer candidate. Then they extracted features from such spammers and actively detect malicious accounts in social networks in a supervised manner.

In order to obtain labels to build training datasets, various methods have been used. Most approaches fall into three categories, i.e., manual labeling, honeypot, and suspension list. Manual labeling is the most direct way to get labels. Normally tweets about a topic are collected, and human annotators are hired to tell whether each tweet is misinformation. For example, a Twitter dataset consisting of more than 10,400 tweets based on five topics is labeled by two annotators [46]. Since manual labeling is often expensive, it is unaffordable to obtain ground truth on a large scale. An automatic alternative is to set up honeypot accounts [57], where several accounts are created with specific profiles tempting attackers to send misinformation. Spreaders can then be identified accurately. However, since honeypot accounts wait to be attacked, the process usually takes time. In addition, honeypot accounts can only help identify malicious accounts (positive data), where labels of regular accounts are inaccessible. In order to remedy it, some accounts are randomly selected

TABLE 5.1 Features of Different Processes of Obtaining Ground Truth

Method	Expenses	Time	Distribution
Manual Labeling	High	Medium	Real
Honeypot	Low	Long	Fake
Suspended Users	High	Short	Fake

TABLE 5.2 Statistics of Datasets

Country	Suspended	Regular	Ratio
Libya	7,061	87,474	7.47%
Syria	40,109	474,741	8.45%
Yemen	3,239	41,331	7.84%

to be used as negative data. The third kind of method is using the suspension list. Since social media websites regularly ban malicious accounts, such suspended user lists can be used as a gold standard [23, 54]. The list is usually publicly available and contains accounts on a large scale, which is proper for evaluation. However, it can only identify malicious accounts and thus fails to reveal the real cutoff between malicious and regular information. We summarize features of different processes of obtaining ground truth in Table 5.1 in terms of expenses of time, cost and truthfulness of distribution.

In order to economically obtain datasets which keep in line with real distribution, we introduce a method which is based on given topics. We first set a topic and compile a list of related keywords, and extract all tweets containing the keywords [30]. In particular, we collected Twitter accounts who post with Arab Spring hashtags from February 3, 2011 to February 21, 2013. The employed hashtags are #gaddafi, #benghazi, #brega, #misrata, #nalut, #nafusa and #rhaibat. Several geographic bounding boxes are used to capture tweets from Libya,[5] Syria[6] and Yemen.[7] The statistics of the three datasets are illustrated in Table 5.2.

As shown in the Table 5.2, real misinformation datasets are often skewed. Such skewness has been overlooked by existing misinformation detection algorithms. Since rare category analysis [21] has been proven to be effective in solving such problems, it will be interesting to apply related methods to help expose misinformation. An alternative way is to apply ranking algorithms, which has been used for fraud detection for mobile applications [61] and system faults detection [15], where the dataset is also skewed.

---

[5]Southwest Lat/Lng: 23.4/10.0; Northeast Lat/Lng: 33.0, 25.0
[6]Southwest Lat/Lng: 32.8/35.9; Northeast Lat/Lng: 37.3, 42.3
[7]Southwest Lat/Lng: 12.9/42.9; Northeast Lat/Lng: 19.0, 52.2

5.4 MISINFORMATION INTERVENTION

As mentioned in Section 5.1, rumors about Ebola kept spreading widely even after some official intervention took place. Effectively reducing negative effect of misinformation is of great interest for governments and social network service providers. In this section, we introduce two measures toward combating misinformation. The first part examines techniques to detect and prevent misinformation from spreading in an early stage. The second one introduces how a competing campaign could be employed to fight against misinformation.

5.4.1 Malicious Account Detection in an Early Stage

Misinformation spreads quickly on social networks. Although spreaders are blocked once they are found to forward or send rumors, misinformation is already spread by then. It will be favorable if such accounts can be found before they start spamming. In order to mislead social network users in a large scale, malicious programmers create a plethora of accounts which can send information according to certain policies. Profiles of automatic generated accounts may look similar, since they may be created using the same template. Investigation toward spam social profiles reveals that duplication of profiles widely exists between malicious accounts [57]. Instead of using a template, malicious programmers tend to directly copy information from others, some URLs are thus shared by many bots. Through studying geographic distribution of malicious accounts, they also found that such accounts gather in some specific states. More behavioral features of profiles are taken into consideration by Egele et al. [12].

Profile features of malicious accounts are extremely sparse. Many items of a spam profile are empty. Since at least a name has to be available for each account, Lee and Kim propose to reveal the patterns hidden behind malicious accounts [34], so as to filter them in an early age. A problem of modeling account names is the sparseness, since they are even sparser than profiles. To cope with the sparsity issue, they cluster all account names and then analyze on the cluster level. Agglomerative hierarchical clustering is adopted, where the likelihood of two names being generated by an identical Markov chain is used for measuring distance, and characters are used as features. After obtaining clusters of similar account names, a supervised method is adopted to classify whether a name cluster is a group of malicious accounts. Lee and Kim leverage several cluster statistics, such as the length distribution and average edit distance within a group, as features for their Support Vector Machines. Account names have also been quantitatively examined [59]. More features including behavioral ones are further incorporated in such algorithms [5, 33, 51, 62].

5.4.2 Combating Rumors with Facts

The perfect plan of limiting misinformation is to identify and filter malicious accounts before they spread misinformation. However, a potential of such algorithms in reality is the cost of the false positive rate. Since social networks cannot emphasize more on involvement of users, mistakenly blocking regular accounts is unacceptable. A more practical method will be controlling the spread and limiting the influence of misinformation after it is spread.

An effective method of combating rumors is to spread truth. By sending the accurate information, people in a social network can either be saved (if they have been "infected" by the rumor) or be immunized. The key issue of such methods is to choose an optimal subset of users to start it. Budak et al. propose a new diffusion algorithm to model the process. They introduce the Multi-Campaign Independence Cascade Model (MCICM) where two campaigns may coexist [6]. Concretely, as mentioned in Section 5.2.1, most information diffusion models consider the situation where only one topic is being spread. In MCICM, besides misinformation campaign, another "good" campaign tries to reduce the effect of misinformation, which is illustrated in Figure 5.7. As shown in Figure 5.7(a), general information diffusion models aim to predict the optimal seed set which can result in the largest scale of diffu-

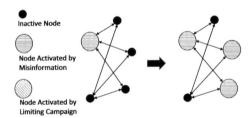

(a) An example of general information diffusion models in social networks, where only misinformation is spread to infect inactive nodes.

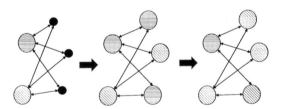

(b) An example of intervention models of misinformation in social networks, where a campaign is used to limit spread of misinformation.

FIGURE 5.7 Illustrative examples of information diffusion and misinformation intervention.

sion, where only one campaign is available. But for misinformation limitation, there are two campaigns at the same time. The aim becomes identifying an optimal set of individuals to be convinced to adopt the competing campaign, which minimizes the effect of the bad campaign eventually. An important assumption needs noting is that once a node has been cured by the positive campaign or being immunized, they can no longer be infected again.

Similar efforts have been paid by Nguyen et al. [44]. They aim to find the smallest set of highly influential nodes whose decontamination with good information helps to contain the viral spread of misinformation. Different from MCICM, which only considers the Independent Cascade Model, they also incorporate the Linear Threshold model. Several interesting patterns have been observed in the investigation. When the good campaign budget is limited, meaning that we can only select a small number of users, influential nodes in larger communities are more effective in competing misinformation. On the other hand, when we can choose more nodes to start with and misinformation has been widespread, choosing influential nodes from small communities can efficiently immunize the whole community. The bridge influencers, which connect between different communities and are expected to have a large impact factor, are not useful for combating misinformation. It is because communities are often with high intra-group propagation probabilities, such bridges are of slim chance to influence them.

Simulation is often used to quantitatively measure rumor intervention methods. Rumors are first assumed to be spread in social networks, and the intervention algorithm is then used to select optimal node set to spread truth. Thus the number of nodes which are inactive for the rumor indicates the effectiveness of intervention. Benchmark datasets include both social networks from online websites,[8] synthetic network and academic collaboration graph.[9]

Social media data is useful for decision-making when some events happen, such as terrorist attacks and disasters. In order to avoid being influenced by false rumors during events, several systems have been developed. The crowdsourcing system[10] depends on active participants. In addition, some Twitter analytic tools are also proposed to help information management during crisis. Kumar et al. try to detect relevant and credible information sources during disasters [31], locations and topics of discussion are extracted as features to analyze their affinity to certain events. Through actively selecting optimal information sources, more and better information can be generated using social media. A problem of their system is that location information is missing for some users. To cope with missing data, they further propose an approach to estimate user location by jointly analyzing prior posts and user profiles [42].

---

[8]http://socialcomputing.asu.edu/
[9]http://research.microsoft.com/en-us/people/weic/projects.aspx
[10]https://veri.ly/

5.5 EVALUATION

In this section, we discuss the evaluation of misinformation detection and intervention, including available benchmark datasets and evaluation metrics.

5.5.1 Datasets

Although there is no agreed way of obtaining labels or benchmark datasets, several datasets are available for evaluating misinformation detection and intervention algorithms, which are obtained from social media sites such as Twitter[11] and Facebook.[12] We list several representative ones below.

Rumor Dataset: Some fact-checking websites have collections of rumors. Crowdsourcing and expert ratings are used for judging the truthfulness of a rumor. In Verily,[13] stories and pictures of questionable veracity are posted, and registered users then discuss and judge whether it is true or false. In PolitiFact,[14] truthfulness of political statements is evaluated, where a "Truth-O-Meter" is assigned to each statement and the rating ranges from "True" to "Pants on Fire". Data on both websites is publicly available. However, connections between these rumors and social media contents are not directly available. Qazvinian et al. propose to employ human annotators to label tweets manually [46]. In Weibo,[15] the content management team[16] will regularly attach labels of false rumors, and such labels, posts and the corresponding diffusion information are available.

Spreader Dataset: As shown in Table 5.1, three methods are used for obtaining misinformation spreader accounts on social media sites. Lee et al. set up several honeypot accounts and captured 23,869 content polluters from Twitter. The corresponding user posts and their social links are available.[17] Authors found 23% of detected polluters are also suspended by Twitter after less than a month, which indicates both methods are effective in finding spammers. Suspension of a Twitter account can be found by using Twitter's API [30].

Misinformation Diffusion Dataset: Simulation is often used for evaluating effectiveness of misinformation intervention. Misinformation and the corresponding fact are simultaneously simulated to spread on social networks, so only social links are needed for evaluation. Nguyen et al. adopted network structures of the author collaboration graph and Facebook users [44], and Budak et al. propose to use regional user graph on Facebook. Besides social

---

[11] http://twitter.com/
[12] http://www.facebook.com/
[13] https://www.veri.ly/
[14] http://www.politifact.com/
[15] http://weibo.com/
[16] http://service.account.weibo.com/
[17] http://infolab.tamu.edu/data/

graphs, networks of customers, videos, web pages and Wikipedia articles[18] could be used for simulation.

5.5.2 Evaluation Metrics

Since misinformation and spreader detection problems are often modeled as binary classification tasks, measures used by supervised learning algorithms can be used as evaluation metrics.

Accuracy: Accuracy measures the similarity between prediction results and real labels. A common practice is to describe accuracy by considering how many errors are made. A widely used measure is Mean Absolute Error (MAE), which is defined as:

$$MAE = \frac{1}{|U|} \sum_{i \in U} |p_i - l_i|, \tag{5.8}$$

where U is the user set and p_i is the prediction result and l_i is the true label. A smaller MAE value represents better performance, meaning that less errors are made.

Precision, Recall and F-measure: Accuracy measures the number of prediction mistakes regardless of positive or negative examples. Since capturing misinformation is more important, precision is often used, which is defined as follows:

$$Precision = \frac{\#TP}{\#TP + \#FP}, \tag{5.9}$$

where $\#TP$ means the number of true positives, representing the number of correctly identified spammers/misinformation; while $\#FP$ means the number of false positives, representing the number of mistakenly identified spammers/misinformation. Since misinformation datasets are often skewed, a high precision can be easily achieved by making less positive predictions. In order to avoid this, recall is used to measure sensitivity:

$$Recall = \frac{\#TP}{\#TP + \#FN}, \tag{5.10}$$

where $\#FN$ the number of means false negatives, representing the number of unidentified spammers/misinformation. F-measure is used to combine both precision and recall, which is defined as follows:

$$F_\beta = (1 + \beta^2) \frac{Precision \cdot Recall}{\beta^2 \cdot Precision + Recall}. \tag{5.11}$$

where β controls the importance of recall. $\beta = 1$ is often normally used, where precision and recall are equally weighted. If β is 2, recall weights twice higher than precision; And if β is 0.5, precision weights higher than recall.

---

[18]http://snap.stanford.edu/data/index.html;http://socialcomputing.asu.edu/pages/datasets

Outcome of Simulation: Misinformation intervention is often modeled as an information diffusion problem, where a subset of nodes is selected to send factual claims. Thus, the final number of nodes immune from rumors can be viewed as effectiveness of the method.

5.6 CONCLUSION AND FUTURE WORK

As the world becomes increasingly connected, social media platforms have made everyone a news source. Misinformation gets issued and repeated more quickly and widely than ever due to the connectivity of social networks, which impact the real world. A false tweet has a negative impact on community or a family, triggers financial panic and even strains diplomatic relations. To cope with the spread of misinformation, we must first understand it. In this chapter, we discuss the distinct aspects of misinformation diffusion in social media, and elaborate existing work of identifying misinformation, its spreaders and intervention methods.

This chapter has discussed some essential issues of misinformation. Benchmark datasets and evaluation metrics are also introduced for misinformation identification and intervention. As remedies for weaknesses of existing approaches, we propose a method to obtain ground truth for spreader detection based on the suspension list, where data distribution is in line with the real world. Since mining misinformation in a social network is an emergent field of study, we also list a number of interesting potential problems for future exploration:

How to seek the provenance of misinformation in social media? The information spread in social media follows a path, i.e., from one user to the other and from one site to other social media sites. For example, a terrorist attack may first be reported on a social media site, then reported by news media and is finally tweeted by more users. Such linking nature enables information to be traceable. Though centrality measures have been studied to find the spreading trace of misinformation within a social media site [19], a global analysis based on different web sites can further facilitate recovering the trace and seeking the real provenance of misinformation.

How to predict the potential influence of misinformation in social media? The verification practices of online information is time-consuming, which makes it almost impossible for service providers and newsrooms to catch up with the speed of social media. Since the budget of competing misinformation is often limited, efforts should be paid on the most destructive rumors. An effective way to estimate potential impact of misinformation will be very useful to control the negative influence.

How to find the vulnerable individuals from social network users? Social network platform consists of various people. Misinformation has different effects on people who are of different levels of vulnerability. Such vulnerability provides the possibility for us to actively avoid weak individuals from being infected. To estimate the level of vulnerability in terms of user profile, misinformation topics and the network structure will be very challenging but useful.

How to exploit data from multiple sources to facilitate misinformation analysis? There are more and more social media platforms. People are usually simultaneously involved in different social network websites. The generation and diffusion may separately start from different platforms, and information exchange also takes place between different websites. It provides a complete picture of misinformation to integrate data from different sources.

Bibliography

[1] Daron Acemoglu, Asuman Ozdaglar, and Ali ParandehGheibi. Spread of (mis) information in social networks. *Games and Economic Behavior*, 70(2):194–227, 2010.

[2] Divyakant Agrawal, Ceren Budak, and Amr El Abbadi. Information diffusion in social networks: observing and affecting what society cares about. In *Proceedings of CIKM*, pages 2609–2610, 2011.

[3] Floyd H Allport and Milton Lepkin. Wartime rumors of waste and special privilege: why some people believe them. *The Journal of Abnormal and Social Psychology*, 40(1):3, 1945.

[4] Gordon W Allport and Leo Postman. *The Psychology of Rumor*. Henry Holt and Company, 1947.

[5] Fabricio Benevenuto, Tiago Rodrigues, Virgilio Almeida, Jussara Almeida, Chao Zhang, and Keith Ross. Identifying video spammers in online social networks. In *International Workshop on Adversarial Information Retrieval on the Web*, pages 45–52. ACM.

[6] Ceren Budak, Divyakant Agrawal, and Amr El Abbadi. Limiting the spread of misinformation in social networks. In *Proceedings of the 20th International Conference on World Wide Web*, pages 665–674. ACM, 2011.

[7] Damon Centola. The spread of behavior in an online social network experiment. *Science*, 329(5996):1194–1197, 2010.

[8] Wei Chen, Laks VS Lakshmanan, and Carlos Castillo. Information and influence propagation in social networks. *Synthesis Lectures on Data Management*, 5(4):1–177, 2013.

[9] Wei Chen, Chi Wang, and Yajun Wang. Scalable influence maximization for prevalent viral marketing in large-scale social networks. In *KDD*, pages 1029–1038. ACM, 2010.

[10] Nicholas DiFonzo and Prashant Bordia. Rumor and prediction: Making sense in the stock market. *Organizational Behavior and Human Decision Processes*, 71(3):329–353, 1997.

[11] Nicholas DiFonzo, Prashant Bordia, and Ralph L Rosnow. Reining in rumors. *Organizational Dynamics*, 23(1):47–62, 1994.

[12] Manuel Egele, Gianluca Stringhini, Christopher Kruegel, and Giovanni Vigna. Compa: Detecting compromised accounts on social networks. In *NDSS*, 2013.

[13] J Elder. Inside a twitter robot factory. *Wall Street Journal*, 821400, 2013.

[14] Hongyu Gao, Jun Hu, Christo Wilson, Zhichun Li, Yan Chen, and Ben Y Zhao. Detecting and characterizing social spam campaigns. In *Proceedings of the 10th ACM SIGCOMM Conference on Internet Measurement*, pages 35–47. ACM, 2010.

[15] Yong Ge, Guofei Jiang, Min Ding, and Hui Xiong. Ranking metric anomaly in invariant networks. *ACM Transactions on Knowledge Discovery from Data (TKDD)*, 8(2):8, 2014.

[16] Malcolm Gladwell. *The Tipping Point: How Little Things Can Make a Big Difference*. Little, Brown, 2006.

[17] Amit Goyal, Wei Lu, and Laks VS Lakshmanan. Simpath: An efficient algorithm for influence maximization under the linear threshold model. In *Data Mining (ICDM), 2011 IEEE 11th International Conference on*, pages 211–220. IEEE, 2011.

[18] Daniel Gruhl, Ramanathan Guha, David Liben-Nowell, and Andrew Tomkins. Information diffusion through blogspace. In *Proceedings of the 13th International Conference on World Wide Web*, pages 491–501. ACM, 2004.

[19] Pritam Gundecha, Zhuo Feng, and Huan Liu. Seeking provenance of information using social media. In *Proceedings of the 22nd ACM International Conference on Information & Knowledge Management*, pages 1691–1696. ACM, 2013.

[20] Aditi Gupta, Hemank Lamba, Ponnurangam Kumaraguru, and Anupam Joshi. Faking sandy: Characterizing and identifying fake images on twitter during hurricane sandy. *WWW '13 Companion*, pages 729–736, 2013.

[21] Jingrui He. *Rare category analysis*. PhD thesis, Carnegie Mellon University, Pittsburgh, PA, 2010.

[22] Xia Hu, Jiliang Tang, Huiji Gao, and Huan Liu. Social spammer detection with sentiment information. In *Proceedings of the IEEE International Conference on Data Mining*, ICDM'14. IEEE, 2014.

[23] Xia Hu, Jiliang Tang, and Huan Liu. Online social spammer detection. In *Twenty-Eighth AAAI Conference on Artificial Intelligence*, 2014.

[24] Tom N Jagatic, Nathaniel A Johnson, Markus Jakobsson, and Filippo Menczer. Social phishing. *Communications of the ACM*, 50(10):94–100, 2007.

[25] Nitin Jindal and Bing Liu. Review spam detection. In *Proceedings of the 16th International Conference on World Wide Web*, pages 1189–1190. ACM, 2007.

[26] Nitin Jindal and Bing Liu. Opinion spam and analysis. In *Proceedings of the 2008 International Conference on Web Search and Data Mining*, pages 219–230. ACM, 2008.

[27] Natascha Karlova and Karen Fisher. Plz rt: A social diffusion model of misinformation and disinformation for understanding human information behaviour. *Information Research*, 18(1), 2013.

[28] David Kempe, Jon Kleinberg, and Eva Tardos. Maximizing the spread of influence through a social network. In *Proceedings of the Ninth ACM SIGKDD International Conference on Knowledge Discovery and Data Mining*, pages 137–146. ACM, 2003.

[29] William O Kermack and Anderson G McKendrick. A contribution to the mathematical theory of epidemics. In *Proceedings of the Royal Society of London A: Mathematical, Physical and Engineering Sciences*, volume 115, pages 700–721, 1927.

[30] Shamanth Kumar, Fred Morstatter, and Huan Liu. *Twitter Data Analytics*. Springer, 2014.

[31] Shamanth Kumar, Fred Morstatter, Reza Zafarani, and Huan Liu. Whom should i follow?: identifying relevant users during crises. In *Hypertext*, pages 139–147. ACM, 2013.

[32] Kyumin Lee, James Caverlee, and Steve Webb. Uncovering social spammers: social honeypots+ machine learning. In *Proceedings of the 33rd International ACM SIGIR Conference on Research and Development in Information Retrieval*, pages 435–442. ACM, 2010.

[33] Kyumin Lee, Brian David Eoff, and James Caverlee. Seven months with the devils: A long-term study of content polluters on twitter. In *ICWSM*. Citeseer, 2011.

[34] Sangho Lee and Jong Kim. Early filtering of ephemeral malicious accounts on twitter. *Computer Communications*, 54:48–57, 2014.

[35] Todd Leopold. In today's warp-speed world, online missteps spread faster than ever. *CNN.com*, 2012.

[36] Huayi Li, Zhiyuan Chen, Bing Liu, Xiaokai Wei, and Jidong Shao. Spotting fake reviews via collective positive-unlabeled learning. In *ICDM*, pages 899–904. IEEE, 2014.

[37] Bruce R Lindsay. Social media and disasters: Current uses, future options, and policy considerations. *CRS Report for Congress*, pages 7–5700, 2011.

[38] Victor Luckerson. Fear, misinformation, and social media complicate ebola fight. *Tech Report*, 2014.

[39] Benjamin Markines, Ciro Cattuto, and Filippo Menczer. Social spam detection. In *International Workshop on Adversarial Information Retrieval on the Web*, pages 41–48. ACM, 2009.

[40] Marcelo Mendoza, Barbara Poblete, and Carlos Castillo. Twitter under crisis: Can we trust what we rt? In *Proceedings of the First Workshop on Social Media Analytics*, pages 71–79. ACM, 2010.

[41] Baharan Mirzasoleiman, Ashwinkumar Badanidiyuru, Amin Karbasi, Jan Vondrak, and Andreas Krause. Lazier than lazy greedy. *arXiv preprint arXiv:1409.7938*, 2014.

[42] Fred Morstatter, Nichola Lubold, Heather Pon-Barry, Jürgen Pfeffer, and Huan Liu. Finding eyewitness tweets during crises. *arXiv preprint arXiv:1403.1773*, 2014.

[43] Dung T Nguyen, Nam P Nguyen, and My T Thai. Sources of misinformation in online social networks: who to suspect. In *Military Communications Conference, MILCOM*, pages 1–6, 2012.

[44] Nam P Nguyen, Guanhua Yan, My T Thai, and Stephan Eidenbenz. Containment of misinformation spread in online social networks. In *Proceedings of the 4th Annual ACM Web Science Conference*, pages 213–222. ACM, 2012.

[45] Onook Oh, Kyounghee Hazel Kwon, and H Raghav Rao. An exploration of social media in extreme events: Rumor theory and twitter during the haiti earthquake 2010. In *ICIS*, page 231, 2010.

[46] Vahed Qazvinian, Emily Rosengren, Dragomir R Radev, and Qiaozhu Mei. Rumor has it: Identifying misinformation in microblogs. In *EMNLP*, pages 1589–1599, 2011.

[47] Jacob Ratkiewicz, Michael Conover, Mark Meiss, Bruno Gonffalves, Snehal Patil, Alessandro Flammini, and Filippo Menczer. Truthy: mapping the spread of astroturf in microblog streams. In *Proceedings of the WWW'11, Companion Volume*, pages 249–252. ACM, 2011.

[48] Christine Roberts. Social media users spreading false information about sandy hook massacre could face charges, say police. *New York Daily News*, 2012.

[49] Scott Shane and Ben Hubbard. Isis displaying a deft command of varied media. *New York Times*, 31, 2014.

[50] Long Song, Raymond YK Lau, and Chunxiao Yin. Discriminative topic mining for social spam detection. *Pacific Asia Conference on Information Systems*, 2014.

[51] Gianluca Stringhini, Christopher Kruegel, and Giovanni Vigna. Detecting spammers on social networks. In *Proceedings of the 26th Annual Computer Security Applications Conference*, pages 1–9. ACM, 2010.

[52] Jeannette Sutton, Leysia Palen, and Irina Shklovski. Backchannels on the front lines: Emergent uses of social media in the 2007 southern california wildfires. In *Proceedings of the 5th International ISCRAM Conference*, pages 624–632. Washington, DC, 2008.

[53] David Talbot. Preventing misinformation from spreading through social media. *MIT Technology Review*, 2013.

[54] Kurt Thomas, Chris Grier, Dawn Song, and Vern Paxson. Suspended accounts in retrospect: an analysis of twitter spam. In *Proceedings of the 2011 ACM SIGCOMM Conference on Internet Measurement Conference*, pages 243–258. ACM, 2011.

[55] Farida Vis. Twitter as a reporting tool for breaking news: Journalists tweeting the 2011 uk riots. *Digital Journalism*, 1(1):27–47, 2013.

[56] Farida Vis. To tackle the spread of misinformation online we must first understand it. *Guardian Comment Network*, 2014.

[57] Steve Webb, James Caverlee, and Calton Pu. Social honeypots: Making friends with a spammer near you. In *CEAS*, 2008.

[58] Reza Zafarani, Mohammad Ali Abbasi, and Huan Liu. *Social Media Mining: An Introduction*. Cambridge University Press, 2014.

[59] Reza Zafarani and Huan Liu. 10 bits of surprise: Detecting malicious users with minimum information. *CIKM'15. ACM*.

[60] Yao Zhao, Yinglian Xie, Fang Yu, Qifa Ke, Yuan Yu, Yan Chen, and Eliot Gillum. Botgraph: Large scale spamming botnet detection. In *NSDI*, volume 9, pages 321–334, 2009.

[61] Hengshu Zhu, Hui Xiong, Yong Ge, and Enhong Chen. Discovery of ranking fraud for mobile apps. *Knowledge and Data Engineering, IEEE Transactions on*, 27(1):74–87, 2015.

[62] Yin Zhu, Xiao Wang, Erheng Zhong, Nathan Nan Liu, He Li, and Qiang Yang. Discovering spammers in social networks. In *AAAI*, 2012.

CHAPTER 6

Rumor Spreading and Detection in Online Social Networks

Wen Xu and Weili Wu

CONTENTS

6.1 INTRODUCTION

The rising popularity of online social networks has made information generating and sharing much easier than ever before, due to the ability to publish content to large, targeted audiences. Such networks enable their participants to simultaneously become both consumers and producers of content, shifting the role of information broker from a few dedicated entities to a diverse and distributed group of individuals. While this fundamental change allows information propagating at an unprecedented rate, it also enables unreliable or unverified information spreading among people, such as rumors. For instance, the misinformation of swine flu was observed in Twitter tweets at the outset of the large outbreak in 2009 [1], or the wide spread of the false report that President Obama was killed on the hacked Fox News' Twitter feed in July 2011 [2].

More generally, sharing rumors and gossip can also build and maintain social ties, as individuals provide early information to peers, express common perspectives and affiliations, and cope with uncertain circumstances. Online communication technologies are often neutral with respect to the veracity of the information: they can facilitate the spread of both true and false information. Nonetheless, the actions of the individuals in the network (e.g., propagating a rumor, referring to outside sources, criticizing or retracting claims) can determine how rumors spread with different truth values, verifiability, and topic spread.

In order for online social networks to serve as a trustworthy channel for disseminating important information, it is crucial to have effective strategies to understand, detect and limit the viral effect of rumors and misinformation. In this chapter, we introduce the following topics regarding rumor spreading in online social networks:

First, understand annotations of rumor and why rumor propagates so fast in online social networks (Section 6.2). Since rumors and non-rumors can spread over the same network, observing a large corpus of such rumors allows studying both common patterns and heterogeneity in their propagation. This includes variation in propagation of rumors of differing veracity: Do true or false rumors spread faster and further? Or are rumors with complex, disputed, or unknown truth values most contagious? Since the same communication technologies are used to spread non-rumors, rumor cascades can be compared with other types of cascades over a common network for propagation.

Second, in Section 6.3, we introduce a fundamental problem of interests: given a particular network structure and identities of infected individuals, how to determine the original source of the rumor diffusion process. In practice, this could indicate the source of various information regarding a natural disaster, leaked classified documents, or a pernicious lie. There is a substantial amount of research around rumors in this field, ranging from psychological studies to computational analyses.

Third, all kinds of false information, especially rumor information, have permeated almost every corner of social networks. Therefore, automatic assessment of information credibility has received considerable attention in recent years. In Section 6.4, we introduce how to distinguish between rumor messages and normal messages in online social networks, especially in Twitter and similar social media websites. Rumor detection is usually modeled as a classification problem using machine learning based approaches.

Finally, Section 6.5 will summarize this chapter and discuss potential directions.

6.2   UNDERSTANDING RUMOR CASCADES

Social networks such as Facebook and Twitter are reshaping the way people take collective actions. They have played a crucial role in the recent uprisings of the 'Arab Spring' and the 'London riots'. It has been argued that the instantaneous nature of these networks influenced the speed at which the events were unfolding [13].

It is quite remarkable that social networks spread news so fast. Both the structure of social networks and the process that distributes the news are not designed with this purpose in mind. On the contrary, they are not designed at all, but have evolved in a random and decentralized manner.

Rumor propagation, one of the basic mechanisms in social networks, is different from traditional methods, leading to that the relationship between people affects the spreading and the spreading process affects the relationship between people in turn. In social media, the ease of information dissemination through weak ties, people's trust of information from their friends, and small network diameter together create an environment where information can spread quickly throughout the world. To deeply understand the mechanism of fast rumor spreading, we first look into important structural properties of existing large social networks and then simulate rumor spreading process on networks having different properties.

6.2.1   Structure Properties of Social Networks

Social networks arise in a variety of contexts. They are formed by people, who are connected by knowing each other, Facebook members by agreeing on being friends in Facebook, scientific authors by having a joint publication, or actors appearing in the same movie. Despite the diversity, the networks share common features. A well-known observation is the small world effect. Milgram's small world experiments [35] show that any two individuals are connected through only six intermediates on average. For the World Wide Web, Albert et al. [9] predicted that the network diameter (maximum distance between two nodes in the graph) is only 19. Several experimental studies such as [7] revealed another intrinsic property of social networks: the histogram of the node connectivity follows power-law distribution, that is, the number of nodes with k neighbors is inversely proportional to a polynomial of k.

Barabasi and Albert [12] suggested a preferential attachment model to simulate real-world networks that show the power-law property. The preferential attachment model has been successfully used to deduce many interesting properties of social networks. Famous structural results prove a small diameter of such graphs [15], determine their degree distribution [10], show high expansion properties [33], and a high robustness against random damage, but a vulnerability against malicious attacks [3]. Algorithmic works show that in such networks, viruses spread more easily than in many other network topologies [36], or that gossip-based decentralized algorithms can approximate averages better [48].

6.2.2   Why Rumor Spreads so Fast?

Theoretical Analysis on Simulated Social Networks. In 2009, [19] studied the performance of rumor spreading in the classic preferential attachment model of Bollob. It is proved that in these networks: (a) The standard PUSH-PULL strategy delivers the message to all nodes within $O(log^2 n)$ rounds with high probability; (b) by themselves, PUSH and PULL require polynomially many rounds. The results are under the assumption that m, the number of new links added with each new node, is at least 2. If $m = 1$, the graph is disconnected with high probability, so no rumor spreading strategy can work.

In 2012, [37] also analyzed the popular push-pull protocol for spreading a rumor on random graphs that have a power law degree distribution with an arbitrary exponent $\beta > 2$. Initially, a single node receives a rumor. In each succeeding round, every node chooses a random neighbor, and the two nodes share the rumor if one of them already knows it.

Their main findings reveal a striking dichotomy in the performance of the protocol that depends on the exponent of the power law. In specific, if $2 < \beta < 3$, then the rumor spreads to almost all nodes in $\theta(loglog n)$ rounds with high probability. On the other hand, if $\beta > 3$, then $\Omega(log n)$ rounds are necessary.

Thus the exponent $\beta = 3$ is a critical point, such that when β crosses this point there is an exponential speedup of the synchronous push-pull protocol. It is believed that this is a universal phenomenon and for both versions of the push-pull protocol, ultrafast dissemination of the rumor occurs when the underlying graph is a random graph that has power law degree distribution with exponent $\beta \in (2, 3)$.

Further Findings. In 2012, [11] analyzed the rumor spreading process on preferential attachment graphs introduced by Barabasi and Albert [12]. It assumes that the rumor is sufficiently interesting so that people learn it when talking to someone knowing it. This is substantially different to the probabilistic virus spreading model [36], where the probability of becoming infected is proportional to the number of neighbors being infected.

Two types of rumor spreading mechanisms have been regarded in the literature. In the push model, only nodes that know the rumor contact neighbors to inform them. In contrast, to capture the effect of gossiping in social networks, it seems more appropriate for uninformed nodes to also actively ask for new information. It therefore uses the push-pull model of Demers et al. [5], in which all nodes regularly contact a neighbor and exchange all information they have. It is assumed that nodes choose their communication partners uniformly at random from their neighbors, however, excluding the person they contacted just before.

In this model, the spread of a single piece of information is initially present at a single node. For simplicity, the rumor spreading process is synchronized, that is, the process takes place at discrete points of time and in each time step, each node contacts a neighbor to exchange information. This is clearly a simplification over the real-world scenario where users act at different speeds, but in sufficiently large networks these differences balance out and thus assuming an average speed used by all nodes does not make a substantial difference.

The communication process is different in each social network. The push-pull model naturally captures best a personal communication between two individuals as by phone or exchanging text messages, emails or other directed communications. Many online social networks allow other ways of communication like posts on user's personal pages, possibly resulting in his friends to be notified of the post when they next log in, and them forwarding the news given that it is sufficiently interesting. Such form of communication can be modelled only by more complicated mechanisms than the push-pull protocol.

It is mathematically proved that rumors in such networks as preferential attachment graphs spread much faster than in many other network topologies — even faster than in networks having a communication link between any two nodes (complete graphs). A key observation in the mathematical proof and a good explanation for this phenomenon is that small-degree nodes quickly learn a rumor once one of their neighbors knows it, and then again quickly forward the news to all their neighbors. This in particular facilitates sending a rumor from one large-degree node to another.

What does this mean for our everyday life? It partially explains why social networks are observed to spread information extremely rapidly even though this process is not organized centrally and the network is not designed in some intelligent way. Crucial is the fruitful interaction between hubs, which have many connections, and average users with few friends. The hubs make the news available to a broad audience, whereas average users quickly convey the information from one neighbor to another.

Analysis on Real Social Networks. In [4], Friggeri et al. referenced known rumors from Snopes.com, a popular website documenting memes and urban legends, and tracked the propagation of thousands of rumors appearing on Facebook. They examined the cascades resulting from individuals resharing the photo, finding that some rumors proceeded to thrive in the environment, broadcasting from one friend to the next. These cascades ran deep, deeper than the average photo reshare cascade of similar size, and elicited different responses depending on their veracity. False rumors were frequently uploaded, and also frequently snoped.

However, it was the true rumors that were most viral and elicited the largest cascades. Although reshares of a rumor that have been snoped are several times more likely to be deleted, the cascade overall easily continues to propagate, as there are many more non-snoped reshares than snoped ones. For false and mixed rumors, a majority of reshares occurs after the first snopes comment has already been added. This points to individuals likely not noticing that the rumor was snoped, or intentionally ignoring that fact.

They further find the popularity of rumors — even ones that have been circulating for years in various media such as email and online social networks — tends to be highly bursty. A rumor will lie dormant for weeks or months, and then either spontaneously or through an external jolt will become popular again. Sometimes the rumors die down on their own, but in one particular case of a rumor claiming that Facebook would start charging a fee, we observed the rumor being dwarfed by an antidote more powerful than the truth: humor.

Yiran et al. [55] studied rumor spreading on an real online social platform called Renren and got the following conclusions. Firstly, the greater the degree of initial rumor node, the faster the rate of spread and diffusion getting to peak rapidly. Secondly, although the different degree of initial node does affect the stable value, the tendency of each density is approximately consistent. Also, the social community structure does have certain influence on rumor spreading.

Understanding rumor cascades in real social networks is still in the preliminary phase. The bursty nature of rumors remains a mystery. Furthermore, it is unclear how individuals change their attitudes toward rumors. These questions will be further investigated in the future.

6.3 RUMOR SOURCE DETECTION: GRAPH THEORY BASED APPROACH

6.3.1 Introduction

Work on rumor source detection is related to information spreading. Many studies on the problem of information propagation are inspired from the more common issue of contagion and generally use models for viral epidemics in populations such as the susceptible-infected-recovered (SIR) model. On this subject, research has focused on the effects of the topological properties of the network on inferring the source of a rumor in a network. Shah and Zaman [50, 49, 51] were the first to study systematically the problem of infection sources estimation which considers a Susceptible-Infected (SI) model, in which there is a single infection source, and susceptible nodes are those with at least one infected neighbor, while infected nodes do not recover.

Subsequently, [28, 31] consider the multiple sources estimation problem under an SI model; [57] studies the single source estimation problem for the Susceptible-Infected-Recovered (SIR) model, where an infected node may recover but can never be infected again; and [30] considers the single source estimation problem for the Susceptible-Infected-Susceptible (SIS) model, where a recovered node is susceptible to be infected again.

Although all the works listed above answer some fundamental questions about information source detection in large-scale networks, they assume that a complete snapshot of the network is given while in reality a complete snapshot, which may have hundreds of millions of nodes, is expensive to obtain. Furthermore, these works assume homogeneous infection across links and homogeneous recovery across nodes, but in reality, most networks are heterogeneous. For example, people close to each other are more likely to share rumors and epidemics are more infectious in the regions with poor medical care systems. Therefore, it is important to take sparse observations and network heterogeneity into account when locating information sources.

In [29, 58, 54], detecting information sources with partial observations in which only a fraction of nodes (observers) can be observed has been investigated. The work in [40] assumes that for each of the observers, the knowledge of the first infected time and from which neighbor the infection is received are given. This assumption is impractical in some cases. For example, it is usually hard to know from which neighbor the infection is coming from in a contagious disease spreading within a community. In [21], the authors have considered the detection rate of the rumor centrality estimator when a priori distribution of the source node is given. Several other source locating algorithms have also been proposed recently, including an eigenvalue-based estimator [41], a fast Monte Carlo algorithm [8], and a dynamic message-passing algorithm under the SIR model [6].

In Section 6.3.2, we consider detecting multiple rumors from a deterministic point of view by modeling it as the set resolving set (SRS) problem [56]. Let G be an undirected graph on n vertices. A vertex subset K of G is SRS of G if any different detectable node sets are distinguishable by K. The problem of Multiple Rumor Source Detection (MRSD) will be defined as finding an SRS K with the smallest cardinality in G. Using an analysis framework of submodular functions, we propose a highly efficient greedy algorithm for MRSD problem on general graphs, which is polynomial time under some reasonable constraints, that is, there is a constant upper bound r for the number of sources. Moreover, we show that our natural greedy algorithm correctly computes an SRS with provable approximation ratio of at most $(1 + r \ln n + \ln \log_2 \gamma)$, given that γ is the maximum number of equivalence classes divided by one node-pair. This is the first work providing explicit approximation ratio for the algorithm solving minimum SRS. Therefore the introduced framework suggests a robust approach for MRSD independent of diffusion models in networks.

6.3.2 Detecting Multiple Rumor Sources in Networks with Partial Observations

Suppose there is more than one rumor source in the network; the problem is how to detect all of them based on limited information about network structure and the rumor infected nodes. If each rumor source initiates a different rumor, then the problem can be decoupled to the detection of each rumor source independently. Thus, we assume that one rumor is initiated at a lot of different locations. We place some nodes $v \in K \subseteq V$ as the observers which has a clock that can record the time at which the state of v is changed (e.g., knowing a rumor, being infected or contaminated). Typically, the time when the single source originates is unknown. The monitors/observers can only report the times when they receive the information, but no information about senders (i.e., we do not know who infects whom in epidemic networks or who influences whom in social networks). The information is diffused from the sources to any vertex through the shortest paths in the network, i.e., as soon as a vertex receives the information, it sends the information to all its neighbors simultaneously, which takes one time unit. Our goal is to select a subset K of vertices with minimum cardinality such that the source can be uniquely located by the infected times of vertices in K and network structure. This problem is equivalent to finding a minimum Set Resolving Set (SRS) in networks defined in our models.

In this section, we originally propose the concept of Set Resolving Set (SRS) problem and give the formal definition of it. Based on SRS, we then present a novel approach for locating multiple information sources on general graphs with partial observations of the set of infected nodes at the observation time, without knowing the neighbors from which the infection is received. Our method is robust to network heterogeneity and the number of observed infected nodes. To the best of our knowledge, this chapter is the first work to study Multiple Rumor Source Detection (MRSD) problem via SRS.

Moreover, we show that our objective function for detecting multiple rumor sources in networks is monotone and submodular. By exploiting the submodularity of the objective, we develop an efficient greedy approximation for MRSD problem, which is theoretically proved to have a $(1 + r \ln n + \ln \log_2 \gamma)$ — approximation ratio in real world, given that γ is the maximum number of equivalence classes divided by one node-pair. These guarantees are important in practice, since selecting nodes is expensive, and we desire solutions which are not too far from the optimal solution.

The following section is organized as follows. In Section 6.3.3, we present the SRS based model and give a formal problem formulation. In Section 6.3.4, we then develop a greedy algorithm, and prove its approximation ratio. To confirm the effectiveness of our algorithm, in Section 6.3.5, the performance of our algorithm is evaluated in networks which exemplify different structures.

6.3.3   The Model

We start by describing the model and problem statement of Multi-Rumor-Source detection. In the process, we will give the definition of set resolving set (SRS), which is the basis of the model.

If a node u is a rumor source, then we use $s(u)$ to denote the time that it initiates the rumor. If u is not a rumor source, then $s(u) = \infty$. For two nodes u and v, the distance between them is denoted as $d(u, v)$. The time that a rumor initiated at node u is received by node v is $r_u(v) = s(u) + d(u, v)$. For a set of rumor sources $A \subseteq V$, the time that the rumor from A is received by node v is $r_A(v) = \min\{r_u(v) \colon u \in A\}$.

Definition 6.1 (Set Resolving Set (SRS)) Let K be a node subset of V. Two node set $A, B \subseteq V$ are *distinguishable* by K if there exist two nodes $x, y \in K$ such that

$$r_A(x) - r_A(y) \neq r_B(x) - r_B(y).$$

For a node set $A \subseteq V$, a node $x \in A$ is detectable if A and $A \setminus \{x\}$ are distinguishable by V. Node set A is *detectable* if every node in A is detectable. Let $\mathcal{D}$ be the family of detectable node sets. Node set $K \subseteq V$ is an SRS if any different detectable node sets $A, B \in \mathcal{D}$ are distinguishable by K.

> MULTI-RUMOR-SOURCE DETECTION problem (MRSD): find an SRS K with the smallest cardinality.

The following theorem characterizes the condition under which a node set is detectable. The idea behind the condition is as follows: when a rumor is initiated at a node x after x can receive the same rumor from some other nodes, then one cannot tell whether the rumor is initiated by x or x merely relays the rumor.

Theorem 6.1 *A node set A is detectable if and only if for every node $x \in A$,*

$$s(x) < r_{A \setminus \{x\}}(x). \tag{6.1}$$

Proof 6.1 *Suppose there is a node $x \in A$ such that $s(x) \geq r_{A \setminus \{x\}}(x)$. Then, there is a node $z \in A \setminus \{x\}$ such that $s(x) \geq r_z(x) = s(z) + d(z, x)$. For any node $y \in V$, $r_x(y) = s(x) + d(x, y) \geq s(z) + d(z, x) + d(x, y) \geq s(z) + d(z, y) = r_z(y)$.*

Hence, $r_A(y) = \min\{r_x(y), r_{A \setminus \{x\}}(y)\} = r_{A \setminus \{x\}}(y)$. It follows that $r_A(y_1) - r_A(y_2) = r_{A \setminus \{x\}}(y_1) - r_{A \setminus \{x\}}(y_2)$ for any nodes $y_1, y_2 \in V$, and thus A and $A \setminus \{x\}$ are not distinguishable by V. This finishes the proof for the necessity.

To show the sufficiency, notice that $s(x) < r_{A \setminus \{x\}}(x)$ implies that

$$\begin{aligned} r_A(x) &= \min\{r_x(x), r_{A \setminus \{x\}}(x)\} = \min\{s(x), r_{A \setminus \{x\}}(x)\} \\ &= s(x) < r_{A \setminus \{x\}}(x). \end{aligned} \tag{6.2}$$

For any node $y_1 \in A$, choose $y_2 \in A$ such that $s(y_2) = \min_{y \in A \setminus \{y_1\}}\{s(y)\}$. Then

$$r_{A \setminus \{y_1\}}(y_2) = s(y_2) = r_A(y_2). \qquad (6.3)$$

This is because of property (6.2) and the observation $s(y_2) = r_{y_2}(y_2) \geq r_{A \setminus \{y_1\}}(y_2) = \min_{y \in A \setminus \{y_1\}}\{s(y) + d(y, y_2)\} \geq \min_{y \in A \setminus \{y_1\}}\{s(y)\} = s(y_2)$. Also by (6.2), we have

$$r_A(y_1) < r_{A \setminus \{y_1\}}(y_1). \qquad (6.4)$$

Combining (6.3) and (6.4), we have

$$r_A(y_1) - r_A(y_2) < r_{A \setminus \{y_1\}}(y_1) - r_{A \setminus \{y_1\}}(y_2).$$

So, A and $A \setminus \{y_1\}$ are distinguishable by y_1 and y_2. The sufficiency follows from the arbitrariness of y_1.

Remark 1 If the starting time for all nodes is a constant, then condition (6.1) is satisfied at all nodes. So, this condition does occur in the real world.

Lemma 1 *Let A, B be two detectable node sets with $A \setminus B \neq \emptyset$. Then for any node $x \in A \setminus B$ and any node $y \in B$, node sets A and B are distinguishable by x and y.*

Proof 6.2 *Suppose the lemma is not true, then there exists a node $x \in A \setminus B$ and a node $y \in B$ such that*

$$r_A(x) - r_A(y) = r_B(x) - r_B(y). \qquad (6.5)$$

Since both A and B are detectable, we see from property (6.2) that

$$r_A(x) = s(x) \text{ and } r_B(y) = s(y).$$

Combining these with (6.5), we have

$$s(x) - r_A(y) = r_B(x) - s(y) \leq r_y(x) - s(y) = d(y, x). \qquad (6.6)$$

Then,

$$r_x(y) = s(x) + d(y, x) \leq r_A(y) \leq r_x(y). \qquad (6.7)$$

It follows that the inequalities in (6.6) and (6.7) become equalities, that is,

$$r_A(y) = r_x(y) \text{ and } r_B(x) = r_y(x).$$

But then,
$r_A(x) - r_A(y) = s(x) - r_x(y) = -d(x, y) < d(y, x) = r_y(x) - s(y) = r_B(x) - r_B(y)$,

contradicting (6.5). The lemma is proved.

As a consequence of Lemma 1, we have the following theorem.

Theorem 6.2 *Node set V is an SRS.*

Theorem 6.2 shows that V is a trivial solution to the MRSD problem. In next section, we shall present an approximation algorithm for the problem.

6.3.4 The Algorithm

In this section, we present a greedy algorithm for MRSD. The algorithm starts from $\mathcal{T} = \emptyset$, and iteratively adds into $\mathcal{T}$ node-pairs with the highest efficiency (which will be defined later) until all sets can be distinguished by some node-pair in $\mathcal{T}$. The output of the algorithm is $K = \bigcup_{T \in \mathcal{T}} T$.

6.3.4.1 Potential Function

The efficiency of a node-pair is related with a potential function f defined as follows. Two detectable node sets A and B are *equivalent* under $\mathcal{T}$, denoted as $A \equiv_{\mathcal{T}} B$, if A and B are not distinguishable by any node-pair in $\mathcal{T}$. Under $\equiv_{\mathcal{T}}$, detectable node sets $\mathcal{F}$ is divided into equivalence classes. The equivalence class containing detectable node set A is denoted as $[A]_{\mathcal{T}}$. Suppose the equivalence classes under $\equiv_{\mathcal{T}}$ are $\mathcal{F}_1, \ldots, \mathcal{F}_k$. Define $\pi(\mathcal{T}) = \prod_{i=1}^{k} |\mathcal{F}_i|!$ and

$$f(\mathcal{T}) = -\log_2 \pi(\mathcal{T}). \tag{6.8}$$

For a node-pair $T = \{x, y\}$, let

$$\Delta_T f(\mathcal{T}) = f(\mathcal{T} \cup \{T\}) - f(\mathcal{T}).$$

We shall show that f is monotone increasing and submodular. The proof idea is similar to the one in [14] which studies group testing. The difference is that in [14], only elements need to be distinguished. While in this paper, distinguishing sets needs more technical details. The following is a technical result of combinatorics (see Figure 6.1(a) for an illustration of its conditions).

	b_1	b_2	$\cdots$	b_q
a_1	h_{11}	h_{12}	$\cdots$	h_{1q}
a_2	h_{21}	h_{22}	$\cdots$	h_{2q}
$\vdots$	$\vdots$	$\vdots$	$\ddots$	$\vdots$
a_p	h_{p1}	h_{p2}	$\cdots$	h_{pq}

(a)

	$\mathcal{F}\mathcal{T}_1^{(i)}$	$\mathcal{F}\mathcal{T}_2^{(i)}$	$\cdots$	$\mathcal{F}\mathcal{T}_q^{(i)}$
$\mathcal{F}\mathcal{S}_1^{(i)}$	$\mathcal{F}_{11}^{(i)}$	$\mathcal{F}_{12}^{(i)}$	$\cdots$	$\mathcal{F}_{1q}^{(i)}$
$\mathcal{F}\mathcal{S}_2^{(i)}$	$\mathcal{F}_{21}^{(i)}$	$\mathcal{F}_{22}^{(i)}$	$\cdots$	$\mathcal{F}_{2q}^{(i)}$
$\vdots$	$\vdots$	$\vdots$	$\ddots$	$\vdots$
$\mathcal{F}\mathcal{S}_p^{(i)}$	$\mathcal{F}_{p1}^{(i)}$	$\mathcal{F}_{p2}^{(i)}$	$\cdots$	$\mathcal{F}_{pq}^{(i)}$

(b)

FIGURE 6.1 (a) Illustration for the conditions in Lemma 2. (b) Refinement of equivalence class $\mathcal{F}_i$ by adding S and T.

Lemma 2 *Suppose* $\{h_{ij}\}_{i=1,\ldots,p}^{j=1,\ldots,q}$ *is a set of nonnegative integers. For* $i = 1,\ldots,p$, $a_i = \sum_{j=1}^{q} h_{ij}$. *For* $j = 1,\ldots,q$, $b_j = \sum_{i=1}^{p} h_{ij}$. *Furthermore,* $\sum_{i=1}^{p} a_i = \sum_{j=1}^{q} b_j = g$. *Then*

$$\frac{g!}{\prod_{j=1}^{q} b_j!} \geq \frac{\prod_{i=1}^{p} a_i!}{\prod_{i=1}^{p} \prod_{j=1}^{q} h_{ij}!}. \tag{6.9}$$

Proof 6.3 *Consider the expansion of the following multi-variable polynomial:*

$$(x_{11} + \cdots + x_{1q})^{a_1} \cdots (x_{p1} + \cdots + x_{pq})^{a_p}$$

$$= \left(\sum_{a_{11}+\cdots+a_{1q}=a_1} \frac{a_1!}{\prod_{j=1}^{q} a_{1j}!} x_{11}^{a_{11}} \cdots x_{1q}^{a_{1q}} \right) \cdots$$

$$\left(\sum_{a_{p1}+\cdots+a_{pq}=a_p} \frac{a_p!}{\prod_{j=1}^{q} a_{pj}!} x_{p1}^{a_{p1}} \cdots x_{pq}^{a_{pq}} \right)$$

$$= \sum \frac{\prod_{i=1}^{p} a_i!}{\prod_{i=1}^{p} \prod_{j=1}^{q} a_{ij}!} x_{11}^{a_{11}} \cdots x_{1q}^{a_{1q}} \cdots x_{p1}^{a_{p1}} \cdots x_{pq}^{a_{pq}},$$

where the sum is over all nonnegative integers $\{a_{ij}\}_{i=1,\ldots,p}^{j=1,\ldots,q}$ *satisfying* $\sum_{j=1}^{q} a_{ij} = a_i$ *for* $i = 1,\ldots,p$. *Setting* $x_{1j} = \cdots = x_{pj} = x_j$ *for* $j = 1,\ldots,q$ *in the above equation, we have*

$$(x_1 + \cdots x_q)^{a_1+\cdots+a_p}$$

$$= \sum \frac{\prod_{i=1}^{p} a_i!}{\prod_{i=1}^{p} \prod_{j=1}^{q} a_{ij}!} x_1^{a_{11}+\cdots+a_{p1}} \cdots x_q^{a_{1q}+\cdots+a_{pq}}. \tag{6.10}$$

On the other hand,

$$(x_1 + \cdots x_q)^{a_1+\cdots+a_p}$$

$$= (x_1 + \cdots x_q)^{g} = \sum_{r_1+\cdots r_q=g} \frac{g!}{\prod_{j=1}^{q} r_j!} x_1^{r_1} \cdots x_q^{r_q}. \tag{6.11}$$

Comparing the coefficients of $x_1^{b_1} \cdots x_q^{b_q}$ *in (6.10) and (6.11), we have*

$$\frac{g!}{\prod_{j=1}^{q} b_j!} = \sum \frac{\prod_{i=1}^{q} a_p!}{\prod_{i=1}^{p} \prod_{j=1}^{q} a_{ij}!}, \tag{6.12}$$

where the sum is over all nonnegative integers $\{a_{ij}\}_{i=1,\ldots,p}^{j=1,\ldots,q}$ *satisfying* $\sum_{j=1}^{q} a_{ij} = a_i$ *for* $i = 1,\ldots,p$ *and* $\sum_{i=1}^{p} a_{ij} = b_j$ *for* $j = 1,\ldots,q$. *Since* $\{h_{ij}\}_{i=1,\ldots,p}^{j=1,\ldots,q}$ *satisfy these restrictions, the righthand side of (6.9) is one term contained in the righthand side of (6.12). Then, the Lemma follows.*

We shall use the following characterization of monotonicity and submodularity.

Lemma 3 ([22] Lemma 2.25) *Let f be a function defined on all subsets of a set U. Then f is submodular and monotone increasing if and only if for any two subsets $R \subseteq S \subseteq U$ and any element $x \in U$,*

$$\Delta_x f(R) \geq \Delta_x f(S).$$

Lemma 4 *The function f defined in (6.8) is submodular and monotone increasing.*

Proof 6.4 *To use Lemma 3, we are to show that for any families of node-pairs $\mathcal{T}_1 \subseteq \mathcal{T}_2$ and any node-pair T,*

$$\Delta_T f(\mathcal{T}_1) \geq \Delta_T f(\mathcal{T}_2). \tag{6.13}$$

In fact, it suffices to prove (6.13) for the case that $|\mathcal{T}_2 \setminus \mathcal{T}_1| = 1$. Then, induction argument will yield the result for the general case. So, in the following, we assume that $\mathcal{T}_2 = \mathcal{T}_1 \cup \{S\}$, where S is a node-pair. In this case, (6.13) is equivalent to

$$\frac{\pi(\mathcal{T}_1)}{\pi(\mathcal{T}_1 \cup \{T\})} \geq \frac{\pi(\mathcal{T}_1 \cup \{S\})}{\pi(\mathcal{T}_1 \cup \{S, T\})}. \tag{6.14}$$

Suppose the equivalence classes under $\equiv_{\mathcal{T}}$ are $\mathcal{F}_1, \ldots, \mathcal{F}_k$. Notice that for any detectable node set A, $[A]_{\mathcal{T} \cup \{S\}} \subseteq [A]_{\mathcal{T}}$, that is, adding one node-pair results in a refinement of equivalence classes. Also notice that for any detectable node set A,

$$[A]_{\mathcal{T} \cup \{S,T\}} = [A]_{\mathcal{T} \cup \{S\}} \cap [A]_{\mathcal{T} \cup \{T\}}.$$

Hence we may assume (see Figure 6.1(b) for an illustration) that for each $i = 1, \ldots, k$,

(a) equivalence classes under $\mathcal{T} \cup \{S, T\}$ which are contained in $\mathcal{F}_i$ are $\{\mathcal{F}_{s,t}^{(i)}\}_{s=1,\ldots,l_i}^{t=1,\ldots,m_i}$;

(b) For $s = 1, \ldots, l_i$, let $\mathcal{FS}_s^{(i)} = \bigcup_{t=1}^{m_i} \mathcal{F}_{s,t}^{(i)}$. Equivalence classes under $\equiv_{\mathcal{T} \cup \{S\}}$ contained in $\mathcal{F}_i$ are $\{\mathcal{FS}_s^{(i)}\}_{s=1}^{l_i}$;

(c) For $t = 1, \ldots, m_i$, let $\mathcal{FT}_t^{(i)} = \bigcup_{s=1}^{l_i} \mathcal{F}_{s,t}^{(i)}$. Equivalence classes under $\equiv_{\mathcal{T} \cup \{T\}}$ contained in $\mathcal{F}_i$ are $\{\mathcal{FT}_t^{(i)}\}_{t=1}^{m_i}$.

Taking $a_l = |\mathcal{FS}_l^{(i)}|$, $b_j = |\mathcal{FT}_j^{(i)}|$, $h_{lj} = |\mathcal{F}_{lj}^{(i)}|$, and $g = |\mathcal{F}_i|$, the conditions of Lemma 2 are satisfied, and thus

$$\frac{|\mathcal{F}_i|!}{\prod_{j=1}^{q} |\mathcal{FT}_j^{(i)}|!} \geq \frac{\prod_{l=1}^{p} |\mathcal{FS}_l^{(i)}|!}{\prod_{l=1}^{p} \prod_{j=1}^{q} |\mathcal{F}_{lj}^{(i)}|!},$$

which is exactly the desired inequality (6.14).

Lemma 5 *Suppose node-pair T divides $\mathcal{F}$ into k equivalence classes. Then*

$$\Delta_T f(\emptyset) \le |\mathcal{F}| \log_2 k.$$

Proof 6.5 *Suppose the equivalence classes under $\equiv_T$ have cardinalities $n_1, \ldots, n_k$, respectively. Then*

$$\Delta_T f(\emptyset) = f(\{T\}) - f(\emptyset) = \log_2\left(\frac{|\mathcal{F}|!}{\prod_{i=1}^k n_i!}\right) \le \log_2\left(k^{|\mathcal{F}|}\right) = |\mathcal{F}| \log_2 k,$$

where the inequality can be seen by setting $x_1 = \cdots = x_k = 1$ in the following equation:

$$(x_1 + \cdots + x_k)^{|\mathcal{F}|} = \sum_{n_1 + \cdots + n_k = n} \frac{|\mathcal{F}|!}{\prod_{i=1}^k n_i!} x_1^{n_1} \cdots x_k^{n_k}.$$

The lemma is proved.

6.3.4.2 The Algorithm and Its Approximation Ratio

As stated at the beginning of Section 6.3.4, an SRS will be derived from a family $\mathcal{T}$ of node-pairs such that

node-pairs in $\mathcal{T}$ can distinguish all detectable node sets.   (6.15)

Call any family of node-pairs as a *test family*, and call a test family satisfying condition (6.15) as a *valid test family*.

Lemma 6 *Suppose $\mathcal{T}$ is a valid test family. Let $K = \bigcup_{T \in \mathcal{T}} T$ and x be an arbitrary node in K. Then $\widetilde{\mathcal{T}} = \{(x, y) \colon y \in K \setminus \{x\}\}$ is also a valid text family.*

Proof 6.6 *Observe that if two detectable node sets A, B are distinguished by $\{y, z\} \in \mathcal{T}$, then they can be distinguished by either $\{x, y\}$ or $\{x, z\}$. The lemma follows.*

Notice that all node-pairs in $\widetilde{\mathcal{T}}$ have a common element. We call such a test family as a *canonical test family*. Notice that $\bigcup_{T \in \mathcal{T}} T = \bigcup_{T \in \widetilde{\mathcal{T}}} T = K$. Hence $\mathcal{T}$ and $\widetilde{\mathcal{T}}$ are equivalent in the sense that they produce a same SRS. As a consequence, to find an SRS, it suffices to consider canonical test families, that is, to find a node x and a valid test family $\mathcal{T}_x \subseteq \mathcal{P}_x = \{\{x, y\} \colon y \in V \setminus \{x\}\}$.

In order to analyze the approximation ratio, we have to compare the size of the approximation solution with that of an optimal one. Since we do not know which node is in an optimal solution, we have to 'guess'. To be more concrete, for each node $x \in V$, the algorithm finds a valid test family $\mathcal{T}_x \subseteq \mathcal{P}_x$. Let $K_x = \bigcup_{T \in \mathcal{T}_x} T$. The final output of the algorithm is $K = \arg\min_{x \in V} |K_x|$. The details of the algorithm for MRSD is described in Algorithm 3.

Algorithm 3 Greedy Algorithm for MRSD

Input: A graph $G = (V, E)$.

Output: A node set K which is an SRS.

    for all $x \in V$ **do**

        Set $\mathcal{T}_x \leftarrow \emptyset$.

        while there exists a node-pair $T \in \mathcal{P}_x$ such that $\Delta_T f(\mathcal{T}_x) > 0$ **do**

            select node-pair $T \in \mathcal{P}_x$ with the maximum $\Delta_T f(\mathcal{T}_x)$.

            $\mathcal{T}_x \leftarrow \mathcal{T}_x \cup \{T\}$.

        end while

        $K_x = \bigcup_{T \in \mathcal{T}_x} T$.

    end for

    Output $K \leftarrow \arg\min\{|K_x| : x \in V\}$.

Lemma 7 *A test family $\mathcal{T}$ is valid if and only if $\Delta_T f(\mathcal{T}) = 0$ for any node-pair T.*

Proof 6.7 *First, we make some observation. Suppose the equivalence classes under $\mathcal{T}$ are $\mathcal{F}_1, \ldots, \mathcal{F}_k$. For each $i = 1, \ldots, k$, $\mathcal{F}_i$ is refined under $\mathcal{T} \cup \{T\}$ into equivalence classes $\mathcal{F}_1^{(i)}, \ldots, \mathcal{F}_{l_i}^{(i)}$. Then*

$$\Delta_T f(\mathcal{T}) = \log_2 \left(\frac{\prod_{i=1}^{k} |\mathcal{F}_i|}{\prod_{i=1}^{k} \prod_{j=1}^{l_i} |\mathcal{F}_j^{(i)}|} \right)$$
$$= \log_2 \left(\prod_{i=1}^{k} \frac{|\mathcal{F}_i|}{\prod_{j=1}^{l_i} |\mathcal{F}_j^{(i)}|} \right). \tag{6.16}$$

Notice that $|\mathcal{F}_i| / \prod_{j=1}^{l_i} |\mathcal{F}_j^{(i)}|$ is the number of ways to put $|\mathcal{F}_i|$ balls into l_i labeled boxes such that the j-th box contains $|\mathcal{F}_j^{(i)}|$ balls ($j = 1, \ldots, l_i$). So,

$$|\mathcal{F}_i| / \prod_{j=1}^{l_i} |\mathcal{F}_j^{(i)}| \tag{6.17}$$

is a positive integer which equals 1 if and only if $l_i = 1$.

Notice that $l_i = 1$ implies that adding node-pair T into $\mathcal{T}$ does not incur a strict refinement of $\mathcal{F}_i$.

If $\mathcal{T}$ is a valid test family, then every equivalence class has cardinality 1, and thus $f(\mathcal{T}) = 0$. Combining this with the fact that f is a non-positive monotone increasing function, we see that the maximum value of f is zero and thus $\Delta_T(\mathcal{T}) = 0$ holds for any node-pair T.

If $\mathcal{T}$ is not a valid test family, then there exist two different detectable node sets A, B which can not be distinguished by $\mathcal{T}$. Since $A \neq B$, we may assume that $A \setminus B \neq \emptyset$. By Lemma 1, A, B can be distinguished by a node-pair $\{y, z\}$

with $y \in A \setminus B$ *and* $z \in B$. *Then by Lemma 6, A, B can be distinguished by $T = \{x, y\}$ or $\{x, z\}$. In this case, at least one equivalence class under T is refined by adding T. In other words, there is an $i \in \{1, \ldots, k\}$ such that $|\mathcal{F}_i| / \prod_{j=1}^{l_i} |\mathcal{F}_j^{(i)}| > 1$. Then by (6.16), $\Delta_T(\mathcal{T}) > 0$. The lemma is proved.*

Theorem 6.3 *Suppose γ is the maximum number of equivalence classes divided by one node-pair. Then, Algorithm 3 correctly computes an SRS with approximation ratio at most $1 + \ln\left(|\mathcal{F}| \log_2 \gamma\right)$.*

Proof 6.8 *By Lemma 7, we see that every $\mathcal{T}_x$ computed in the algorithm is a valid test family. The correctness follows.*

To analyze the approximation ratio, suppose K^* is an optimal solution to MRSD and x is a node in K^*. Let $\mathcal{T}^* = \{\{x, y\} : y \in K^* \setminus \{x\}\}$.

Consider the test family $\mathcal{T}_x$ produced by the greedy algorithm for node x. We claim that every node pair T chosen in line 4 of the algorithm satisfies

$$\Delta_T f(\mathcal{T}_x) \geq 1. \tag{6.18}$$

By expression (6.16), this is equivalent to show

$$\prod_{i=1}^{k} \frac{|\mathcal{F}_i|}{\prod_{j=1}^{l_i} |\mathcal{F}_j^{(i)}|} \geq 2. \tag{6.19}$$

Since every T taken in line 4 of the algorithm has $\Delta_T f(\mathcal{T}_x) > 0$, which is equivalent to $\prod_{i=1}^{k} \frac{|\mathcal{F}_i|}{\prod_{j=1}^{l_i} |\mathcal{F}_j^{(i)}|} > 1$, we see that at least one $|\mathcal{F}_i| / \prod_{j=1}^{l_i} |\mathcal{F}_j^{(i)}|$ is greater than 1, and thus is at least 2. Inequality (6.19) follows from this observation and property (6.17). Claim (6.18) is proved.

We shall use Theorem 3.7 in [22], which says, using terminologies here, that as long as (6.18) is true, then

$$|\mathcal{T}_x| \leq \left(1 + \ln \frac{f(\mathcal{T}^*) - f(\emptyset)}{|\mathcal{T}^*|}\right) \cdot |\mathcal{T}^*|. \tag{6.20}$$

By a property of submodular function (see [22] Lemma 2.23),

$$\sum_{T \in \mathcal{T}^*} \Delta_T f(\emptyset) \geq \Delta_{\mathcal{T}^*} f(\emptyset) = f(\mathcal{T}^*) - f(\emptyset).$$

Combining this with Lemma 5,

$$
\begin{aligned}
&\frac{f(\mathcal{T}^*) - f(\emptyset)}{|\mathcal{T}^*|} \\
&\leq \frac{\sum_{T \in \mathcal{T}^*} \Delta_T f(\emptyset)}{|\mathcal{T}^*|} \leq \max_{T \in \mathcal{T}^*} \{\Delta_T f(\emptyset)\} \leq |\mathcal{F}| \log_2 \gamma.
\end{aligned} \tag{6.21}
$$

Combining (6.20), (6.21) with $|K_x| = |\mathcal{T}_x| - 1$ and $|K^*| = |\mathcal{T}^*| - 1$, we have

$$|K_x| \leq \left(1 + \ln\left(|\mathcal{F}| \log_2 \gamma\right)\right)\left(|K^*| - 1\right) + 1 \leq \left(1 + \ln\left(|\mathcal{F}| \log_2 \gamma\right)\right)|K^*|.$$

The approximation ratio follows since the algorithm chooses a node x_0 with $|K_{x_0}| = \min_{y \in V} |K_y| \leq |K_x|$.

Remark 2 Notice that in a worst case, the number of detectable node sets is $\Theta(2^n)$. In fact, if the starting time for all nodes is a constant, then by Remark 1, every nonempty node set is detectable, and thus $|\mathcal{F}| = 2^n - 1$. In such a case, the approximation ratio is $(1 + n \ln 2 + \ln \log_2 \gamma)$, which is no better than a trivial bound n. However, in the real world, it is reasonable to assume that the number of rumor-sources is at most a constant number r, and only those detectable node sets of cardinality at most r are considered. In this case, $|\mathcal{F}| = O(n^r)$, and the approximation ratio is $(1 + r \ln n + \ln \log_2 \gamma)$.

Remark 3 Notice that $\gamma \leq 2D + 1$, where D is the diameter of the graph. To see this, suppose $T = \{x, y\}$ is a node-pair, A is a node set, and $r_A(x) - r_A(y) = c$, then a node set B belongs to equivalence class $[A]_{\{T\}}$ if and only if $r_B(x) - r_B(y) = c$. Notice that c has at most $2D + 1$ different values, namely, $\{-D, -(D-1), \ldots, -1, 0, 1, \ldots, D-1, D\}$. So, one node-pair divides $\mathcal{F}$ into at most $2D + 1$ equivalence classes. In a social network, D is a small constant. So, the third term $\ln \log_2 \gamma$ in the above approximation ratio is not large.

6.3.5 Simulation Results

In this section we experimentally evaluate our greedy algorithm for MRSD, in particular its effectiveness in finding rumor sources — how many sources it identifies, whether it correctly identifies and its scalability.

As discussed in the introduction, the existing proposals for identifying rumor sources consider significantly different problems settings than we do. The rumor centrality of Shah and Zaman [49, 51] can only discover one rumor source, while estimators proposed in [28] consider a completely different infection model from ours. As such it is not meaningful to compare performances, and therefore here we only consider the greedy algorithm for MRSD.

In our study we conduct simulations on synthetic networks exemplifying different types of structure — including geometric trees, regular trees and small-world networks. In general, we set the rumor sources, simulate diffusion process, and record the times of monitors when they received the rumors. Then, given the times and network structure, we try to infer the the number rumor sources and where they are.

As described in Section 6.3.3, the diffusion model is implemented as a discrete event in Java. Each hop takes one time unit. Note that the cascade starts from all rumor sources at the same time stamp. The number of rumor sources is set as k. For each k, we perform large number of simulation runs to get high precession.

A. Effectiveness of greedy in identifying How Many

The number of infection sources k are chosen to be 1, 2, 3 and 4. For each type of network and each number of infection sources, we perform 1000 simulation runs with 500 monitors. The estimation results for the number of infection sources in different scenarios are shown in Figure 6.2. It can be seen that our algorithm correctly finds the number of infection sources more than

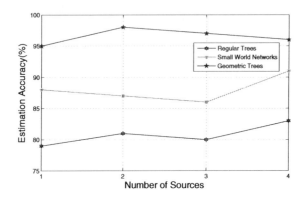

FIGURE 6.2 Estimating the number of rumor sources.

95% of the time for geometric trees, and more than 86% of the time for regular trees. The accuracy of about 79% for small-world networks is slightly lower than that for the tree networks, as the node pair for a small-world network is estimated based on the BFS heuristics, thus additional errors are introduced into the procedure. It also shows the power of our approach, as we can easily identify the true number of seeds for most cases using a principled approach.

B. Effectiveness of greedy in identifying Which Ones

To quantify the performance of identified rumor sources, we propose error distance. Error distance is defined as the average distances between the estimates and the respective rumor sources. To be specific, we match the estimated source nodes with the actual sources so that the sum of the error distances between each estimated source and its match is minimized. If we have incorrectly estimated the number of infection sources, we neglect the extra number of found nodes since here we only focus on the error distance between correct sources. In Figure 6.3, we see that the proposed algorithm finds rumor sources that have small error distance on average. Note that the reported results here is also based on 1000 trials. For geometric trees, the average error distance lies between 1.4 to 0.6 hop. For regular trees, the error distance decreases from 1.2 to 0.65 hops. For small-world networks, the value is between 1.6 to 0.8. In general, the average error distance is less than 2 hops. Moreover, as the number of monitors increases, error distance will start to drop.

C. Scalability

Figure 6.4 demonstrates the the average computation time of greedy after running it on increasingly larger infected graphs (as the complexity depends on the size of the monitors). We use small-world network graph with $k=2$. The statistics of running time is based on 10 runs for each graph. As we can see,

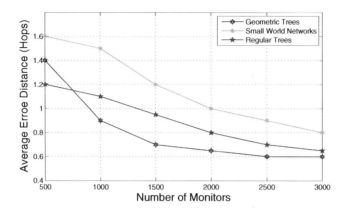

FIGURE 6.3 Estimating the average error distance between the identified source and the actual source.

the running-time is linear on the number of edges of the infected graph. Thus, overall our algorithm scales well with high performance in solution quality.

6.3.6 Discussion

In Section 6.3.2 we discussed finding multiple rumor sources, the challenging problem of identifying the nodes from which an infection in a graph started to spread. We first gave the definition of set resolving set(SRS) and proposed

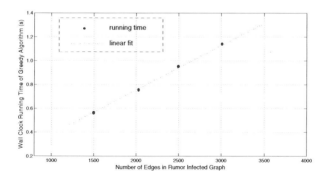

FIGURE 6.4 Wall-clock computation time (in seconds) by our greedy algorithm for increasingly larger infected graphs. $k = 2$. Each point is an average of 10 runs.

to employ minimum SRS for identifying the set of rumor sources from which the rest of nodes in the graph can be distinguished correctly. In this framework, the inference is based only on knowledge of the infected monitors and the underlying network structure. We have designed a highly efficient greedy algorithm using submodularity analysis and theoretically proved the performance ratio to be $1 + \ln\left(|\mathcal{F}| \log_2 \gamma\right)$, given that γ is the maximum number of equivalence classes divided by one node-pair.

Several improvements and future directions are possible. One direction is to extend our methodology to different applications, including influence maximization, rumor blocking etc. and see how the proposed methodology leads to deeper insights. Another promising direction is to tackle the MRSD problem in different diffusion models, such as models with transmission probabilities between nodes considered or models without submodularity property.

6.4 RUMOR DETECTION: MACHINE LEARNING BASED APPROACH

Rumor is often viewed as an unverified account or explanation of events circulating from person to person and pertaining to an object, event, or issue in public concern. DiFonzo and Bordia emphasise the need to differentiate rumors from similar phenomena such as gossip and urban legends. They define rumors as unverified and instrumentally relevant information statements in circulation that arise in contexts of ambiguity, danger or potential threat and that function to help people make sense and manage risk.

Bordia et al. [16] propose that transmission of rumor is probably reflective of a "collective explanation process". Since there is often not enough resource to manually identify rumors or misinformation from the huge volume of fast evolving data, it has become a critical problem to design systems that can automatically detect misinformation and disinformation. Current media environment is suitable to the emergence and propagation of rumors that are not limited to insignificant subjects: rumors can have major consequences on political, strategic or economical decisions. Increasingly, they are triggered off on purpose for various reasons: campaigns can be carried out in order to discredit a company, endanger strategic choices or question political decisions. Therefore research on rumor detection has great significance on Web security issues [39].

6.4.1 Natural Language Processing

Social network analysis about studying rumors often focus on machine learning techniques such as building classifiers, sentiment analysis, Twitter data mining and so on. Work in this area includes [27, 46, 23, 42]. Leskovec et al. use the evolution of quotes reproduced online to identify memes and track their spread overtime [27]. Ratkiewicz et al. [46] created the Truthy system, identifying misleading political memes on Twitter using tweet features, including hashtags, links and mentions. Other projects focus on highlighting disputed claims on the Internet using pattern matching techniques [23]. Qazvinian et al. [42] explore the effectiveness of three categories of features: content-based, network-based, and microblog-specific memes for correctly identifying rumors in microblogs. In these introduced research work, a complete set of social conversations (e.g., tweets) that are actually about the rumor need to be retrieved first.

Sentiment classification is one of the many language processing techniques that are developed in this area, however, more sophisticated techniques such as speech-act classification and the quantification of formality and sophistication of the language used in tweets are also developed. There has been extensive research done on speech act (also known as dialogue act) classification in computational linguistics, e.g., [32, 24]. There are two major annotated corpora used for speech act annotation which all of the research listed use. The Switchboard-DAMSL [20] or SWBD, and the Meeting Recorder Dialog Act [43] or MRDA. SWBD provides an annotation scheme for labelling dialog or speech acts from phone conversations. It also contains labelled speech act data collected from telephone conversations. Similarly, the MRDA corpus provides an annotation scheme and labelled speech act data for face-to-face meetings with multiple parties.

Unfortunately, these annotation schemes and annotated datasets do not map well to Twitter, given the noisy and unconventional nature of the language used on the platform. As far as we know, there is no publicly available dataset of labelled speech acts for Twitter. Zhang et al. proposed supervised [44] and semi-supervised [45] speech act classification. However, they limit their features to a set of words, n-gram phrases and symbols and do not take into account the rich syntactic structure of the tweets in their classification.

Recent advances in Twitter parsers and part-of-speech taggers have made it possible to extract the syntactic structure of tweets with relative ease, without having to normalize the texts as was suggested by Kaufmann and Kalita [26]. In [52], they utilized new tools to create a set of novel syntactic and semantic features. These features are used to train a supervised speech act classifier, using a manually annotated dataset of a few thousand tweets. This combined set of semantic and syntactic features help to achieve state-of-the-art performance for Twitter speech-act classification.

6.4.2 Towards Information Credibility

There have appeared some recent studies on analyzing rumors and information credibility on Twitter. Castillo et al. [17] focus on automatically assessing the credibility of a given set of tweets. They analyze the collected microblogs that are related to "trending topics", and use a supervised learning method (decision tree) to classify them as credible or not credible. Qazvinian et al. [42] focus on two tasks: the first task is classifying those rumor-related tweets that match the regular expression of the keyword query used to collect tweets on

Twitter monitor. The second task is analyzing the users' believing behavior about those rumor-related tweets. They build different Bayesian classifiers on various subsets of features and then learn a linear function of these classifiers for retrieval of those two sets. Mendoza et al. [34] use tweets to analyze the behavior of Twitter users under bombshell events such as the Chile earthquake in 2010. They analyze users' retweeting topology network and find the difference in the rumor diffusion pattern on Twitter environment and on traditional news platforms.

Semantic classification combined with propagation patterns. Wu et al [25] study the problem of automatic detection of false rumors on Sina Weibo, the popular Chinese microblogging social network. One key insight is that most false rumors can be identified not only by what the false rumor says, but also by the way people respond to it and who these people are. The propagation patterns, combined with the topics of the thread and the sentiment of the responses, can give strong indications whether the original message is the truth or fiction. In this chapter, a graph-kernel based hybrid SVM classifier is proposed which captures the high-order propagation patterns in addition to semantic features such as topics and sentiments. The new model achieves a classification accuracy of 91.3% on randomly selected Weibo dataset.

Deception detection for online news. Chen et al [18] analyze two types of problematic news practice in modern journalism. First, headline/body dissonance: both headlines present the story as fact, while the article bodies simply report (unverified) claims. Second, questioning headlines: using a question as a headline creates the impression that the claim is credible, though it may not be true. As the Internet continues to break down barriers to content creation and dissemination, the line between user generated content and traditional media content has become increasingly blurred. When information is decontextualized from its source, alternative methods are required to verify and judge the trustworthiness of news reporting.

As an important development at an intersection of library and information science (LIS), natural language processing (NLP), big data and journalism, fake news detection (of the three identified types) holds promise in automated news verification and online content credibility assessment. Rubin et al. [47] separate the task of fake news detection into three, by type of fake: (a) serious fabrications (uncovered in mainstream or participant media, yellow press or tabloids); (b) large-scale hoaxes; (c) humorous fakes (news satire, parody, game shows). Serious fabricated news may take substantial efforts to collect case by case. Journalistic fraudsters may face harsh consequences for dishonest reporting, and are likely to exhibit cues of deception akin to verbal leakages in other contexts (such as law enforcement or CMC). Large-scale hoaxing attacks are creative, unique, and often multi-platform, which may require methods beyond text analytics (e.g., network analysis). Humorous news provides a steady stream of data, but their writers' intentions to entertain, mock, and be absurd may interfere with binary text classification techniques, especially if algorithms pick up cues of believability, sensationalism, or humor instead of cues for deception.

Claim check in presidential debates. Hassan et al [38] present a supervised learning based approach to automatically detect check-worthy factual claims from presidential debate transcripts. They construct a labeled dataset of spoken sentences by presidential candidates during 2004, 2008 and 2012 presidential debates. Each sentence is given one of three possible labels: it is not a factual claim; it is an unimportant factual claim; it is an important factual claim. They train and test several multiclass classification models using several supervised learning methods, including Multinomial Naive Bayes Classifier (NBC), Support Vector Classifier (SVM) and Random Forest Classifier (RFC)on the labeled dataset. Preliminary experiment results show that the models achieved 85% precision and 65% recall in classifying check-worthy factual claims.

Real-time Rumor Debunking on Twitter. In 2015, Liu et al. [53] propose the first real time rumor debunking algorithm for Twitter. They concentrate on identification of a rumor as an event that may comprise of one or more conflicting microblogs. They use beliefs of the crowd, along with traditional investigative journalism features on top of language, user, propagation and other meta features. They show that it can beat baseline methods and even professionals by a significant margin even when as little as five tweets about an event are available.

6.5 CONCLUSION

This chapter contains three parts: first, we give a concise overview of most important theoretical results and algorithms on rumor propagation mechanisms on large social networks, which helps us to understand why rumor spreads so fast in online social networks.

Second, after understanding rumor diffusion process, we discuss how to find the source of a rumor spreading with limited information of network structure and the rumor infected nodes, which is an important and challenging research problem in networks. In specific, we develop an efficient set resolving set based algorithm to detect multiple rumor sources from a deterministic point of view. This is the first work providing explicit approximation ratio for the algorithm solving minimum set resolving set. The introduced framework suggests a robust approach for multiple rumor source detection independent of diffusion models in networks.

Thirdly, we describe machine learning based methodology to detect and verify rumors, false claims, negative news etc in social media automatically, which has profound meaning in practical field. The problems we focus on are central in diverse areas: from presidential elections to commercial marketing, from modern journalism to cyber security, from computer science to social science. Our emphasis is on theoretical analysis behind each topic, and guidelines for the practitioner.

Bibliography

[1] *http://www.pcworld.com/article/163920/swine-flu-twitter.*

[2] *http://www.theguardian.com/news/blog/2011/jul/04/fox-news-hacked-twitter-obama-dead.*

[3] A. M. Frieze A. D. Flaxman and J. Vera. Adversarial deletion in a scale-free random graph process. *Comb., Probab. and Comput.*, 16:261–270, 2007.

[4] D. Eckles A. Friggeri, LA Adamic and J. Cheng. Rumor Cascades. *AAAI Conference on Weblogs and Social Media (ICWSM)*, 2014.

[5] C. Hauser W. Irish J. Larson S. Shenker H. E. Sturgis D. C. Swinehart A. J. Demers, D. H. Greene and D. B. Terry. Epidemic algorithms for replicated database maintenance. *Operating Systems Review*, 22:8–32, 1988.

[6] H. Ohta A. Y. Lokhov, M. Mezard and L. Zdeborova. Inferring the origin of an epidemy with dynamic message-passing algorithm. *arXiv preprint arXiv:1303.5315*, 2013.

[7] L. A. Adamic, O. Buyukkokten, and E. Adar. A social network caught in the web. *First Monday*, 8:6, 2003.

[8] A. Agaskar and Y. M. Lu. A fast monte carlo algorithm for source localization on graphs. *SPIE Optical Engineering and Applications*, 2013.

[9] R. Albert, H. Jeong, and A.L. Barabasi. The diameter of the world wide web. *Nature*, 401:130, 1999.

[10] J. Spencer B. Bollobas, O. Riordan and G. Tusnady. The degree sequence of a scalefree random graph process. *Random Structures and Algorithms*, 18:279–290, 2001.

[11] M. Fouz B. Doer and T. Friedrich. Why rumors spread so quickly in social networks. *ACM*, 55:70–75, 2012.

[12] A.-L. Barabasi and R. Albert. Emergence of scaling in random networks. *Science*, 286:509–512, 1999.

[13] P. Beaumont. The truth about twitter, facebook and the uprisings in the arab world, feb 2011. *http://www.theguardian.com/world/2011/feb/25/twitter-facebook-uprisings-arab-libya.*

[14] P. Berman, B. DasGupta, and M. Kao. Tight approximability results for test set problems in bioinformatics. *Journal of Computer and System Sciences*, 71:145–162, 2005.

[15] B. Bollobas and O. Riordan. The diameter of a scale-free random graph. *Combinatorica*, 24:5–34, 2004.

[16] P. Bordia and N. DiFonzo. Problem solving in social interactions on the internet: Rumor as social cognition. *Social Psychology Quarterly*, 67(1):33–49, 2004.

[17] C. Castillo, M. Mendoza, and B. Poblete. Information credibility on twitter. *WWW*, pages 675–684, 2011.

[18] Conroy N. J. Chen, Y. and V. L. Rubin. News in an Online World: The Need for an Automatic Crap Detector. *The Proceedings of the Association for Information Science and Technology Annual Meeting (ASIST2015), Nov. 6-10, St. Louis*, 2015.

[19] Lattanzi S. Chierichetti, F. and Panconesi A. Rumor Spreading in Social Networks. *LNCS*, 5556:375–386, 2009.

[20] E. Shriberg D. Jurafsky and D. Biasca. Switchboard swbd-damsl shallowdiscourse-function annotation coders manual. *Institute of Cognitive Science Technical Report*, pages 97–102, 1997.

[21] W. Dong, W. Zhang, and C. W. Tan. Rooting out the rumor culprit from suspectss. *IEEE Int. Symp. Information Theory (ISIT)*, pages 2671–2675, 2013.

[22] D.-Z. Du, K.-I Ko, and X. Hu. *Design and Analysis of Approximation Algorithms*. Springer, New York, 2012.

[23] R. Ennals, D. Byler, J. M. Agosta, and B. Rosario. What is disputed on the web? *Proceedings of the 4th Workshop on Information Credibility (WICOW)*, pages 67–74, 2010.

[24] Y. Liu J. Ang and E. Shriberg. Automatic dialog act segmentation and classification in multiparty meetings. *ICASSP*, 1:1061–1064, 2005.

[25] S. Yang K. Wu and K. Q. Zhu. False rumors detection on sina weibo by propagation structures. *IEEE International Conference on Data Engineering, ICDE*, 2015.

[26] M. Kaufmann and J. Kalita. Syntactic normalization of twitter messages. *International Conference on Natural Language Processing*, Kharagpur, India, 2010.

[27] J. Leskovec, L. Backstrom, and J. Kleinberg. Meme-tracking and the dynamics of the news cycle. *Proceedings of the 15th ACM SIGKDD International Conference on Knowledge Discovery and Data Mining (KDD)*, pages 497–506, 2009.

[28] W. Luo and W. P. Tay. Identifying multiple infection sources in a network. *Proc. Asilomar Conf. Signals, Systems and Computers*, 2012.

[29] W. Luo and W. P. Tay. Estimating infection sources in a network with incomplete observations. *Proc. IEEE Global Conference on Signal and Information Processing (GlobalSIP)*, pages 301–304, 2013.

[30] W. Luo and W. P. Tay. Finding an infection source under the sis model. *IEEE Int. Conf. Acoustics, Speech, and Signal Processing (ICASSP)*, 2013.

[31] W. Luo, W. P. Tay, and M. Leng. Identifying infection sources and regions in large networks. *IEEE Trans. Signal Process*, 61:2850–2865, 2012.

[32] C.-Y. Lin M. Jeong and G. G. Lee. Semi-supervised speech act recognition in emails and forums. *Proceedings of the 2009 Conference on Empirical Methods in Natural Language Processing*, 3:1250–1259, 2009.

[33] C. Papadimitriou M. Mihail and A. Saberi. On certain connectivity properties of the internet topology. *J. Comput. Syst. Sci.*, 72:239–251, 2006.

[34] M. Mendoza, B. Poblete, and C. Castillo. Twitter under crisis: can we trust what we rt? *Proceedings of the First Workshop on Social Media Analytics (SOMA)*, pages 71–79, 2010.

[35] S. Milgram. The small world problem. *Psychology Today*, 2(60), 1967.

[36] J. T. Chayes N. Berger, C. Borgs and A. Saberi. On the spread of viruses on the internet. *16th ACM-SIAM Symposium on Discrete Algorithms (SODA)*, pages 301–310, 2005.

[37] K. Panagiotou N. Fountoulakis and T. Sauerwald. Ultra-fast rumor spreading in social networks. *23rd Annual ACM-SIAM Symposium on Discrete Algorithms (SODA)*, pages 1642–1660, 2012.

[38] C. Li N. Hassan and M. Tremayne. Detecting check-worthy factual claims in presidential debates. *CIKM*, 2015.

[39] F. Nel, M. J. Lesot, P. Capet, and T. Delavallade. Rumour detection and monitoring in open source intelligence: understanding publishing behaviours as a prerequisite. *Proceedings of the Terrorism and New Media Conference*, 2010.

[40] P. C. Pinto, P. Thiran, and M. Vetterli. Locating the source of diffusion in large-scale networks. *Phys. Rev. Lett.*, 109:068–702, 2012.

[41] B. A. Prakash, J. Vreeken, and C. Faloutsos. Spotting culprits in epidemics: How many and which ones? *IEEE Int. Conf. Data Mining (ICDM)*, pages 11–20, 2012.

[42] V. Qazvinian, E. Rosengren, D. R. Radev, and Q. Mei. Rumor has it: Identifying misinformation in microblogs. *Proceedings of the 2011 Conference on Empirical Methods in Natural Language Processing*, pages 1589–1599, 2011.

[43] H. Carvey R. Dhillon, S. Bhagat and E. Shriberg. Meeting recorder project: Dialog act labeling guide. *ICSI, Berkeley, CA, Tech. Rep.*, pages TR–04–002, 2004.

[44] D. Gao R. Zhang and W. Li. What are tweeters doing: Recognizing speech acts in twitter. *Analyzing Microtext*, 2011.

[45] D. Gao R. Zhang and W. Li. Towards scalable speech act recognition in twitter: tackling insufficient training data. *Proceedings of the Workshop on Semantic Analysis in Social Media*, pages 18–27, 2012.

[46] J. Ratkiewicz, M. Conover, M. Meiss, B. Goncalves, S. Patil, A. Flammini, and F. Menczer. Truthy: mapping the spread of astroturf in microblog streams. *Proceedings of the 20th International Conference Companion on WWW*, pages 249–252, 2011.

[47] Chen Y. Rubin, V. L. and N. Conroy. Deception Detection for News: Three Types of Fakes. *Proceedings of the Association for Information Science and Technology Annual Meeting (ASIST)*, 2015.

[48] B. Prabhakar S. P. Boyd, A. Ghosh and D. Shah. Randomized gossip algorithms. *IEEE Transactions on Information Theory*, 52:2508–2530, 2006.

[49] D. Shah and T. Zaman. Finding sources of computer viruses in networks: Theory and experiment. *Proc. ACM Sigmetrics*, 15:5249–5262, 2010.

[50] D. Shah and T. Zaman. Rumors in a network: Who's the culprit? *IEEE Transactions on Information Theory*, 57(8):5163–5181, 2011.

[51] D. Shah and T. Zaman. Rumor centrality: A universal source detector. *SIGMETRICS*, pages 199–210, 2012.

[52] S. Vosoughi. Automatic detection and verification of rumors on twitter. Ph.D. dissertation, Massachusetts Institute of Technology, 2015.

[53] Q. Li R. Fang X. Liu, A. Nourbakhsh and S. Shah. Real-time rumor debunking on twitter. *Proceedings of the 24th ACM International Conference on Information and Knowledge Management. ACM*, 2015.

[54] W. Xu and H. Chen. Scalable Rumor Source Detection under Independent Cascade Model in Online Social Networks. *IEEE the 11th International Conference on Mobile Ad-hoc and Sensor Networks*, pages 236–242, 2015.

[55] G. Yiran and M. Fanrong. Rumor spreading in the online social network: A case of a Renren account. *Third International Conference on Digital Manufacturing and Automation, ICDMA, China*, pages 751–754, 2012.

[56] W. Wu Z. Zhang, W. Xu and D.-Z. Du. A novel approach for detecting multiple rumor sources in networks with partial observations. *Journal of Combinatorial Optimization*, pages 1–15, 2015.

[57] K. Zhu and L. Ying. Information source detection in the sir model: A sample path based approach. *Information Theory and Applications Workshop (ITA)*, pages 1–9, 2013.

[58] K. Zhu and L. Ying. A robust information source estimator with sparse observations. *Computational Social Networks*, 1:3–23, 2014.

IV

Applications

CHAPTER 7

A Survey on Multilayer Networks and the Applications

Huiyuan Zhang, Huiling Zhang and My T. Thai

CONTENTS

N ETWORK theory is one of the most fundamental and important sciences to help us discover and analyze existing complex systems such as social network, smart grid, biological networks and so on. In the past decades, research on networks has exploded in a wide range of areas. However, up until recently, most of research attention was given to an individual network in which all interactions are conducted in a single layer network, while neglecting that entities interact with each other can encompass multiple networks, and the interactions can also diffuse from one network to another. To better understand such complex systems, it is necessary to generalize traditional network system to a more complicated system in which multiple layers are taken into account.

In this survey, a comprehensive review on multiple network systems will be given in order to improve our understanding of the complicated patterns, relationships and dynamics through each layer. We discuss a general formulation for multiple networks, and list wildly used multiple layer networks and how to generalize monoplex network to multiple layer network. With above information, we review recent works of how to model the dynamics and represent it in multiple networks as well as synchronize the diffusion process in each layer. We also survey a variety of applications such as community structure, cascading failures and connected components. An outlook and future direction is also given at the end of this survey.

7.1 INTRODUCTION

Network science is a fundamental tool for studying and investigating complex systems in a wide range of areas, such as computer networks, biological networks, social networks and telecommunication networks. One of the most widely used approaches is to take an abstraction of the complex system, in which every system entity is considered as a *node* (or vertex), and the iteration/relationship among entities is modeled as a *edge* (or link). Although this kind of abstraction is simple, main infrastructure and key information of the

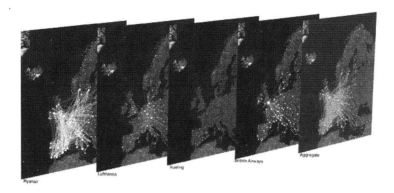

FIGURE 7.1 Multiple layer network embedded in geographical regions. This is the networks of European airports, where each layer represents an airline for the first four layers, and the last layer is the aggregate network [1].

system could be reserved for further analysis, and thus this approach has been using in almost every scientific research area.

The last decade has witnessed the burst development in information science, and more and more scientists paid their attention to *big data*, with the goals of finding the ultimate representation to model the dynamics and explaining what we have observed in such system. As previous complex network research has mostly conducted, each system unit is characterized into a network node, and unit-unit interaction or relationship is represented by a single edge. However, this kind of simple representation is not able to fully capture the details or properly model some real world scenarios, which leads to incorrect descriptions of some real world phenomena. For example, consider a social network system, where nodes of networks are a set of users, and links represent their social relationship. An initial attempt to model this system can treat each user account equally as a node, and friendship among users as links in a single network. But this kind of representation is far different from the real situation. Since real world users can participate in more than one social network such as Facebook, Twitter and Google+. More examples can be found in other areas, such as networks of European airports shown in Figure 7.1, where the geographical information has been embedded into multiple layer networks, in which each layer represents a different airline.

Therefore, it is essential to move forward and look into more complicated and general models beyond simple graphs and investigate into more complicated but realistic multilayer systems. To represent systems consisting of multiple networks, we introduce concept of *layer* into our picture. There are two approaches to generalize the traditional single layer network to multiple layer network: The first is to allow nodes to connect subset of edges from different layer of networks, such as multiplex networks [2, 3], independent networks [4], and multidimensional networks [5, 6]; Another way is letting edges connect more than two nodes, such as hypernetworks [7, 8, 9]. Representation of their structure can use the generalized graph theory based approach, tensor-decomposition methods [10, 11], singular value decomposition (SVD) [12]. Some other networks system cannot be represented as a traditional graph have been investigated from a data-mining perspective. For example, heterogeneous (information) networks [13] take into account multiple types of nodes and edges.

The success of new scientific areas can be assessed by their potential in contributing to new theoretical approaches and in applications to real-world problems. Complex networks have fared extremely well in both of these aspects, with their sound theoretical basis developed over the years and with a variety of applications [14]. The research and efforts devoted in multilayer networks have raised a great expectation, as they are more complex than traditional network representation and have the capability of depicting real-world systems with higher precision and dimensions. The applications of multilayer networks theory can be seen in social, scientific and technological, spatial, and economical networks.

In this survey, we review the recent literature on multilayer networks and present a general definition that can be used to represent most of the complicated systems. Additionally, we classify numerous multilayer network system according to their constraints and properties. We also survey the diffusion models in multilayer networks, and the dynamics processes on the underlying networks. Then list of applications of on multilayer network has been introduced. Finally, we conclude this survey and discuss future work.

7.2 NETWORK REPRESENTATION

In this section, we first present a general definition for multilayer networks, which can be used for most types of complex systems that consist of multiple layer networks. Then we review the existing literature and discuss several different kinds of multilayer networks and their representations. Then we also have discussions of the advantages and limitations regarding all mentioned representations.

A network can be represented by $G = (V, E)$, where V is the set of nodes, and $E \subset V \times V$ is the set of edges. Normally, an edge $(u, v) \in E$ links two nodes u and v (Edges in hypergraphs are allowed to link more than two nodes, we will discuss more in Section 7.2.3.7). And a node $u \in V$ can associate any subset of edges $\{(u, v)|v \in V\}$. If a node does not link to any edge, we call it an isolate node. The adjacency can be described in two aspects: a pair of nodes u and v connected by an edge (u, v) are said to be adjacent to each other; on the other hand, for two edges (u, v) and (w, v) that incident to the same node v are also said to be adjacent to each other.

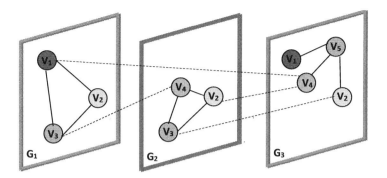

FIGURE 7.2 An example of a multilayer network.

To represent a complicated system which consists of multiple networks, we introduce a new concept *layer* into network structure. Let $\mathcal{G} = \{G_i\}_{i=1}^m$ denote a sequence of m layers(networks). Rather than consider it has m isolated networks, we take into account the connections across different layers, which is more meaningful for real-world applications as well as research interests.

7.2.1 General Representation

To construct the most general framework, we first extend the definition of node by allowing it to present in any subset of layers. That is, for a node $v \in V_M$, $\{v|v \in V_i, i = \alpha_1, \cdots \alpha_d\}$, V_i indicates the presence of node v in layer G_i. Thus edges can encompass pairwise connections among all possible combinations of nodes from different layers. For example, in Figure 7.2, node v_2 appears in all layers from G_1 to G_3. The connectivity can be extended through v_2 in $\mathcal{G}$ as v_2 connects to v_1 and v_3 in layer G_1, and connects to v_4 in G_2. Furthermore, v_2 is adjacent to v_5 in G_3. Thus, v_3 is known to be incident to all other nodes in V_M. In addition to nodes, we generalize edges by allowing two end points of one edge (u, v) to belong to different layers. For instance, for a node u, an multilayer network edge (u, v) can be defined as $\{(u, v)|v \in V_i, i = 1, \cdots, m\}$. In this way, we bring the interconnected edges which are across different layers in to picture, and those edges make the connectivity of this system more stronger.

Considering the sequence of layers $\{G_i\}_{i=1}^m$, we first construct a space by assembling all layers using a Cartesian product of $G_1 \times \cdots \times G_m$. Since a node can present in any subset of layers, for each presence of a node in one layer, we need to consider all combinations of nodes and layers, thus resulting $\mathcal{V} =\subseteq V_1 \times \cdots \times V_m$, which is called *node space*. An equivalent expression is $\mathcal{V} = V_M \times G_1 \times \cdots \times G_m$. And we can also obtain that $V_M \subseteq \mathcal{V}$. Therefore, a node v can be represented by $(v, \alpha_1, \cdots, \alpha_d)$, where α_i indicates the appearance.

Normally, an edge is linking two nodes, with the consideration of directions, we can treat the first node as the starting point and the second node is the ending point. Thus the edge set of a multilayer network is defined as a set of pairs of nodes from all possible combinations as $E_M \subseteq V_M \times V_M$.

For a multilayer networks $\mathcal{G} = (V_M, E_M)$, with $G_i = (V_i, E_i)$, it can be defined as

$$V_M = \bigcup_{i=1}^{m} V_i, E_M = \left(\bigcup_{i=1}^{m} E_i \right) \cup \left(\bigcup_{i \neq j}^{m} E_{ij} \right) \tag{7.1}$$

where the node set V_M is obtained by taking the unions of all nodes presented in each layer. And edge set is the union of inner connected links (where both endpoints belong to the same layer) and interconnected links (where two points of an edge belong to different layers.)

7.2.2 Adjacency Representation

The adjacent matrix representation for single layer networks is powerful since there are numerous theories, methods and approaches that have been developed and studied. Following above definition, for each network layer $G_k, k = 1, \cdots, m$, the adjacent matrix will be denoted by $A_k = (a_{ij}^k)$, and the set of nodes $V_k = \{v_1^k, \cdots, v_{|V_k|}^k\}$, where in a single layer network, A_{G_k} is defined as:

$$a_{ij}^k = \begin{cases} 1 & if (v_i, v_j) \in V_k \times V_k \\ 0 & otherwise. \end{cases}$$

for $1 \leq i, j \leq |V_k|$ and $1 \leq k \leq M$.

For inter connected edges, the matrix is defined as

$$a_{ij}^{pq} = \begin{cases} 1 & if (v_i^p, v_j^q) \in V_p \times V_q \\ 0 & otherwise. \end{cases}$$

To apply those research results to the study of multilayer networks, one easy approach is to represent the whole system with a supra-adjacency matrix. Such representation of multilayer networks have yielded some insights for investigating for information diffusion [15], epidemic spreading [16] and synchronizability [17]. In addition, supra-adjacency matrix representation is also convenient for studying walks, paths.

As illustrated in Figure 7.2, we can link different layers of networks through inter-connect edges of the same nodes, and then map all layers in the system into one super network, thus obtaining a corresponding supra-adjacent matrix [18, 15].

Given a multilayer network system G_M, the element in its supra-adjacent matrices A_G is defined as:

$$a_{ij} = \begin{cases} 1 & if a_{ij}^k = 1 \ for \ 1 \leq k \leq M \\ 0 & otherwise. \end{cases}$$

For the degree of node v on the aggregated topological network, we have

$$d(i) = \sum_j a_{ij}$$

And $\overline{A_G}$ can be written as a block matrix

$$\begin{pmatrix} A_{G_1} & I & \cdots & I \\ I & A_{G_2} & \cdots & I \\ \cdots & \cdots & \cdots & \cdots \\ I & I & I & A_{G_m} \end{pmatrix}$$

where A_{G_i} is the adjacent matrix of network G_i, and I is identity matrix.

Note that the behaviors of the whole network system G_M and the super network denoted by $\overline{G_M}$ may be different, since a single node in G_M has more than one corresponding node in $\overline{G_M}$. The reason is that in $\overline{G_M}$, the whole node set is the disjoint union of nodes in $G_1, G_2, \cdots, G_M$. Therefore, the properties and behavior of a multiplex G_M can be viewed as a type of non-linear quotient of the properties of $\overline{G_M}$.

7.2.3 Network Types

In this subsection, we present the basic structural notions for several types of widely studied multilayer networks as shown in Figure 7.3. We show how to demonstrate those complicated systems by using the above-mentioned formulations into multilayer networks. Most of the ways of representing these network structures as general multilayer networks only cover a subset of all of the possible multilayer networks, and these subsets can be characterized by the constraints that they satisfy or by the properties of their own constructions.

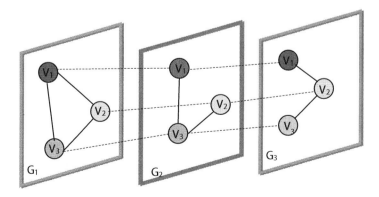

FIGURE 7.3 An example of a multilayer network.

7.2.3.1 Multiplex Network

A multiplex network [2, 3] $G_M = (V_M, E_M)$ with m layers is a set of layers networks $G_i, i \in \{1, 2, \cdots, m\}$, where each layer can be directed, undirected, weighted or unweighted graph. And all layers have exactly the same nodes. We can represent this network system as a multilayer network generalized definition as $V_1 = V_2 = \cdots = V_m$, and $E_{ij} = \{(v, v); v \in V_M\}$ for $1 \leq i \neq j \leq m$.

7.2.3.2 Independent Networks

In interdependent networks[4], nodes in two or more monoplex networks are adjacent to each other via edges which are called dependency edges. For example, consider a system consists of an electrical grid and a computer network as a pair of interdependent networks, and for the nodes in computer network which represent routers can depend on power stations in the power grid network. In practice, if there exist some nodes from one layer of the network depending on control nodes in a different layer, then the dependency will be the additional edges link nodes from different layers. And in this representation, the interconnection structure is called mesostructure [19]. Similarly to the previous case, we can consider an interdependent (or layered) network as a multilayer network by identifying each network with a layer.

7.2.3.3 Interconnected Networks

Interconnected or interacting networks [20] are a family of networks $\{G_1, G_2, ...G_k\}$ that interact with each other, they can be modeled as a multilayer system, in which the inter connection edges E_{ij} across layers corresponding to the iterations between two networks G_i and G_j. However, different from independent networks, edges that connect different networks do not need indicate dependency relations. Note that both of independent networks and interconnected networks are equivalent to *node-colored* networks [21], "color" here is more likely as label. In a node-colored network $G = (V_C, E_C, C, f)$, where V_C and E_C are the node and edge set and C is a set of possible colors, and $f : V_C \to C$ is a function that map color to each node.

7.2.3.4 Multidimensional Networks

Similar to the above introduced node-colored networks, a multidimensional network [5, 6] is a edge-labeled network $G = (V_D, E_D, D)$, where D is a set of labels representing the dimensions, and E_D is a set of labeled edges. For example, consider a triple tuple $(u, v, d) \in E_D$ where $u, v \in V_D$ and $d \in D$, which represents one edge in the network. It is assumed that given a pair of node and one particular label, there is only one such edge in the network. Thus, for each pair of nodes (u, v), there will be at most $|D| = d$ edges connect them. A multidimensional network $G = (V_D, E_D, D)$ can be modeled

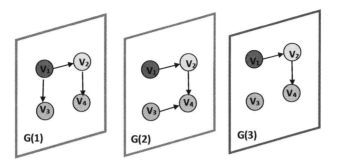

FIGURE 7.4 An example of temporal network.

as a multiplex network by mapping each label to a layer. In a multiplex network representation, it can be modeled as $\{G_1, G_2, ...G_{|D|}\}$, where for each $d \in D$, $G_d = (V_d, E_d)$, with $V_d = V$ and $E_d = \{(u,v) \in V \times V; (u,v,i) \in E, \text{ and } i = d\}$.

7.2.3.5 Multilevel Networks

A multilevel network [22] is a network $G = (V, E, S)$, where $S = \{S_1, S_2, ...S_m\}$ is a family of subgraphs $S_i = (V_i, E_i)$, $i = 1, 2...m$ of G such that

$$V = \bigcup_{j=1}^{m} V_j, E = \bigcup_{j=1}^{m} E_j$$

7.2.3.6 Temporal Networks

A temporal graph $G(t)$, $t = 1, \cdots, T$, can be viewed as multiple layers graph with each layer representing a snapshot of the graph in time t as shown in Figure 7.4. Notice that t is a discrete time step, not a continuous parameter. And $E_{\alpha\beta} = \emptyset$ if $\beta \neq \alpha + 1$, while

$$E_{\alpha,\alpha+1} = \{(e, e) | e \in E_\alpha \cap E_{\alpha+1}\}$$

7.2.3.7 Hypernetworks

All of the above introduced graphs have a common characteristic: edges in the graph connect exactly 2 nodes. A natural generalization of the framework leads us to the hypernetworks [7, 8, 9], where edges can connect more than 2 nodes as shown in Figure 7.5. For example, a node in layer i can be connected to any node in layer j. Then we obtain the definition of hypernetwork, given a pair $\mathcal{H} = (V, H)$, where V is the node set of cardinality larger than 1 and $H = \{H_1, H_2, \cdots, H_M\}$ is a family of non-empty subsets of V, each of them is called a hyperlink of $\mathcal{H}$.

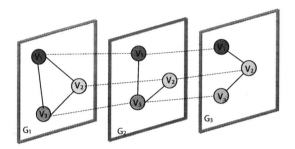

FIGURE 7.5 An example of Hypernetworks.

7.3 DYNAMICS IN MULTILAYER NETWORKS

One of the main reasons to study dynamical systems on networks is to improve the understanding of how connectivity affects dynamical processes on networks. This task can be very complicated, and especially when studying dynamics on multilayer networks. It is very important to develop a deep understanding of such dynamics as well as design strategies to achieve desired outcomes. It has been illustrated that dynamical processes that have been studied on single layer networks exhibit different behaviors in multilayer systems or by aggregating layers.

7.3.1 Diffusion Spreading in Multilayer Networks

Social media provides a platform for spreading diffusion such as social influence, cascading failures or epidemic diseases. So far, there has been considerable interest in studying diffusion behaviors for single layer networks. Since multiple layers can have much stronger connectivity of the underlying networks, they can also have important effects on dynamics spreading process. We will briefly talk about different types of the diffusion to give motivation of multilayer networks modeling. More detailed discussions will be provided in the application section.

Social Influence. Social influence is the change of behavior that is influenced by others through social iterations. Previously, interactions between people was limited to face-to-face communication. With the development of technology, online social networks (OSNs) have been treated as a new major communication medium for information sharing and discovery. Such engagement of online users fertilizes the land for information propagation to a degree which has never been achieved before. OSNs such as Facebook, Twitter and Google Plus+ have been growing steadily in the last decade. And two-thirds of online users are using social networks. There are over one billion active Facebook users, 200 million twitters and more than 40 million Google+ subscribers. With the effect of word-of-mouth, the influence could spread out all over OSNs. For example, a Facebook user, Mike, makes a post about a new movie that he just watched and this post will appear on his friends' walls. Very shortly, some of his friends comment on his post or forward this post and friends of Mike's friends may continue to propagate Mike's review of the movie. In this way, information posted by Mike passes to other Facebook users. Other examples could be Gangnam Style, a South Korean song released in July 2012, became the first video reaching 1 billion views on YouTube as of December 21, 2012. Within one year of its first release, it has been viewed more than 1.745 billion times.

Influence maximization (IM) [23] is one of the fundamental problems in the study of social influence. Since people are likely to be affected by decisions of their friends and colleagues, some researchers and marketers have investigated social influence and the word-of-mouth effect in promoting new products and designing profitable marketing strategies. Suppose that with the knowledge of individuals' preference and their influence on each other, and we would like to promote a new product that will be adopted by a large amount of users in this network. The strategy of viral marketing is to select a small number of influential members within this network at the beginning, and then by convincing them to adopt the new product and utilizing the social influence effect users advertise and recommend the product to their friends, we can trigger widespread adoptions.

Along with the fast development of all social networks, especially for OSNs, users are participating in more than one network. Recently, researchers have started to explore multiplex networks. Yagan [24] and Liu [25] studied the connection between offline and online networks. Shen [26] investigated propagation in multiplex online social networks with consideration of the interest and engagement of users. The authors combined all networks into one network by representing an overlapping user as a super node. Zhang et al. [27] studied the least cost influence maximization problem across multiple social networks.

Cascading Failures. One of the most attractive fields for studying the multilayer system is the independent system, where each layer of the network has its unique functionality, and nodes in one layer are independent of nodes in other layers. When two or more networks are independent, a failure occurring in one part of the network can propagate and affect dynamics of other layers. This leads to an iterative process of cascading failures, which reveals that the interdependent networks can be much more fragile than single layer networks.

Cascading failure [4, 28] is not uncommon in power grids. Electrical power grids have firstly attracted many researchers to study this problem. Each layer in an independent system has its own nature, for example in Figure 7.6, in which the independent system consists of a power network, a transportation network and a telecommunication network. When a node failure happens on v_1 in the power network, it triggers a cascading failure in transportation and telecommunication layers, which leads to more failed nodes.

The increased fragility of interdependent networks attracts many scientists to investigate it, and henceforth opens a lot of research questions. Among them, the most important one is how to design an optimal strategy to min-

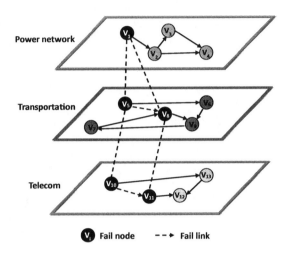

FIGURE 7.6 Cascade failure in independent networks.

imize the dramatic effect of cascading failures while increasing the network resilience to any random failures happening in the network. In the presence of the interdependency, [29] gives a way to estimate the robustness of independent networks by calculating the size of their *mutually connected giant components* (MCGC) when a random damage affects a fraction $1 - p$ of the nodes in the system. After the random damage occurs and propagates back and forth, the largest component remains in the system is called MCGC.

Spreading of Disease. The analysis of the spreading of diseases and the design of contention policies have capitalized most of the literature in the field of network science [30]. In addition, the study of the spreading of infectious diseases on top of networks also gives insight on other dynamical processes of interest, such as the information and misinformation spreading in social networks [31]. Thus, the recent interest in multilayer networks has provided a natural way to extend and improve our understanding of the basics of spreading dynamics in real world multilayer systems.

7.3.2 Diffusion Models in Multilayer Networks

One of the most general issues on complex systems is the study of transport process along with the underlying network typologies. These studies involve studying the dynamics and the flows of spreading process. Traditionally, researchers study the diffusion process by using diffusion models. Empirical studies of diffusion in social networks began in the middle of the twentieth century. Currently, there are a variety of diffusion models arising from the economics and sociology communities. The most popular models are Linear Threshold model and Independent Cascading model, which are widely used in studying the social influence problems. Besides those two well-known models, there are many variations and extensions reflecting more complicated real-world situations. In this subsection, we give an overview of the widely used models that characterize the transmission behavior.

It is traditional to study spreading processes using diffusion models. Usually, each node in the network is defined as a state, e.g., *activated* or *inactive* or *susceptible* and *infected*. In addition, each edge is associated with an edge weight represents some natural property like contact frequency, influence from on node to the other and so on. The nodes always have either continuous or discrete update rules that govern how the states change. Among all those existing diffusion models, there are three most widely-used models, which are known as Threshold models, Cascading models and epidemic model.

We begin with introducing the first topological based diffusion models, which are widely used diffusion models have been adopted by a lot of researchers. Formally, a network system is represented as a graph G, which can be either a directed or undirected graph according to its real application and network property. In graph G, each vertex $v \in V$ represents an individual user/entity. In a directed graph, an edge $(u, v) \in E$ represents u has an influence on v; in an undirected graph, an edge (u, v) represents mutual influence between u and v. Particularly, an undirected graph can be viewed as a directed graph by treating each edge as a bidirectional edge with the same influence on both direction. In addition, let $N(v)$ denote vs neighbors in an undirected graph, let $N^{in}(v)$ and $N^{out}(v)$ denote the sets of incoming neighbors (or in-neighbors) and outgoing neighbors (or out-neighbors), respectively.

7.3.2.1 Threshold Model

Threshold models are especially useful in a structural analysis of collective action, an approach that most rational theorists have avoided. Sudden changes in the level of production of a particular public good does not necessarily reflect similar changes in the overall preferences of the actors. What really matters is the distribution of thresholds and the social connections through which members could have chances to learn about the others.

Linear Threshold (LT) model has been extensively used in studying diffusion models among the generalizations of threshold models. In this model, each node v has a threshold θ_v, and for every $u \in N(v)$, (u, v) has a non-negative weight $w_{u,v}$ such that $\sum_{u \in N(v)} w_{u,v} \leq 1$. Given the thresholds and an initial set of active nodes, the process unfolds deterministically in discrete steps. At time t, an inactive node v becomes active if

$$\sum_{u \in N^a(v)} w_{u,v} \geq \theta_v$$

where $N^a(v)$ denotes the set of active neighbors of v. Every activated node remains active, and the process terminates if no more activation are possible. The threshold in this model is related to a linear constraint of edge weight, and hence get the name for the model. It is important to note that given the thresholds in advance, the diffusion process is deterministic, but we can still inject the randomness by randomizing the individual threshold. For example, the thresholds selected by Kempe et al. [23] are uniformly distributed over the interval [0,1], which intends to capture the lack of knowledge of their values.

The first attempt of generalizing the linear diffusion to multilayer networks is done by Gomez [32]. The time-continuous equations for the linear diffusion in a multiplex composed of M networked layers (each of them has one representation of each of the N nodes) are:

$$\frac{dx_i^\alpha}{dt} = D_\alpha \sum_{j=1}^{N} w_{ij}^\alpha (x_j^\alpha - x_j^\alpha) + \sum_{\beta=1}^{M} w_{\alpha\beta}^\alpha (x_j^\beta - x_j^\alpha) \qquad (7.2)$$

where $x_i^\alpha(t)$ ($i = 1, \cdots, N$ and $\alpha = 1, \cdots, M$) denotes the state of node i in layer α. Generally, the diffusion coefficients are different for each of the intralayer diffusive processes D_α with $\alpha = 1, \cdots, M$ and for each of the interlayer diffusion dynamics $D_{\alpha\beta}$ with $\alpha, \beta = 1, \cdots, M$. In Equation 7.2, the first term in the right side accounts for the intralayer diffusion, while the second one represents those interlayer processes. Being a multiplex, the latter ones take place between the replicas of a given node in each of the layers.

7.3.2.2 Cascading Model

Inspired by the work on interacting particle systems and probability theory, dynamic cascade models are considered for the diffusion process. In the cascade models, the dynamics is captured in a step-by-step fashion: at time t, when a node v first becomes active, it has a single chance to influence each previously inactive neighbor u at time $t + 1$. And it successfully turns u to be activated with a probability $p(u, v)$. In addition, if multiple neighbors of u become active at time t, their attempts to activate u are sequenced in an arbitrary order. If one of them say w succeeds in time t, then u becomes active in time $t + 1$; however, whether w succeeds or not, it cannot make any more attempts in the following time steps. Similar to the threshold models, the process terminates until no more new activation happens.

Each edge $(u, v) \in E$ is associated with an influence probability p_{uv}. When a node u becomes active, it gets a single chance to activate every currently inactive outgoing neighbor v, succeeding with a probability p_{uv}.

7.3.2.3 SIR Model

This model is one of the simplest and is favored by researchers who study disease spreading and information-spreading processes [33]. For many large-scale spreading processes, one important step toward making models more realistic is to study them on a large population structure instead of on a single network. In such a structure, each node is a completely mixed population that is adjacent to other populations via the edges in a network. Epidemic processes on networks of networks (e.g., interconnected networks, node-colored networks, etc.) are natural extensions of completely mixed meta population models. Several authors have studied an SIR model on two-layer networks. For example, focal ideas have included the correlations of the intra-layer degrees of nodes that are adjacent across layers, the strength of coupling (i.e., the number of inter-layer edges) between the two networks, and the identification of influential spreaders by computing k-shells.

7.3.3   Network Aggregation and Synchronization

An intuitive way to examine systems with multiplexity is to construct a monoplex network by aggregating data from the different layers of a multiplex network and then study the resulting monoplex network. One way to construct an aggregated network (which is also known as a superposition network, overlapping network, or overlay network) is to define edge weights between two nodes in the resulting monoplex network as a linear combination of the weights between those same nodes from each of the layers.

However, simply taking the linear combination to construct the monplex network may fail to reverse necessary information from the individual networks. Given above mentioned popular diffusion models, Dung et al.[27] proposed several network aggregation schemes which can better keep the topological information as well as node and edge properties.

Clique Lossless Aggregation Scheme In LT-model, the first issue is solved by introducing dummy nodes for each user u in networks that it does not belong to. These dummy nodes are isolated. Now the vertex set V^i of ith network can be represented by $V^i = \{u_1^i, u_2^i, \ldots, u_n^i\}$ where $U = \{u_1, u_2, \ldots, u_n\}$ is the set of all users. u_p^i is called the *representative vertex* of u_p in network G^i. In the new representation, there is an edge from u_p^i to u_q^i if u_p and u_q are connected in G^i. Now we can union all k networks to form a new network G. The approach to overcome the second challenge is to allow nodes $u^1, u^2, \ldots, u^k$ of a user u to influence each other, i.e. adding edge (u^i, u^j) with weight $\theta(u^j)$. When u^i is influenced, u^j is also influenced in the next time step as they are actually a single overlapping user u, thus the information is transferred from network G^i to G^j. But an emerged problem is that the information is delayed when it is transferred between two networks. Right after being activated, u^i will influence its neighbors while u^j needs one more time step before it starts to influence its neighbors. It would be better if both u^i and u^j start to influence their neighbors in the same time. For this reason, new *gateway vertex* u^0 is added to G such that both u^i and u^j can only influence other vertices through u^0. In particular, all edges (u^i, v^i) $((u^j, z^j))$ will be replaced by edges (u^0, v^i) $((u^0, z^j))$. In addition, more edges are added between u^0, u^i, and u^j to let them influence each other, since the connection between gateway and representative vertices of the same user forms a clique, so we call it clique lossless coupling scheme. A simple example of the clique lossless coupling scheme is

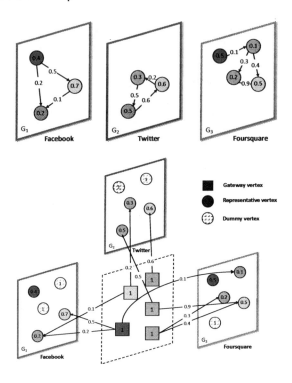

FIGURE 7.7 An example of the *clique lossless coupling scheme.* An instance of multiplex networks with 4 users. Each user is represented by vertices of the same color with different thresholds in different networks, e.g., green user has thresholds of 0.3 and 0.2 in G^2 and G^3. The influence of gateway vertices on represenative vertices represent the influence between users in multiplex networks. (See color ebook.)

illustrated in Figure 7.7. After forming the topology of the coupled network, we assign edge weights and vertex thresholds as following:

Vertex thresholds. All dummy vertices and gateway vertices have the threshold of 1. Any remaining representative vertex u_p^i has the same threshold as u_p in G^i, i.e., $\theta(u_p^i) = \theta^i(u_p)$.

Edge weights. If there is an edge between user u and v in G^i, then the edge (u^0, v^i) has weight $w(u^0, v^i) = w^i(u, v)$. The edges between gateway and representative vertices of the same user u are assigned as $w(u^i, u^j) = \theta(u^j)$, $\forall \ 0 \le i, j \le k, i \ne j$ to synchronize their state together.

Star Lossless Aggregation Scheme. Note that the large volume of extra edges is due to the direct synchronization between each pair of representative vertices of u in *clique lossless coupling scheme,* so we can reduce it by using indirect synchronization. In the new coupling scheme, we create one intermediate vertex u^{k+1} with threshold $\theta(u^{k+1}) = 1$ and let the active

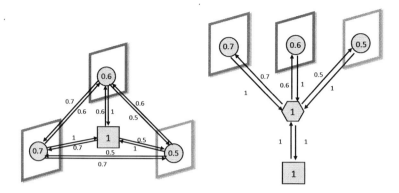

FIGURE 7.8 Synchronization of *Clique and star lossless coupling scheme.* The connection between gateway and representative vertices of the same user.

state propagate from any vertex in $u^1, u^2, \ldots, u^k$ via this vertex. Specifically, the synchronization edges are established as follows: $w(u^i, u^{k+1}) = 1$ and $w(u^{k+1}, u^i) = \theta(u^i)\ 1 \leq i \leq k$; $w(u^{k+1}, u^0) = w(u^0, u^{k+1}) = 1$. The synchronization strategy of *star lossless coupling scheme* is illustrated in Figure 7.8. Now, the number of extra edge for each user is $2(k+1)$ and the size of the coupled network is reduced as shown in the following proposition.

Although those two aggregation schemes can better preserve the valuable information about an inherently multilayer system, they generate considerable redundant edges and nodes, which leads to increasing the running time of their solutions. Thereby, if the time complexity of the solution comes in the first priority, lots of other aggregation schemes may choose to dismiss some information.

Extensions to other diffusion models. In this section, we show that we can design lossless coupling schemes for some other well-known diffusion models in each component network. As a result, the most influential users can be identified under these diffusion models. We are particularly interested in two well-known stochastic diffusion models, namely, Stochastic Threshold and Independent Cascading models [23].

- *Stochastic Threshold model.* This model is similar to the Linear Threshold model but the threshold $\theta^i(u^i)$ of each node u^i of G^i is a random variable in the range $[0, \Theta^i(u^i)]$. Node u^i will be influenced when $\sum_{v^i \in N_{u^i}^-, v \in A} w^i(v^i, u^i) \geq \theta^i(u^i)$

- *Independent Cascading model.* In this model, there are only edge weights representing the influence between users. Once node u^i of G^i is influenced, it has a single chance to influence its neighbor $v^i \in N^+(u^i)$ with probability $w^i(u^i, v^i)$.

For both models, we use the same approach of using gateway vertices, representative vertices and the synchronization edges between gateway vertices and their representative vertices. The weight of edge (u^i, u^j), $0 \leq i \neq j \leq k$ will be $\Theta(u^j)$ for Stochastic Threshold model and 1 for Independent Cascading model. Once u^i is influenced, u^j will be influenced with probability 1 in the next time step. The proof for the equivalence of the coupling scheme is similar to ones for LT-model.

7.4 NETWORK STRUCTURE AND MEASUREMENTS

Given a complex system, knowing the role of a node, an edge or component of a graph is of great importance, thus identifying the critical nodes is one of the fundamental problems in studying network structures. Among all existing results, node degree and betweenness are widely used centrality measurements. In this section, we discuss the apply of those measurements from monoplex network to complex network system.

7.4.1 Node Degree

The degree of node is the most common measurement of a node, which is denoted by $d(v)$ for any node v in the single layer network, which represents the number of links adjacent to this node. In multilayer networks $\mathcal{G} = \{G_i\}_{i=1}^m$, the degree of a node $u \in V_M$ is defined as a vector:

$$d(u) = (d(u)^1, \cdots, d(u)^m),$$

where $d(u)^i, i = 1, \cdots, m$ is the degree of node u in the layer i. Since most of the centrality measurements is used for obtaining a ranked list in order to further study their roles in terms of the structural importance. Although this vector type definition is a natural extension of node degree in the multilayer network, it can not help producing a ranked list of all nodes accordingly. One possible way is to use a aggregated node degree [34] defined as below:

$$\overline{d(u)} = \sum_{i=1}^m d(u)^i$$

7.4.2 Betweenness

Betweenness is originally introduced as a centrality measure which quantifies the importance of a vertex relative to other vertices in a graph. For a node u, the *betweenness centrality* $b(u)$ is defined as:

$$b(u) = \sum_{s \neq t} \frac{\delta_{st}(u)}{\delta_{st}}$$

where δ_{st} is the number of shortest paths going from s to t and $\delta_{st}(i)$ is the number of shortest paths going from s to t through the node i. Vertices with a higher betweenness than others are more important in the graph. However, for a lattice, the betweenness centrality is maximal at the barycenter of all nodes and we thus expect for real networks an interesting interplay between the degree of the node and its distance to the barycenter [35].

In a complex network system, taking into account that the shortest paths might not be able to obtained. Instead a search algorithm is used for navigation, the betweenness is defined in terms of the probability of it being visited by the search algorithm. This generalization, which is proposed based on random walks by Newman in [36].

7.4.3 Clustering and Transitivity

Multilayer networks are essentially characterized by a small set of parameters in which the clustering coefficient is an important quantity that gives information about local clustering. Networks are often clustered by nature, and degree distribution, where high-degree nodes are suppressed by long-distance costs [37]. This observation underlines the need for appropriate metrics for the analysis and modeling of networks where constraints play an important role [38]. For a node i of degree k_i, its clustering coefficient is defined as

$$c(i) = \frac{E_i}{k_i(k_i - 1)/2}$$

where E_i is the number of edges among the neighbors of i. In weighted representation of a spatial network, where the edges are differentiated by their relative importance, or weight, rather than an indication of their presence or absence, the *weighted clustering coefficient* is expressed rather differently as in [39]:

$$c^w(i) = \frac{1}{s_i^w(k_i - 1)} \sum_{j,h} \frac{w_{ij} + w_{ih}}{2} a_{ij} a_{ih} a_{jh}$$

where $s_i^w(k_i - 1)$ is a normalization factor, and a_{ij} value comes from adjacency matrix. This coefficient is a measure of the local cohesiveness that takes into account the importance of the clustered structure on the basis of the amount of traffic or interaction intensity actually found on the local triplets.

7.4.4 Walks and Paths

The metric structure of a multilayer network is related to the topological distance between nodes, written in terms of walks and paths in the graph. So, in order to extend the classical metric concepts to the context of multilayer networks, it is necessary to establish first the notions of path, walk and length.

Given a multilayer network $\mathcal{G} = \{G\}_{i=1}^m$, a *walk* is defined as a non-empty sequence of length $q - 1$ as $\{v_1^{\alpha_1}, e_1, v_2^{\alpha_2} e_2, \cdots, v_q^{\alpha_q} e_q, \}$ of nodes and edges, with $\alpha_1, \cdots, \alpha_q \in \{1, 2, \cdots, m\}$ and $e_1, \cdots, e_q \in E_M$. If there exists $v_i^{\alpha_i} = v_j^{\alpha_j}$

where $i \neq j$, this walk is said to be *closed*. If the edges are weighted, the length of the walk is defined as the sum of the inverse of the corresponding weights.

A *path* $\{v_1^{\alpha_1}, v_2^{\alpha_2}, \cdots, v_q^{\alpha_q}\}$ between two nodes $v_1^{\alpha_1}$ and $v_q^{\alpha_q}$ is a walk through the nodes in $\mathcal{M}$ in which each node is visited only once. A *cycle* is a closed path starting and ending at the same node. If it is possible to find a path between any pair of its nodes, a multilayer network $\mathcal{M}$ is said to be connected; otherwise it is called disconnected. However, different types of reachability may be considered in multilayers network systems. The length of a path is usually defined as the number of edges in the path. However, taking into account the connection in multilayer networks, we have two kinds of edges, one is inter-layer edge and the other is intra-layer edge. Thus, the definition of path length will be changed according the practical meaning to determine the equivalence of those two type of edges.

7.4.5 Matrices and Spectral Properties

Adjacency matrices and their spectral properties play an important role which is directly related to a number of dynamical processes in a multilayer network environment. Given a multilayer network $\mathcal{G}$, we could define the following adjacency matrices: the adjacency matrix $A^{[\alpha]}$ of each layer G_α, the adjacency matrix $\overline{A_\mathcal{G}}$ of the projection network $\text{proj}(\mathcal{G})$ and the supra-adjacency matrix $A_\mathcal{G}$.

Using some results from interlacing on eigenvalues of quotients of matrices, it was proven that if $\lambda_1 \leq \cdots < \lambda_N$ is the spectrum of the supra-adjacency matrix $A_\mathcal{G}$ of an undirected multilayer network and $\mu_1 \leq \cdots < \mu_{n_\alpha}$ is the spectrum of the adjacency matrix $A^{[\alpha]}$ of layer G_α, then for every $1 \leq k \leq n_\alpha$, we have

$$\lambda_k \leq \mu_k \leq \lambda_{k+N-n_\alpha} \tag{7.3}$$

The spectral properties of Laplacian matrices of a network also provides insights into its structure and dynamics. The Laplacian matrix $\mathcal{L}_G = \mathcal{L}$ (also called supra-Laplacian matrix) of a multiplex $\mathcal{G}$ is defined as the $MN \times MN$ matrix of the form:

$$\mathcal{L} = \begin{pmatrix} D_1 L^1 & \cdots & 0 \\ 0 & \cdots & 0 \\ \cdots & \cdots & \cdots \\ 0 & 0 & D_M L^M \end{pmatrix} \tag{7.4}$$
$$+ \begin{pmatrix} \sum_\beta D_{1\beta} I & \cdots & -D_{1M} I \\ -D_{21} I & \cdots & -D_{2M} I \\ \cdots & \cdots & \cdots \\ -D_{M1} I & \cdots & \sum_\beta D_{N\beta} I \end{pmatrix}$$

In the above equation, $L^\alpha, 1 \leq \alpha \leq M$ is the usual $N \times N$ Laplacian matrix of the network layer α with elements $L_{ij} = s_i^\alpha \delta_{ij} - w_{ij}^\alpha$ where s_i^α is the strength of node i in layer α, $s_i^\alpha = \sum_j w_{ij}^\alpha$. I represents the $N \times N$ identity matrix and D is the diagonal matrix. In [40], the authors proved that the diffusion dynamics is strongly related to spectral properties of $\mathcal{L}$. More specifically, if $\lambda_1 \leq \cdots \leq \lambda_N$ is the spectrum of the Laplacian matrix $\mathcal{L}$ of an undirected multilayer network and $\mu_1 \leq \cdots < \mu_{n_\alpha}$ is the spectrum of the laplacian matrix L^α of layer G_α, then for every $1 \leq k \leq n_\alpha$

$$\mu_k \leq \lambda_{k+N-n_\alpha}$$

7.5 APPLICATIONS

The success of new scientific areas can be assessed by their potential in contributing to new theoretical approaches and in applications to real-world problems. Multilayer networks have fared extremely well in both aspects, with their sound theoretical basis developed over the years and with a variety of applications. The research efforts devoted in multilayer networks have raised a great expectation, as they are more complex than traditional network representation and have the capability of depicting real-world systems with higher precision and dimensions.

Nevertheless, this section provides a comprehensive review of the applications of multilayer networks, and discusses how they have been applied to real data to obtain useful insights. The applications of multilayer networks theory is organized into four main categories: social, scientific and technological, transportation, and economical networks.

7.5.1 Social Networks

The idea of studying the way social interactions develop on multiple layers dates back to the 1970s. The first written contribution of such approaches was probably introduced by Erving Goffman in 1974, along with the theory of *frame analysis* [41]. According to this research method, any communication between individuals (or organizations) is constructed (or *framed*) in order to maximize the probability of being interpreted in a particular manner by the receiver. Such framing may differ according to the type of relations between the involved individuals, several of them potentially overlapping in a single communication: thus, the output of multiple framings can be interpreted as a multilayer structure.

The needs of understanding social impacts and relations increase in the following years motivated by a series of problems. To name but a few, Simon proposed a model of generating highly skewed distribution functions in [42], the famous small-world effect, came into being from Milgram's social experiments [43], the careful analysis on multilayer social structure by Greiger and Pattison [44], a quantitative analysis of multilayer social networks is performed by [45]. The motivation for understanding "social networks" increased in the following years, especially with analysis of empirical data. However, the collected data are subjected to criticism because of bias in data, disunity and location dependent. Benefited by the World Wide Web popularity, tools like blogs, photoblogs, emails, and social network sites are more widespread, promising a large amount of data samples with less biased features. In the following sections, we will focus on describing the contributions on social networks between human and non-human relationships.

7.5.2 Computer Science Networks

Computer science is a relatively recent area. While its fundamental topics involve computer architecture, data storage and processing, and system control, it has become essential for developments in a variety of areas. Complex network theory has been considered for boundary shape analysis and image processing. The shape boundary characterization approach models a shape into a small-world network and use degree and joint degree measurements to extract the shape signature or descriptor which is able to characterize the shape boundary [46]. Costa [47] suggested an image segmentation approach where an image was mapped into a network. To obtain segmented objects, a community identification method was applied.

7.5.3 Transportation Networks

In airline networks, airports are considered as nodes, and flights connecting different airports represent edges. In addition, different networks usually interconnect with each other, thus a multilayer approach is a natural choice. Recently, there have been two papers that try to address the multimodal problem in transportation networks. The first paper [48] proposes a two-layer structure by merging the world wide port and airport networks. The goal is to study the global robustness against random attacks. Inspired by previous works [49], a similarity between the layers is assessed by means of two metrics, i.e., the inter degree-degree correlation and the interclustering coefficient. The simulations results reveal that as the networks become more intersimilar, the system becomes significantly more robust to random failure, as one network is able to back-up the other network as per need.

The road networks and railway networks deserve special attention in our daily life since they directly influence our travel times and costs. Over the past years, we have witnessed a huge increase of the number of vehicles and trains, which resulted in more traffic and sometimes jams as the capacity of the network is reached. In the second publication [50], the authors study the Indian air and railway transportation networks. In railway networks, the nodes are represented by stations and the edges indicate railway connections. The paper uses a multilayer structure to model both networks, where the pairs of nodes belonging to different layers. From the analysis, it is indicated that the heterogeneity of the two networks leads to a good performance of the global network in terms of navigability. This is because the airport network is small and presents a scale-free structure while the rail network is much larger with a topology constrained by geography.

As for studies of the individual transportation networks, a multilayer structure is often used to model different aspects of the transportation process or by taking into account of different service providers.

7.5.4 Power Grids

The power grid is an electric power transmissions system, which is one of the most complex human-made networks. It comprises transmission lines and substations, which include generators, transmission substations, and load centers which deliver the electricity to consumers [51]. The first studies in the power transmission systems relied on creating simple dynamical models [52, 53]. These models simulate each component of the network to understand the blackout dynamics of the whole system. When one transmission line or station failed, the power flow burdens are shared by the other lines and stations. However, new failures may happen due to overflow, leading to a cascading effect. During the analysis of the topology of these networks, it was shown that the removal of highly connected nodes can lead to blackouts of certain regions of the networks [54, 55]. Overall, the power transmission systems are of high clustering coefficient and the degree distribution in an exponential form.

7.5.5 Economical Networks

In a broad sense, economical networks include trade networks, currency, wealth, and organizational networks.

The International Trade Network (ITN) is defined as the graph of all import/export relationships between world countries. Traditional network studies have considered the ITN at the aggregate level, in which an edge represents a presence of a trade relationship irrespective of the commodity. In recent years, the introduction of the multilayer network concept has enabled more precise studies based on the import and export relationships for a given commodity, or merchandise class. The models introduced in [56] consider the network of 97 layers with presence of 162 countries from 1992 to 2003. In these works, the topological metrics between different layers have been studied and it is indicated that commodity-specific communities have a degree of granularity which is lost in the aggregate approach.

The authors in [57] build a model to investigate the effects of network topology on the evolution of a dynamic process. It is specifically designed for wealth distribution to display the small-world effect. Their results indicate that the wealth distribution depends on the probability of rewiring edges and fraction of rewiring edges. A similar study was performed by [58] using an

TABLE 7.1   Different networks and applications

Network Category	Social	Scientific	Spatial	Economical
Multiplex Net	✓	✓	✓	✓
Independent Net	✓			✓
Interconnected Net	✓		✓	
Multidimensional Net	✓			✓
Multilevel Net	✓	✓		✓
Temporal Net		✓		✓
Hypernetworks		✓	✓	

additive stochastic process. They have shown that the shape of the wealth distribution was defined by the degree distribution of the network used.

Finally, it is worthwhile to provide a summary of applications of multilayer networks with respect to application field, network category, and model type. Please refer to Table 7.1 for more details.

7.6   CONCLUSIONS

The study of multilayer networks and of frameworks like multiplex networks and interconnected networks in particular has drawn a lot of attention recently. Most real and engineering systems include multiple subsystems and layers of connectivity, and the demand for a deep understanding of multilayer systems necessitates generalizing "traditional" network theory. Ignoring such information can yield misleading results, so new schemes and solutions are needed to be designed. One future research direction is to have better models and diagnostics of the diffusion processes, in which we may see interesting phenomenon that may only happen in multilayer networks. Moreover, the increasing availability of empirical data for fundamentally multilayer systems makes it possible to develop and validate the proposed general frameworks for the study of networks.

In the present chapter, we discussed the history of research on multilayer networks and related frameworks, and we reviewed the recent work in this area. Numerous similar ideas have been developed in parallel, for instance, a very wealth of ideas generated in subjects like sociology and biology, which we have not covered much in this chapter since our focus in mainly on the social influence and engineering aspect.

We presented a general framework for studying multilayer networks and constructed a dictionary of terminology to relate the numerous existing notions to each other. We then provided a thorough discussion to compare, contrast, and translate between related notions such as multilayer networks, multiplex networks, interdependent networks, networks of networks, and many others. We also introduce two aggregation schemes to couple several individual networks into a monoplex network, where most of the valuable information can be preserved as much as possible. In addition, some generalized approaches of network aggregations have been also covered. Then, we reviewed attempts at generalizing single-layer network diagnostics, methods, models, and dynamical systems to multilayer settings. An important theme that has developed in the literature is the importance of multiplexity-induced correlations. For example, such correlations can have significant effects on the speed of transmission of diseases and ideas as well as on the robustness of systems to failure. We expect to see many more available and interesting multilayer data sets in the near future, which can better help scholars to develop new theories, methods, and diagnostics for gaining insight into multilayer networks. The study of multilayer networks is very exciting, and we look forward to what the next several years will bring.

Bibliography

[1] Manlio De Domenico, Mason A Porter, and Alex Arenas. Muxviz: a tool for multilayer analysis and visualization of networks. *Journal of Complex Networks*, page cnu038, 2014.

[2] Jesus Gomez-Gardenes, Irene Reinares, Alex Arenas, and Luis Mario Florja. Evolution of cooperation in multiplex networks. *Scientific reports*, 2, 2012.

[3] Zhaofeng Li and Yichuan Jiang. Cross-layers cascade in multiplex networks. In *AAMAS*, pages 269–276, 2014.

[4] Zhen Chen, Wen-Bo Du, Xian-Bin Cao, and Xing-Lian Zhou. Cascading failure of interdependent networks with different coupling preference under targeted attack. *Chaos, Solitons & Fractals*, 80:7–12, 2015.

[5] Michele Berlingerio, Michele Coscia, Fosca Giannotti, Anna Monreale, and Dino Pedreschi. Foundations of multidimensional network analysis. In *ASONAM*, pages 485–489, 2011.

[6] Michele Coscia. *Multidimensional network analysis*. PhD thesis, Ph. D. thesis, Universita Degli Studi Di Pisa, Dipartimento di Informatica, 2012.

[7] Regino Criado, Miguel Romance, and M Vela-Perez. Hyperstructures, a new approach to complex systems. *International Journal of Bifurcation and Chaos*, 20(03):877–883, 2010.

[8] Claude Berge. *Hypergraphs: Combinatorics of Finite Sets*. Elsevier Science Publishers, North-Holland, Amsterdam, volume 45. 1984.

[9] JA Rodrjguez. On the laplacian spectrum and walk-regular hypergraphs. *Linear and Multilinear Algebra*, 51(3):285–297, 2003.

[10] Daniel M Dunlavy, Tamara G Kolda, and W Philip Kegelmeyer. Multilinear algebra for analyzing data with multiple linkages. *Graph Algorithms in the Language of Linear Algebra*, pages 85–114, 2011.

[11] Tamara G Kolda and Brett W Bader. Tensor decompositions and applications. *SIAM Review*, 51(3):455–500, 2009.

[12] Carla D Martin and Mason A Porter. The extraordinary svd. *The American Mathematical Monthly*, 119(10):838–851, 2012.

[13] Deng Cai, Zheng Shao, Xiaofei He, Xifeng Yan, and Jiawei Han. Community mining from multi-relational networks. In *PKDD*, pages 445–452. 2005.

[14] Luciano da Fontoura Costa, Osvaldo N Oliveira Jr, Gonzalo Travieso, Francisco Aparecido Rodrigues, Paulino Ribeiro Villas Boas, Lucas Antiqueira, Matheus Palhares Viana, and Luis Enrique Correa Rocha. Analyzing and modeling real-world phenomena with complex networks: a survey of applications. *Advances in Physics*, 60(3):329–412, 2011.

[15] Sergio Gomez, Albert Diaz-Guilera, Jesus Gomez-Gardenes, Conrad J Perez-Vicente, Yamir Moreno, and Alex Arenas. Diffusion dynamics on multiplex networks. *Physical Review Letters*, 110(2):028701, 2013.

[16] Faryad Darabi Sahneh, Caterina Scoglio, and Fahmida N Chowdhury. Effect of coupling on the epidemic threshold in interconnected complex networks: A spectral analysis. In *ACC, 2013*, pages 2307–2312, 2013.

[17] Albert Sole-Ribalta, Manlio De Domenico, Nikos E Kouvaris, Albert Diaz-Guilera, Sergio Gomez, and Alex Arenas. Spectral properties of the laplacian of multiplex networks. *Physical Review E*, 88(3):032807, 2013.

[18] Emanuele Cozzo, Mikko Kivelä, Manlio De Domenico, Albert Sole, Alex Arenas, Sergio Gomez, Mason A Porter, and Yamir Moreno. Clustering coefficients in multiplex networks. *arXiv preprint arXiv:1307.6780*, 2013.

[19] Adam J Meuler, Marc A Hillmyer, and Frank S Bates. Ordered network mesostructures in block polymer materials. *Macromolecules*, 42(19):7221–7250, 2009.

[20] Jonathan F Donges, H CH Schultz, Norbert Marwan, Yong Zou, and Juergen Kurths. Investigating the topology of interacting networks. *The European Physical Journal B-Condensed Matter and Complex Systems*, 84(4):635–651, 2011.

[21] Alexei Vazquez. Spreading dynamics on heterogeneous populations: multitype network approach. *Physical Review E*, 74(6):066114, 2006.

[22] Jeffrey A Davis and James D Meindl. Compact distributed rlc interconnect models-part ii: Coupled line transient expressions and peak crosstalk in multilevel networks. *Electron Devices, IEEE Transactions on*, 47(11):2078–2087, 2000.

[23] David Kempe, Jon Kleinberg, and Eva Tardos. Maximizing the spread of influence through a social network. In *Proceedings of the Ninth ACM SIGKDD International Conference on Knowledge Discovery and Data Mining*, pages 137–146, 2003.

[24] Osman Yağan, Dajun Qian, Junshan Zhang, and Douglas Cochran. Information diffusion in overlaying social-physical networks. In *Information Sciences and Systems (CISS), 2012 46th Annual Conference on*, pages 1–6, 2012.

[25] Xingjie Liu, Qi He, Yuanyuan Tian, Wang-Chien Lee, John McPherson, and Jiawei Han. Event-based social networks: linking the online and offline social worlds. In *KDD*, pages 1032–1040, 2012.

[26] Yilin Shen, Thang N Dinh, Huiyuan Zhang, and My T Thai. Interest-matching information propagation in multiple online social networks. In *CIKM*, pages 1824–1828, 2012.

[27] Huiyuan Zhang, Dung T Nguyen, Soham Das, Huiling Zhang, and My T Thai. Least cost influence maximization across multiple social networks, 24(2), pages 929-939, 2015.

[28] Huiling Zhang, Yilin Shen, and My T Thai. Robustness of power-law networks: its assessment and optimization. *Journal of Combinatorial Optimization*, pages 1–25, 2015.

[29] Sergey V Buldyrev, Roni Parshani, Gerald Paul, H Eugene Stanley, and Shlomo Havlin. Catastrophic cascade of failures in interdependent networks. *Nature*, 464(7291):1025–1028, 2010.

[30] Alexander V Goltsev, Sergey N Dorogovtsev, JG Oliveira, and Jose FF Mendes. Localization and spreading of diseases in complex networks. *Physical Review Letters*, 109(12):128702, 2012.

[31] Huiling Zhang, Md Abdul Alim, My T Thai, and Hien T Nguyen. Monitor placement to timely detect misinformation in online social networks. In *ICC*, pages 1152–1157, 2015.

[32] Sergio Gomez, Albert Diaz-Guilera, Jesus Gomez-Gardenes, Conrad J Perez-Vicente, Yamir Moreno, and Alex Arenas. Diffusion dynamics on multiplex networks. *Physical Review Letters*, 110(2):028701, 2013.

[33] Yubo Wang and Gaoxi Xiao. Effects of interconnections on epidemics in network of networks. In *WiCOM*, pages 1–4, 2011.

[34] Federico Battiston, Vincenzo Nicosia, and Vito Latora. Structural measures for multiplex networks. *Physical Review E*, 89(3):032804, 2014.

[35] Marc Barthelemy. Spatial networks. *Physics Reports*, 499(1):1–101, 2011.

[36] Mark EJ Newman. A measure of betweenness centrality based on random walks. *Social Networks*, 27(1):39–54, 2005.

[37] P. Expert, T. Evans, V. Blondel, R. Lambiotte, and K. Wachter. Uncovering space-independent communities in spatial networks. In *Proceedings of the National Academy of Sciences of the United States of America*, volume 108, pages 7663–7668. 2011.

[38] K. Kosmidis, S. Havlin, and A. Bunde. Structural properties of spatially embedded networks. In *Europhys Lett*, volume 82. 2008.

[39] A. Barrat, M. Barthelemy, R. Pastor-Satorras, and A. Vespignani. The architecture of complex weighted networks. In *Proc Natl Acad Sci*, volume 101, pages 3747–3752. 2004.

[40] Ruben J Sanchez-Garcja, Emanuele Cozzo, and Yamir Moreno. Dimensionality reduction and spectral properties of multilayer networks. *Physical Review E*, 89(5):052815, 2014.

[41] Erving Goffman. *Frame Analysis: An Essay on the Organization of Experience*. Harvard University Press, Cambridge, MA, 1974.

[42] Herbert A Simon. On a class of skew distribution functions. *Biometrika*, 42(3/4):425–440, 1955.

[43] Linton C Freeman. Centrality in social networks conceptual clarification. *Social Networks*, 1(3):215–239, 1978.

[44] Ronald L Breiger and Philippa E Pattison. Cumulated social roles: The duality of persons and their algebras. *Social Networks*, 8(3):215–256, 1986.

[45] Jae Dong Noh and Heiko Rieger. Stability of shortest paths in complex networks with random edge weights. *Physical Review E*, 66(6):066127, 2002.

[46] Luciano da Fontoura Costa. Complex networks, simple vision. *arXiv preprint cond-mat/0403346*, 2004.

[47] Andre Ricardo Backes, Dalcimar Casanova, and Odemir Martinez Bruno. A complex network-based approach for boundary shape analysis. *Pattern Recognition*, 42(1):54–67, 2009.

[48] Roni Parshani, Celine Rozenblat, Daniele Ietri, Cesar Ducruet, and Shlomo Havlin. Inter-similarity between coupled networks. *EPL (Europhysics Letters)*, 92(6):68002, 2011.

[49] Sergey V Buldyrev, Roni Parshani, Gerald Paul, H Eugene Stanley, and Shlomo Havlin. Catastrophic cascade of failures in interdependent networks. *Nature*, 464(7291):1025–1028, 2010.

[50] Arda Halu, Satyam Mukherjee, and Ginestra Bianconi. Emergence of overlap in ensembles of spatial multiplexes and statistical mechanics of spatial interacting network ensembles. *Physical Review E*, 89(1):012806, 2014.

[51] Reka Albert, Istvan Albert, and Gary L Nakarado. Structural vulnerability of the north american power grid. *Physical Review E*, 69(2):025103, 2004.

[52] Ian Dobson, B Carreras, V Lynch, and D Newman. An initial model for complex dynamics in electric power system blackouts. In *hicss*, page 2017, 2001.

[53] B Carreras, V Lynch, M Sachtjen, Ian Dobson, and D Newman. Modeling blackout dynamics in power transmission networks with simple structure. In *hicss*, page 2018, 2001.

[54] Adilson E Motter and Ying-Cheng Lai. Cascade-based attacks on complex networks. *Physical Review E*, 66(6):065102, 2002.

[55] Paolo Crucitti, Vito Latora, and Massimo Marchiori. Model for cascading failures in complex networks. *Physical Review E*, 69(4):045104, 2004.

[56] Matteo Barigozzi, Giorgio Fagiolo, and Diego Garlaschelli. Multinetwork of international trade: A commodity-specific analysis. *Physical Review E*, 81(4):046104, 2010.

[57] Wataru Souma, Yoshi Fujiwara, and Hideaki Aoyama. Small-world effects in wealth distribution. *arXiv preprint cond-mat/0108482*, 2001.

[58] T Di Matteo, T Aste, and ST Hyde. Exchanges in complex networks: income and wealth distributions. *arXiv preprint cond-mat/0310544*, 2003.

CHAPTER 8

Exploring Legislative Networks in a Multiparty System

Jose Manuel Magallanes

CONTENTS

A MULTIPARTY SYSTEM is a particular setting where social network analysis has much to offer, especially in my case, the National Congress of Peru, where much of what is known on legislative networks is based on two-party systems in developed countries. This work is particularly interesting as the Peruvian National Congress is a multiparty representative body with a low rate of re-election, which lives within a weak party system, and interacts with a strong executive branch that makes balance of power difficult to achieve. In a situation like this, I assume legislators need adaptive strategies to prolong their political career. I will try to identify these strategies from the relations legislators establish with their pairs when co-sponsoring bills. The results show that co-sponsoring is an effective way to detect party-switching legislators, identify the variability of party discipline along the legislation sessions, but it is a weak proxy to identify reelection strategies, which may require the inclusion of exogenous factors.

This work particularly deals with technical issues of data collection as accessibility and organization of the legislative data; the importance of theory behind social and political data analysis; and with the possibility of bringing up sound insights not easily discovered without the power and flexibility of network, or graph, theory.

8.1 INTRODUCTION

Peru has a multi-party system with several political parties competing in legislative elections according to a party-list proportional representation system. As a consequence, it is rare for any single political organization to obtain an absolute majority in the Congress of Peru. Overall, Peru's political party system is weak as compared to a very powerful executive branch. There is also a very low rate of re-election; therefore, legislators interested in a long-lasting political career in Congress have to develop adaptive strategies to get re-elected.

It is assumed that one endogenous strategy followed by successful legislators is the establishment of good connections as a way to stay alive in politics, so it would be good to find out more about how this networking pattern differentiates them from the unsuccessful ones (the ones who were not re-elected). I can abstract all these connections as a network of legislators, where the relative position each one has and achieves is not done randomly but strategically during their mandate. As there are many possible networks, I will rely, in this work, on a co-sponsorship network. In such a network, links represent one legislator's support to another one's proposal. The co-sponsorship data was gathered for the National Congress of Peru in the years 2006-2011.

This work is organized into four sections. The first presents the scenario in which this Congress existed; The second presents a review of the literature related to legislative networks; the third presents the construction and analysis of the network; and finally, I present some conclusions and reflections.

8.2 BACKGROUND

8.2.1 Political Scenario

Peru could be considered a country with a democracy not yet fully institutionalized, where the highest constitutional powers (Legislative, Judiciary and Executive branches) do not have a clear balance among them yet; even though many tools are present in the Peruvian Constitution to promote a better balance among them. Nevertheless, making those tools effective would need, among other ingredients, an effective party system, which does not yet exist.

Figure 8.1 clearly shows that some parties merged, some had constant presence, and some disappeared since 1980, the year that democracy was restored after 11 years of military government. That situation reinforces my interest in political relationships, as it is not easy for legislators in one Congress to be part of the next one.

Party in Congress	1980	1985	1990	1992	1995	2000	2001	2006	2011
Partido Aprista Peruano	■	■	■	■	■	■	■	■	■
Acción Popular	■		■		■	■	■		
Frente Nacional de Trabajadores y Campesinos	■		■			■			
Unidad de Izquierda	■	■							
Unidad de Izquierda Revolucionaria	■								
Unidad Democrática Popular	■								
Frente Obrero, Campesino y Estudiantil	■								
Partido Revolucionario de los Trabajadores	■								
Partido Popular Cristiano	■			■					
Solidaridad Nacional						■	■		■
Unidad Nacional							■	■	
Izquierda Unida		■	■						
Convergencia Democrática			■						
Frente Independiente Moralizador			■	■	■	■	■	■	
Cambio 90			■						
Izquierda Socialista			■						
Acuerdo Popular			■						
Frente Democrático			■						
Frente Tacneñista			■						
Movimiento Regionalista Loretano			■						
Renovación Nacional				■	■				
Cambio 90-Nueva Mayoría				■	■				
Coordinadora Democrática				■					
Movimiento Democrático de Izquierda				■					
Frente Popular Agrícola del Perú					■	■			
Convergencia Democrática - País Posible					■	■			
Movimiento Cívico Nacional Obras					■				
Movimiento Independiente Agrario					■				
Perú Posible						■	■	■	
Unión por el Perú						■	■	■	■
Partido Democrático Somos Perú						■	■		
Perú 2000						■			
Avancemos						■			
Renacimiento Andino							■		
Solución Popular							■		
Todos por la Victoria							■		
Frente de Centro								■	
Restauración Nacional								■	
Alianza por el Futuro								■	
Alianza por el Gran Cambio									■
Fuerza 2011									■
Gana Perú									■

FIGURE 8.1 Parties in Congress since 1980.

That situation has given rise to a set of concepts that are the focus of discussion every time the congress is analyzed, namely:

1. Legislators's uncertainty on their political future in their party of origin: Renomination is difficult inside the party, as most parties need to reregister when they had low proportions of votes, which leads to changing party names, opting for electoral alliances, and more recently to inviting "independent" popular figures. The situation is particularly worse for the governing party that loses the next election.

2. Legislators's uncertainty of their followers: In the last two elections (2006 and 2011), newly elected legislators comprised 80% of the Congress, and re-elected legislators only comprised about 10%. Since the 2001 election, the governing party has only achieved at most 20% of the seats it had previously obtained.

3. Lack of party discipline: Most new and/or minority parties have no discipline when voting [10], suggesting that for each important bill proposal, the cost of convincing individual legislators to vote in a certain way is rather high.

4. Party splitting: In this multiparty system, the winning party in the executive branch rarely has the absolute majority in Congress, so minorities play an interesting role. In this case, minority parties, and sometimes the opposition party, split, giving birth to new political groups inside Congress that negotiate their support directly with other political actors within or outside Congress.

5. Party switching: Instead of splitting and forming a group, one legislator can move from one party to another. For the election of 2011, 13 legislators presented for re-election in different parties than they had originally been elected to Congress in; nine of them were from Lima (the capital of Peru which has 30% of the seats in Congress). However, only one of these 13 was re-elected.

8.2.2 Institutional Conditions

The Peruvian National Congress is a unicameral body in charge of the representative, legislative and political control power in Peru. Currently, the Congress consists of 130 members who are elected for a consecutive five-year period, with unlimited possibilities to be re-elected. To be eligible, candidates must be Peruvian citizens, must be older than 25 years old, and must not have their political rights suspended. A legislator has no restrictions to be re-elected, while the President of the Executive is forbidden for immediate re-election. Congress and Presidential elections are always done simultaneously.

In Peru, there is reapportionment but no redistricting. The Congress represents 25 Electoral Districts and the number of its eligible voters determines the number of congressional seats for each district, and a political party needs to win a minimum of five seats in two electoral districts or 4% of nationwide valid votes in order to be represented in Congress.

8.2.3   The 2006-2011 Congress

The National Congress of Peru (NCP) consisted of 120 members during the period of analysis, elected for a five-year period. The 2006 National Elections had 2 election rounds because to be elected President the winner needs more than 50% of votes and no candidate achieved that; however, the NCP legislators were elected in the first round. After the second round, Alan Garca from Partido Aprista Peruano (PAP) won the election with 52.62% to Ollanta Humala from Union por el Peru (UPP) who got 47.38%. No party got the absolute majority in Congress. Besides, 93 out of the 120 were first timers (77%); the party of the President got second in the congress, and his challenger's party in the second round, UPP, got the relative majority in Congress, declaring themselves the opposition. The total result is summarized in Table 8.1.

TABLE 8.1   Results from 2006-2011 election for Congress

Parties	National Votes (%)	Seats
Union por el Peru (UPP)	21.154	45
Partido Aprista Peruano (PAP)	20.586	36
Unidad Nacional (UN)	15.331	17
Alianza por el Futuro (AF)	13.095	13
Frente del Centro (FC)	7.07	5
Peru Posible (PP)	4.105	2
Restauracion Nacional (RN)	4.019	2
Alianza Para el Progreso	2.31	0
Frente Independiente Moralizador	1.455	0
Fuerza Democratica	1.427	0
Justicia Nacional	1.406	0
Partido Socialista	1.248	0
Movimiento Nueva Izquierda	1.238	0
Avanza Pais	1.141	0
Concertacin Descentralista	0.854	0
Frente Popular Agricola del Peru	0.791	0
Renacimiento Andino	0.702	0
Con Fuerza Peru	0.664	0
Peru Ahora	0.432	0
Reconstruccion Democratica	0.268	0
Proyecto Pais	0.2	0
Resurgimiento Peruano	0.191	0
Y se llama Peru	0.185	0
Progresemos Peru	0.13	0

In this situation the governing party, PAP, needed to develop some strategies to ensure governability during its presidential term. The PAP is a long established party, and the only one with high party discipline [10]; so, it was not expected that it could lose members to other parties. PAP needed to get the support from the minority parties, from some legislators of the opposition party or hope that the latter splits, so that the opposition would weaken.

Fortunately, PAP had many tools on its favor. As the Political Constitution of Peru gives no power to Congress to propose public spending or investment, the executive branch has many mechanisms to capture the attention of legislators who may have made electoral promises that were in fact out of their reach, thus creating fertile ground for pork barrel politics and party switching [21].

8.3   CO-SPONSORSHIP AS A NETWORK

It is clearly difficult to find a social activity that can not be represented as a network. In politics, and particularly inside the Congress, there are many ways one could identify a set of relationships that resemble a network, but not every network can serve my purposes in this case, as we need to encounter a valid relationship of strategic networking that is less affected by confounding factors. For instance, co-partisan relationships can be abstracted using voting on roll-calls; however, confounding factors such a gate-keeping authority, log-roll, and selection biases in the type of legislative initiatives that reach the plenary floor may prevent voting from being a sincere reflection of their own preferences; other option with big data could seek to use joint media appearances and mentions in blogs or any other social media using tool like Google Correlate (www.google.com/trends/correlate), but, even though that is very possible in the United States, it may not have the same validity in countries like Peru where these activities are not only just beginning, but also biased due to Internet penetration, thus limiting the representativeness of the findings. Another interesting option supported in the current literature could be membership to congressional caucuses[20], a sub grouping of legislator in US Congress with shared affinities who team-up to advocate and lobby on issues of mutual interest. However, the caucusing is neither a common practice in Peru nor a widespread institution in the world.

In this situation, a more common and accepted ground for research are co-sponsorship networks, where the bill proposed represents the link and the legislators, presenting and supporting the bill, represent the nodes. Co-sponsorship has begun being analyzed from a social network approach with the tools of computational social science by political scientists. Fowler [5] examines co-sponsorship from 1973 to 2004 in the U.S. Congress concluding that well-connected legislators are more successful at amending legislation and gaining support in floor votes. Gross [7] uses a multi-level approach to analyze co-sponsorship and finds that similarity in ideology, origin of the legislator, and previous collaboration in a committee are significantly associated with co-sponsorship. This principle, 'the homophily principle', structures network ties related to work, advice, support, information transfer, exchange, co-membership, and others. In particular, Bratton and Rouse [3] use network analysis including exponential random graph (ERGM) statistical modeling to pay close attention to different patterns that may explain the co-sponsoring. They found that co-sponsoring reflects a combination of homophily, social identity, and legislative roles proposing that more senior legislators are less likely to co-sponsor the measures introduced by relatively junior members. However, it is worth noticing that all of these studies, and some others [11, 22] have been done considering the party system and legislative institutions in the United States, which is a technical advantage as the Thomas database in the Library of Congress has these data ready to download (http://thomas.loc.gov/home/thomas.php). Having institutions that curate data are important for the growth of big data and network applications. However, that is not the case in many developing countries outside the United States. While few American scholar have been doing interesting research following the hypotheses from the US environment in countries like Argentina and Chile [1], the Congress of Peru lacks a mechanism to make data accessible and lacks procedures to structure the data in a way that could be easily explored and analysed.

As there are diverse interests in the use of co-sponsorship networks, there may be many conflicting opinions as to what the network can say. However, what remains as a mutual agreement, is the fact that these networks carry information one needs so decipher, and that the legislators participating in them are purposive actors whose intentions one needs to uncover. In the next section, I will go in a different direction not yet untouched, seeking to decipher whether co-sponsoring can inform about party-splitting and party switching, and whether I can uncover in the network some individual strategies to get re-elected.

8.4   BILL CO-SPONSORSHIP AND SOCIAL NETWORK ANALYSIS

This section represents the core analytics of this work. I will present the different steps followed to organize the data and look for answers to my research goals.

8.4.1   Organizing the Data

The data for this study was not available for downloading and the National Congress offers no API or related service to get the data. However, in the "law proposals" site (www.congreso.gob.pe/proyectosdeley) anyone can browse each proposal. In this situation, I needed a detailed exploration of the structure of the web pages where each proposal resides, in order to write the scrapping code and make sure I got every proposal. Thus, the general strategy comprised finding a URL that could lead me to every law; recover every field available for each proposal, paying close attention to the HTML structure.

TABLE 8.2   Association rule related to re-election

Rule Found	Support	Confidence	Lift
$Degree_{2006-II}$=medium, $Closeness_{2007-I}$=medium, $Degree_{2009-I}$=medium	0.156	0.842	1.676
$EI\ Seniority_{2007-II}$=medium, $EI\ Seniority_{2009-I}$=medium, $Closeness_{2006-II}$=low	0.151	0.816	1.624
$EI\ Position_{2009-I}$=medium, $Degree_{2006-II}$=medium, $Degree_{2009-I}$=medium	0.161	0.805	1.602
$EI\ Seniority_{2006-II}$=medium, $Degree_{2006-II}$=medium, $Degree_{2009-I}$=medium	0.161	0.805	1.602

In these circumstances, I first explored the contents of the page source and to find the pattern of the links to each bill, and then use each entry to get the data. All 3687 proposals were collected, and each of the key fields for this study was recovered: the list of proponents, the date, the status. Additionally, I needed to visit and get information about every legislator from the National Jury of Elections, whose portal *Infogob* (ww.infogob.com.pe) has historical information of the 130 legislators. It is worth noticing that this Congress has 120 legislators, but some legislators died and others were sanctioned, so the amount of nodes gets to 130. All this work was done in **Python**, making use of *BeautifulSoup* for recovering the contents.

Having the legislators's attributes and every proposal, a social network was built, which is depicted in Table 8.2. As it is shown in Table 8.1, I have a multiparty congress with seven political parties conforming it. For the sake of simplicity, I have worked with three groups, the *opposition* (Union por el Peru), the party that won the Presidential elections or *governing party* (Partido Aprista Peruano), and the other five parties will be considered the *minority.*

The graph in Figure 8.2 uses the Radial Axis Layout in Gephi (www.gephi.org), developed by Groeninger [6], which I decided to use precisely for its capacity to show intra- and inter-group relationships. As it is clear form that graph, this five year period as a whole has made congressmen interact constantly among one another, creating relationships between legislators of different parties and different experience.

The centralization measures are a good and simple way to have a clearer idea of the structure emerging out of the interaction among congressmen. I have computed the very well-know degree, closeness and betweeness measures at node level, representing all three in the Figure 8.3.

I have classified the proposals in five categories: *law, amendment, resolution, declaration* and *urgentMatter*, which are presented in a *session.* Laws produce general legislation, amendments are corrections to the laws, decla-

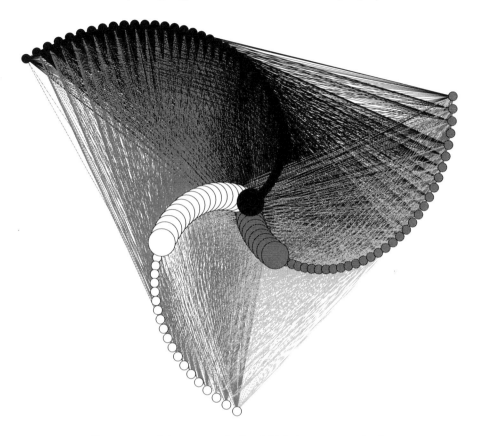

FIGURE 8.2 Cosponsorship network for 2006-2011 period. Opposition is represented in black; governing party in white and minority parties in gray. Small nodes represent first timers and big nodes experienced legislators. The graph has no components and its diameter is *3*, and only two legislators did not sponsor each other in five years: Perez del Solar and Negreiros.

rations are expression of interest from the Congress, and urgentMatter are requests from the executive branch. The production of these proposals is represented in Figure 8.4.

The rest of this chapter will consider only the law proposals, not only due to their relevance, but also to limit the kind of proposals analyzed and ease of understanding, and because the other kinds of proposals are much fewer.

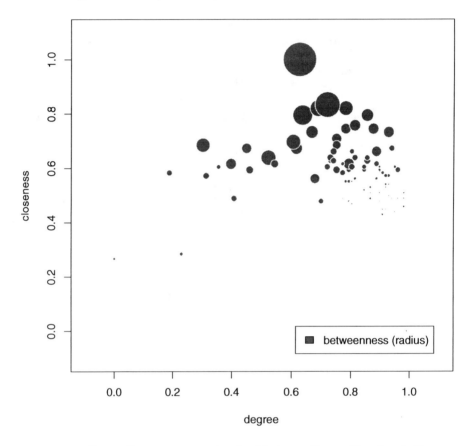

FIGURE 8.3 Centrality measures for legislators; the radius (and diameter) of the circle represent centrality betweeness. All the values have been scaled between 0 and 1. Values were computed in R using igraph.

8.4.2 Re-Election Strategies

Re-election is an interesting topic in political science as it creates debate over many institutional conditions. In the United States, there is an interesting debate over the stagnation of legislators in both the House of Representatives and the Senate. Research on this topic have hypothesized some exogenous and endogenous causes of this phenomenon leading to low political competition in electoral districts. Some research emphasizes the quality of the incumbent [18] and other particular features such as popularity and visibility [14]; researchers have also focused on other possible causes such as accessibility of incumbent to financial resources for their campaigns [9, 15], as well as to the well-known tactics of Gerrymandering [4]and Pork Barrel [16]. Whatever the cause or causes are, the real consequence is that re-election in Congress is above 80% since the 1980s in the United States. Re-election research in Latin America is

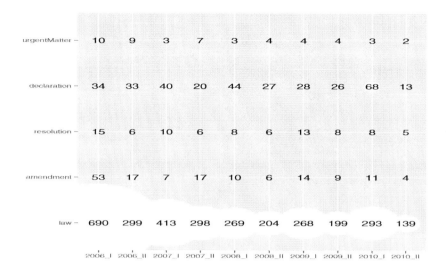

	2006_I	2006_II	2007_I	2007_II	2008_I	2008_II	2009_I	2009_II	2010_I	2010_II
urgentMatter	10	9	3	7	3	4	4	4	3	2
declaration	34	33	40	20	44	27	28	26	68	13
resolution	15	6	10	6	8	6	13	8	8	5
amendment	53	17	7	17	10	6	14	9	11	4
law	690	299	413	298	269	204	268	199	293	139

FIGURE 8.4 Number of proposal per session and classification. There are two sessions per year, and the Congressional year starts in July.

also currently on debate, but mainly considering the President of the executive branch [23, 13], while the debate on this matter for the legislators is yet not visible. In my case, completely different from the US case, re-election is very low (around 10% since the 1990s), see Figure 8.5.

As I assume that the conditions identified are valid, I present a good exercise to find out whether network science can help identify another endogenous condition.

To start, I can reorganize my five-year data in sessions of 6 months, recompute the centrality metrics for each session, to see if there is a pattern that differentiates re-elected from non-re-elected. The findings are shown in Figure 8.6.

A centrality measure will inform of the relative position of the legislator, but will not take into consideration its attributes. So, I will additionally compute the EI Index proposed by Krackhardt and Stern [12] (see Formula 8.1, where EL represents the number of links between nodes that dont share a given attribute or characteristic, and IL represents the number of links between nodes who share that attribute or characteristic), which is the number of ties external to the groups minus the number of ties that are internal to the group divided by the total number of ties. This value can range from 1 to -1.

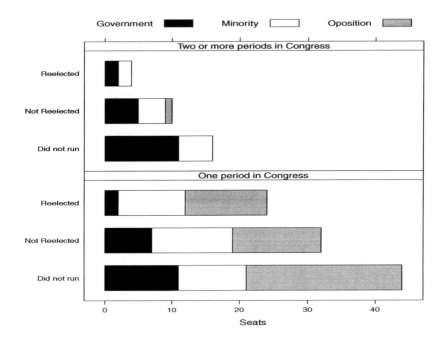

FIGURE 8.5 Reelection of 2006 legislators in 2011 elections by seniority.

In this case, I will use the attributes seniority and position to explore the E-I index for each, per session (see Figure 8.7).

$$EI = \frac{EL - IL}{EL + IL} \qquad (8.1)$$

As I can infer from these graphics there is no clear pathway that reelected legislators as a group followed that differentiates them from the non-reelected. However, boxplot are still aggregating the individual values, so I could also try to uncover some pathway at the individual level making use of a data mining technique known as rule association; in particular, there is the *apriori* function as it is offered in the R package "arules". For that, all the variables were categorized as high (greater than or equal to its third quartile), medium (lower than third and greater than its first quartile) and low (lower than or equal to its first quartile). The results are presented in Table 8.2 for a balanced data set, which needed to be created considering the low percentage of occurrences of reelected cases:

Following the explanation in [8], support is defined as the proportion of rows in the data set, which contain that rule. For example, in rule No 1 above, the value 0.156 means that there are 0.156*120=18.72 legislators that have that rule; the confidence of 0.842 means that 84% of the time that rule

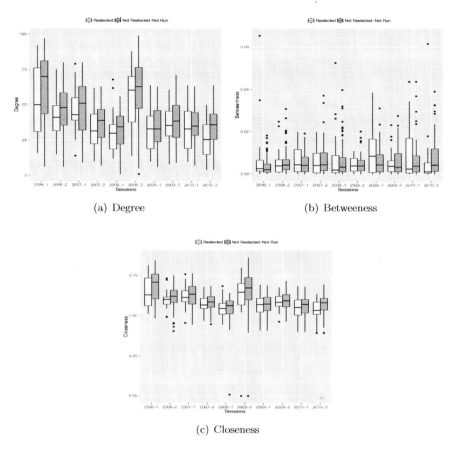

(a) Degree

(b) Betweeness

(c) Closeness

FIGURE 8.6 Centrality measures by re-election status per session.

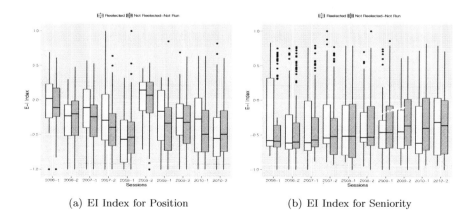

(a) EI Index for Position

(b) EI Index for Seniority

FIGURE 8.7 EI index by re-election status per session.

is found, it coincides with reelection. Finally, the lift of a rule can be interpreted as the deviation of the support of the whole rule from the support expected under independence given the supports of the rule and the outcome, that is, the greater the lift values the stronger the associations.

8.4.3 Party Splitting and Switching

The 2006-2011 Congress suffered party splitting. As legislators start office, they should organize into *political groups*, which are by default their original party. These groups are not informal associations, they are official units entitle to official representation to every decision making committee in the Congress. Only legislators organized into these groups can aspire to become members of the Board. or preside it. However, it could be expected that if we had 7 parties at the beginning (see Table 8.1), the parties with fewer seats should negotiate merging, and so the Congress should have had fewer than 7 groups; but the opposite happened, as the congress had request to create 14 groups and by the end of the Congress (2011), it had 9 groups acting.

Splitting cannot be seen from Figure 8.2, where it seems that there are no particular communities as relationships are very dense. However, a better picture can be obtained if each session is analyzed. In their first session (Figure 8.8), co sponsorship reveals no isolates and shows parties pretty cohesive. As sessions passed by, more parliamentary groups formed, but that does not seem to have changed the co-sponsorship density, which is clear for the first four years (Figures 8.9(a), (b), (c)).

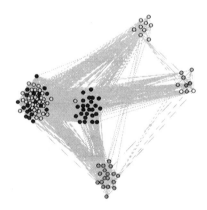

FIGURE 8.8 First session. 2006-I session co-sponsorship. Graph was produced with *DrL* layout from igraph package in R. PAP legislators are in light blue, UPP in red, AF in yellow, RN in orange, UN in green, FC in gray, and PP in white (see Table 8.1 for full names). (See color ebook.)

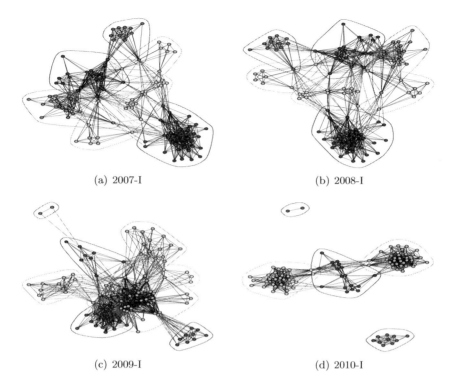

(a) 2007-I (b) 2008-I

(c) 2009-I (d) 2010-I

FIGURE 8.9 Exploring community formation. Communities highlighted are found using walktrap algorithm [19]. Color only denotes the number of communities and their variety of composition. (See color ebook.)

Only in the last year, the co-sponsorship graph split, but not into 12 groups but into 3 (Figure 8.9(d)). That is, even though the Congress had many political groups, that does not alter, for most of the time, the way legislators connected to make laws. This would make the last year with many components an atypical year, if it were not for the fact that legislators were campaigning as the election was in he middle of that current session.

However, the fact of having a congress split does not mean that each group divided itself, but that legislators, as individuals, either found the necessary conditions to abandon his or her original party and be part of another party in the Congress, or created a new parliamentary group.

The detection of legislators that eventually switched parties has been done by multislicing, following [17]:

$$Q = \frac{1}{2\mu} \sum_{ijsr} [(A_{ijs} - \gamma_s \frac{k_{is}k_{js}}{2ms})\delta_{sr} + \delta_{ij}C_{jsr}]\delta(g_{is}, g_{jr}), \qquad (8.2)$$

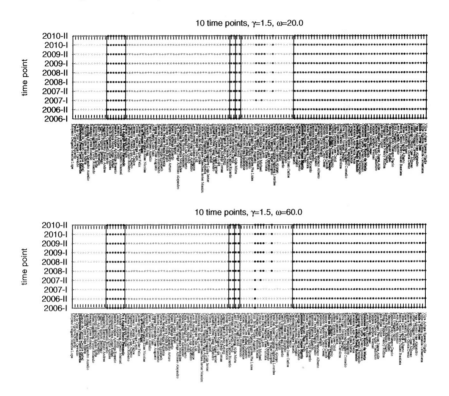

FIGURE 8.10 Party switching of legislators in the 2006-2011 Congress. Each vertical line is the separation of legislators by party: (from left to right) Alianza por el Futuro, Frente de Centro, Partido Aprista Peruano, Peru Posible, Restauracion Nacional, Unidad Nacional, and Union por el Peru.

In Equation 8.2, i and j are legislator indices, and s and r are slice (year) indices. The adjacency tensor $A_{ijs} \neq 0$ if nodes i and j are connected in slice s, and $A_{ijs} = 0$ otherwise. k_{is} is the degree (or strength in weighted networks) of node i in slice s, ms is the number of edges (or sum of weights in weighted networks) in slice s, and γ_s is the resolution parameter in slice s. $C_{jsr} \neq 0$ if slices s and r are connected via node j, and $C_{jsr} = 0$ otherwise. The factor 2μ is used for the normalization condition $Q \in$ [-1,1]. I use the simplest version of interslice connection that $C_{jsr} = \omega$ if two adjacent years s and r share lehgislator j and $C_{jrs} = 0$ otherwise, and $\gamma_s = \gamma$ for all the slices. Therefore, ω as the interslice connection strength and γ as the intraslice resolution parameter are the control parameter plane. As in [17], I have used the Louvain method [2] for maximizing Q from community aggregation.

8.5 DISCUSSION OF RESULTS

This work confirms the usefulness of social network analysis to study the interaction of legislators in multi-party systems. As much of the literature on co sponsorship uses the US Congress as the case of study, this work makes uses of the techniques available to study a different country where many parties get seats, but most legislators know they will not *survive* the next election. In this case, I first focus my attention to discover if co sponsorship can complement the accepted re election strategies which are mostly exogenous and without a network approach. The results obtained clearly show how different network metrics reveal the position that the legislators occupied as time went by, however, as it was seen, the strategy followed by every reelected or no re-elected legislator was similar or not easy to differentiate, which motivated the use of a data mining technique. The results obtained by the association rule algorithm proved that there are some combination of endogenous strategies which included a combination of centrality and homophily (EI index) telling that reelection was achieved by legislators that kept intermediate values in those dimensions. On the other hand, graph theory proved very useful to highlight how the splitting of a party in congress (macro-level) does not correlate with co sponsorship, as this network reported one component during four of the five years a legislator is in office. In the same manner, using the multi slicing technique proved very effective to detect the party switching process, which is done in parallel with party splitting. In general, party switching in Peru is very criticized, it is portrayed by most mass media as a dishonest act since the phenomena started in the 1990s. In this circumstances, switching is a risky strategy but it is nevertheless followed by many legislators. As a by product of this analysis, I could also detect party discipline at the individual level, as there are parties whose legislators never quit (Alianza por el Futuro -Fujimoristas, Frente de Centro, Partido Aprista Peruano).

8.6 FURTHER RESEARCH

I have focused this work on a particular set of proposals — the law proposals mainly because they were the most numerous and also because they addressed the issues of greater impact on the governability of Peru. However, I have not analyzed the other proposals I also collected. For example, I have amendments, which are more sophisticated proposals that may need not only the signature of the proposal but also more dedication on the part of the legislator, since, in case it is accepted for roll-call vote, it would need at least 66% of the votes to be approved. A less conflicting proposal and also the least interesting is the Declaration, which is a symbolic act: congressmen declare some issue as relevant for the nation and the like. However, both of these proposals may present different challenges. It will also be important to study more Congresses. I am already organizing the data available from 1995 which will give me two more Congresses to analyze with the possibility of comparing important structural differences among them. This could be very interesting due to the fact that the legislators from 2001 onward consider themselves as the leaders of the restoration of democracy after the so-called dictatorship during the 1990s; therefore I should expect differences among the 1995-2000 Congress and those that came after. Another interesting strategy would be to carry out ego-network analysis, considering that each case represents an interesting history by itself, however, that may need some further qualitative fieldwork. I now know some more on Congress dynamics. I can clearly see that the Peruvian political class is still learning how to survive in the complex political setting where they are embedded. It may also seem that these legislators are in a "beginner stage" when their inner motivations for political survival are distracting them from building strong political parties. This will not need to continue indefinitely; there will come a time when they realize that keeping this mindset may in fact make survival harder for them; but I cannot anticipate when this will happen.

ACKNOWLEDGMENT

I thank the collaboration of Sang Hon Lee in the multislice technique. I am also grateful to Mason Porter and James Fowler for their interest in this topic and his advice during the organization of the data. I also owe a lot to the different scholar to whom I have discussed about this data: Claudio Cioffi-Revilla, Robert Axtell, Andrew Crooks, Maksim Tsvetovat, William Kennedy, Jeniffer Victor and Bruce Desmarais. Finally, particular thanks to my co researchers Scott Morgensten and Ernesto Calvo in this topic with whom I may soon finish a comparative research study on co sponsorship. There are previous versions of this work with the participation of my colleagues Annetta Burger, Adriana Martinez and Nikhil Murali from George Mason University. I also would like to acknowledge my former student Maria Alejandra Guzman, with whom I started working on this topic in Peru.

Bibliography

[1] Eduardo Aleman and Ernesto Calvo. Explaining Policy Ties in Presidential Congresses: A Network Analysis of Bill Initiation Data. *Political Studies*, 61(2):356–377, June 2013.

[2] Vincent D Blondel, Jean-Loup Guillaume, Renaud Lambiotte, and Etienne Lefebvre. Fast unfolding of communities in large networks. *Journal of Statistical Mechanics: Theory and Experiment*, 2008(10):P10008, October 2008.

[3] Kathleen A. Bratton and Stella M. Rouse. Networks in the Legislative Arena: How Group Dynamics Affect Cosponsorship. *Legislative Studies Quarterly*, 36(3):423–460, August 2011.

[4] John A. Ferejohn. On the Decline of Competition in Congressional Elections. *The American Political Science Review*, 71(1):166–176, March 1977.

[5] James H. Fowler. Legislative cosponsorship networks in the US House and Senate. *Social Networks*, 28(4):454–465, October 2006.

[6] Matt Groeninger. "Circular layout", Gephi Marketplace, March 2, 2013. https://marketplace.gephi.org/plugin/circular-layout/.

[7] Justin H. Gross and Cosma Shalizi. Cosponsorship in the us senate: A multilevel approach to detecting the subtle influence of social relational factors on legislative behavior. *Unpublished Manuscript, Department of Statistics, Carnegie Mellon University*, 2008.

[8] Michael Hahsler, Bettina Grn, and Kurt Hornik. A computational environment for mining association rules and frequent item sets. *Journal of Statistical Software*, 14(15), pages 1–25, 2005.

[9] Harry Henderson. *Campaign and Election Reform*. Library in a book. Facts On File, New York, 2004.

[10] IDEA. *Estudios sobre el Congreso Peruano: grupos parlamentarios, disciplina partidaria y desempeo profesional*. UARM, Instituto Etica y Desarrollo ; IDEA Internacional, Lima, 2009. bibtex: IDEA2009.

[11] Gregory Koger and James H. Fowler. Parties and Agenda-Setting in the Senate, 1973-1998. *SSRN Electronic Journal*, 2007.

[12] D. Krackhardt and R.N. Stern. *Informal Networks and Organizational Crises: An Experimental Simulation*. ILR Reprints. ILR Press, New York State School of Industrial and Labor Relations, Cornell University, 1988.

[13] Kevin Lees. Incumbents Arent Latin Americas Problem | Americas Quarterly, November 2014.

[14] Steven D. Levitt and Catherine D. Wolfram. Decomposing the sources of incumbency advantage in the U.S. House. *Legislative Studies Quarterly*, 22(1):45–60, February 1997.

[15] Michael J. Malbin, editor. *Life after Reform: When the Bipartisan Campaign Reform Act Meets Politics*. Campaigning American style. Rowman & Littlefield, Lanham, MD, 2003.

[16] David R. Mayhew. Congressional elections: The case of the vanishing marginals. *Polity*, 6(3):295–317, April 1974.

[17] Peter J. Mucha, Thomas Richardson, Kevin Macon, Mason A. Porter, and Jukka-Pekka Onnela. Community structure in time-dependent, multiscale, and multiplex networks. *Science*, 328(5980):876–878, 2010.

[18] Ivan Pastine, Tuvana Pastine, and Paul Redmond. Incumbent-Quality Advantage and Counterfactual Electoral Stagnation in the US Senate: Incumbent-Quality Advantage. *Politics*, 35(1):32–45, February 2015.

[19] Pascal Pons and Matthieu Latapy. Computing communities in large networks using random walks (long version). *arXiv:physics/0512106*, December 2005. arXiv: physics/0512106.

[20] Nils Ringe and Jennifer Nicoll Victor. *Bridging the Information Gap: Legislative Member Organizations as Social Networks in the United States and the European Union*. The University of Michigan Press, Ann Arbor, 2013.

[21] Kenneth A. Shepsle and Barry R. Weingast. Political preferences for the pork barrel: A generalization. *American Journal of Political Science*, 25(1):96–111, February 1981.

[22] Wendy K. Tam Cho and James H. Fowler. Legislative success in a small world: Social network analysis and the dynamics of congressional legislation. *The Journal of Politics*, 72(01):124, January 2010.

[23] Daniel Zovatto. Reelection, continuity and hyper-presidentialism in Latin America, The Brookings Institute, February 12, 2014. https://www.brookings.edu/research/opinions/2014/02/12-reelection-continuity-hyperpresidentialism-zovatto.

Index